Confabulations

Creating False Memories
Destroying Families

By Eleanor Goldstein

With Kevin Farmer

Library of Congress Cataloging-in-Publication Data

Goldstein, Eleanor C.
    Confabulations: creating false memories, destroying families /
by Eleanor Goldstein.
              p.335   cm.21.5
    Includes bibliographical references.
    ISBN 0-89777-144-3 : $14.95
1. Adult child sexual abuse victims — United States — Family
relationships — Case studies. 2. Adult child sexual abuse victims —
United States — Psychology — Case studies. 3. Adult child abuse
victims — Psychotherapy — Malicious accusations — Child molesting.
I. Title.
HV6570.2.G65 1992
362.7'64'0973 — dc2092-22933
CIP

Manufactured in the United States

Published by:

 SIRS Books
1100 Holland Drive
Boca Raton, FL 33487
(407) 994-0079

Acknowledgments

Thank you to the families who wrote their stories to share with others in the hopes of stopping this terrible epidemic and retrieving their lost adult daughters.

To Dr. Pamela Freyd, director of FMS Foundation, whose unstinting dedication has brought parents together to share their grief and work together for a resolution of the tragedy that has befallen them.

To the SIRS staff, who worked diligently to make this book a reality. Thanks especially to: Ann Gazourian and Roland Goddu, editors; Michelle McCulloch, who designed and typeset the book; Beth Metz, assistant designer; and Karla Vaillancourt, head of the art department. They, too, were moved by the heartfelt stories as they took shape during the process of putting this book together.

FMS or *False Memory Syndrome* — Refers to a condition in which the person's personality and interpersonal relationships are oriented around a memory that is objectively false but strongly believed in to the detriment of the welfare of the person and others involved in the memory.

Comments referring to the phenomenon of FMS:

The Big Bang that will rock therapy in the 1990s
— *Darrell Sifford,* **Philadelphia Inquirer**

If there exists a Richter scale for psychotherapeutic earthquakes, this one is almost certain to break the needle.
— *John Rosemond, Syndicated columnist*

For further information about FMS contact:

FMS Foundation
3508 Market Street, Suite 128
Philadelphia, PA 19104
(215) 387-1865
1-800-568-8882

Confabulations

Confabulate—
"To replace fact with fantasy in memory."
—Webster's II New Riverside University Dictionary

Confabulation—
"Making up stories to fill in gaps in one's memory."
—Hidden Memories by Robert A. Baker

"People who purportedly recover lost memories are in fact generating not memories of true events but fanciful guesses, fantasies, or plain *confabulations.* Such data would then constitute evidence not of repression but of imagination."

—Elizabeth Loftus,
author of *Witness for the Defense*

"Controlled laboratory studies of age regression have demonstrated a tendency of hypnotized subjects to *confabulate* information spontaneously."

—Sherrill Mulhern, *The Satanism Scare*

Table of Contents

Families' Stories

Introduction

Something really terrible is happening. It could be the worst crisis to ever hit the American family. An epidemic of false accusations is occurring in which adult children are accusing their parents of horrendous acts of sexual abuse, including incest and satanic ritual abuse. These accusations are based on "decades delayed discoveries" coming from "repressed memories."

Typically, a successful, intelligent woman goes to a therapist with a problem – perhaps about marriage, children, an inexplicable illness, an eating disorder. She emerges from therapy with the belief that all of her problems are related to childhood sexual abuse. And after perhaps first accusing a baby sitter, a cousin, a family friend, or a teacher, the parent is accused, not allowed to present a defense and abandoned – perhaps even sued.

Imagine what it is like to have the person you have loved, nurtured, idolized – your child – suddenly turn against you and accuse you of the most horrendous crimes imaginable. That is what is happening in the U.S. today.

There is a growing belief that sexual abuse of all sorts engulfs the nation. Horrendous stories appear every day of abuse in nursery schools, rapes are happening in every community and the most dangerous place of all, according to some, is the home where parents are abusing their children and incest is common.

Celebrities have told their stories of incest and rape and dozens of books have been written; talk shows, newspaper and magazine articles tell the details which horrify us all. We appear to be a nation of depraved sex maniacs.

The statistics are shocking. Repeated over and over again in hundreds of these reports it is claimed that one out of four women and one out of ten men has been sexually abused by age eighteen – most by people they know, 70% by friends and relatives. Imagine what the number means. It means that the worst crimes are being committed regularly by family members. What a horror. The family is insane!

Where do these statistics come from? We contacted the National Committee for the Prevention of Child Abuse. They report that:

> *"while many estimates have been made, the national incidence rate of sexual abuse remains unknown. **The estimate that one in four girls and one in ten boys are abused prior to age eighteen became widely known simply from being repeated.** Retrospective surveys reveal great variation with 6 percent to 62 percent of females and 3 percent to 31 percent of males reporting to have experienced some form of sexual abuse."*

What does this mean? It means that we don't have any valid statistics at all.

Yet mass hysteria is being created by the media which leads us to believe that a large proportion of adults in our society are perpetrators of heinous crimes and our children are in constant danger from almost everyone they might come in contact with, especially family members.

The consequences of this mass hysteria are devastating. Since it is believed that sex abuse is common, therapists, teachers, doctors are looking for it, everywhere. And many are finding it – EVEN WHEN IT DOESN'T EXIST.

With the uncovering of widespread sexual abuse has come an epidemic of false accusations of sexual abuse.

Since sexual abuse of a child is the worst crime we know of — to be falsely accused of such a crime is the worst thing that can happen to a person.

The act of sexual abuse against a child is presumed to be so traumatic that apparently the memory of the experience is often repressed, sometimes for decades. Sometimes memories of sexual abuse occur spontaneously, often with the guidance of a therapist, in a group or in a group therapy seminar. Many therapists believe that the repressed memory never exaggerates. They say the "body remembers, the head may forget." Clients may spend months or years doing the "work" to recall traumatic events in their past. When a memory is dredged out, real or imagined — many therapists say it doesn't matter — the pain is real.

The final result is that hundreds, more likely tens of thousands, of parents have been falsely accused of the most horrendous crimes of sexual abuse against the people they love the most in this world — their children.

These families are devastated and hopeless. The anger, hatred and vilification expressed by adult children against their parents is so great in these situations that reconciliation seems impossible.

But, though the situation appears hopeless, it is with hope that families tell their stories. Hope that people will listen! That the tragedy of false accusations will stop. Above all else they want their daughters back in the family again.

More than 2,000 families responded to an 800 number from October 1991 until October 1992 to seek help in solving this terrible problem. Here are some of their stories. Hoping for reconciliation, names have been changed to protect privacy.

A Father of Three Loses His Daughters

Introduction

I am a fifty-two-year-old father of three daughters. Jane, Cindy, and Caroline are thirty, twenty-nine, and twenty-seven. My wife Maggie and I have been married for thirty-one years. I always thought of us as an exceptionally close family. We are no longer close. Our daughters have become a part of a vast army of "codependents" or "adult children." Maggie and I have become "the family of origin." They are told that contact with us may threaten their recovery.

How did this happen? What is the adult child movement? How could my happy, intelligent, independent, and loving daughters be recruited by a movement that requires that they denounce their parents?

I no longer feel great pride in my daughters. The feeling of pride has been replaced with shame. My fantasy is that in twenty or thirty years, maybe a decade after my death, they'll read this and realize that they were wrong. I hope my grandchildren will read it sooner.

Cindy

The first time Cindy cut us out of her life was when she was a sophomore at a private college. She wrote us asking for money to see a psychiatrist. I wrote back that I thought it a terrible idea. With three in college the next year, I could not afford it. I told her, if she was serious about needing help, she could come home and go into therapy. But I could not afford both college and psychotherapy. My

response made her so angry that she refused to correspond or speak to us for the next year. Her mother continued to write letters. I continued to write checks. Cindy
cashed the checks but did not answer.

After a year, Cindy forgave us. She even thanked her
mother for continuing the flow of letters. She had news for
us. She wanted to come home for Christmas and asked if
she could bring her lesbian lover as a guest. We gave an
immediate yes. And then we worried. What have we done?
That first visit was difficult. We were, without a doubt,
homophobic. I didn't know that word at the time. I am
now a sophisticated Big City resident. I will admit to having been homophobic way back in 1980. But we loved our
daughter. She and her friends would always be welcome.

Over the next six or seven years, we visited her in
California or she visited us in Texas two or three times a
year. I got bored with lesbian issues. I argued vociferously
against Cindy being artificially inseminated by a gay friend.
I didn't like the way she dressed. But these were minor
problems. We enjoyed our times together and we totally
accepted that our daughter was lesbian. We came to love
her last lover who was also named Cindy. Most of the
women had been rejected by their families. We enjoyed
being the enlightened parents who welcomed them into
our family.

Our Cindy dramatically ended that relationship in 1986.
It was a collect call from Cindy, "Dad, I'm in love and it's
with a man." She seemed disappointed when I didn't share
her excitement. I tried to explain that I had gotten used to
her being lesbian and I was concerned for her friend
Cindy. She said that Cindy was taking it hard and would
probably revert to her former alcoholism. I had gotten to
know Cindy # 2 during the two years they were together.

We had had a number of talks. She invited me to read her journal. She was a kind, sensitive, intelligent person. I cared for her.

During one of their visits to Dallas, Cindy and Cindy and I attended an AA meeting. My daughter Cindy announced that she was there because she was a sex addict and she was visiting with her lover and her father who were both alcoholics. That seemed to stun even that room of jaded folks.

I felt a little embarrassed. My daughter Cindy loved it. We were the stars of the meeting.

My Mother

Over the next few years, Cindy made a series of comments at different times that seemed bizarre. I had always been close to my mother. One day Cindy made the comment that the relationship between my mother and me had been "emotionally incestual." This nasty combination of words angered and puzzled me. I told her that incest has a specific meaning and to use it that way was dishonest.

Often, I stopped and picked wildflowers in a field and brought them home to my mother. I told her everything that happened in school each day. I told her the dirty jokes the other boys told, the swear words they used. We shook our heads together and agreed that I was too nice a boy to tell such jokes or use such words. I still have difficulty swearing unselfconsciously.

My mother was always depressed around Christmas. She told me that her loved ones died around Christmas time. She was relieved when the holiday was over.

My mother lost a baby girl, her third child, in 1945. The baby died just a few hours after birth. Mom was kept in the hospital for a few weeks. My father and a couple of uncles drove 1000 miles from Detroit back home to Fordyce, Arkansas. The baby and casket went by rail. After the funeral, on the way home on icy roads, there was a head-on crash with a truck and Dad was killed. It was about three weeks before Christmas.

I was six years old. I became the man of the family. I was also a burden. I woke screaming in terror, often. Sometimes, I dreamed that my mother had died. Other times, it was a dream that was just a feeling. The feeling was that everything was speeded up, and kept happening faster and faster. It was terrifying to me. My mother would have to hold me and comfort me for most of the night. I believe that the dreams only lasted a few months. But I clung to her. She was my world. And I was often her confidant. She shared her worries with me. She talked a great deal about my father. She portrayed him always in heroic terms. I became her audience. I heard many hours of stories about every aspect of her life.

If I was inclined to view myself as a victim, I could, perhaps, see that I had been harmed by this relationship. I have no doubt that a therapist, if I went and confessed feelings of inadequacy, and told my history, would suggest that I had been emotionally abused. But, not being so inclined, I am proud of the little kid that I was in 1945. My mother was a strong person. She needed somebody. I was there. My sister was there. We were wounded. We nurtured and cared for each other. We loved one another for those years and for the rest of our lives. Just being in the presence of either my mother or my sister has been comforting to me for as long as I can remember. I was a lucky man to have that.

New Words
It was several years later that I read the following words

in *Bradshaw on: The Family.* "Emotional sexual abuse results from crossgenerational bonding. I've spoken of enmeshment as a way that children take on the covert needs of a family system. It is very common for one or both parents in a dysfunctional marriage to bond inappropriately with one of their children. The parents in effect use the child to meet their emotional needs. The relationship can easily become sexualized and romanticized."

I admit to an emotional reaction every time I read the above words. The most moderate thought I have had after reading them, is, this man is a troubled, dangerous man. I know I do not like this man.

Adult Child Movement

Cindy was being caught up in a mass movement known variously as: 12-Step Self Help, Codependency, or Adult Children movement. She was being indoctrinated. Her therapist, Adult Child meetings, and her readings were all giving her the same message.

Very succinctly the message is: We live in a compulsive/addictive society. That means that most of us grew up in dysfunctional homes. We were subjected to shame, physical abuse, sexual abuse, poisonous pedagogy, emotional abuse, and incest. These abuses are all interrelated. If you suffered one, you probably suffered others. Often, people don't remember the worst of the crimes committed against them. It may take some time and therapy to remember the worst of the beatings or the pain of the sexual assaults. If you suffer from low self-esteem, if you go through life feeling numb, if you have problems feeling close to anybody, then you are an Adult Child. That means you were abused repeatedly. You were shamed. You were not allowed to blossom. Your "inner child" shriveled in terror.

To combat the horrors of your upbringing you will need to break free from your "family of origin." The only way to find yourself is to accept your status as an Adult Child. A joyous and fulfilling life awaits you. The loving fellowship of the Adult Child group will be your new family.

How could the above obnoxious ideas appeal to a normal person who had had a loving family environment? That is the question that I have been obsessed with for the past year.

Over a period of a year or two, my daughters introduced me to the following words:

dysfunctional family	violated boundaries
inappropriate language	emotional abuse
inner child	denial
emotional incest	self parenting
abusive family	incest
recovery	codependency

It is very strange to read best-selling self-help books and have them evoke very emotional personal memories. I remember the first time that Cindy said we were a dysfunctional family; when Jane wanted to tell her mother about her "inner child"; and Cindy announced that she had parented herself.

Losing All Three

As my children became more and more immersed in the movement, they were taught that Adult Children tended to idealize their parents. They were also taught that resistance to the ideas of the movement is to be expected and is called "denial." In time, all three were able to overcome their tendency to idealize their parents.

When Caroline was married, we had a small wedding in

Dallas, where Maggie and I were living. Maggie was work-ing as a teacher. Caroline and Paul were in Austin. Maggie was working all day. I had more flexible hours, so I handled most of the arrangements for the wedding. Lisa and Cindy flew in from California and Arizona. They had no interest in helping out. In fact, their goals seemed to be to upset the bride and get in the way of the preparations. At one point, Cindy said to me, "Dad, you are acting so responsibly, it's not like you." I didn't have an answer for her. Now I would like to say to her, how do you think mortgage payments were made, and your braces paid for, and those expensive running shoes, and college tuition bills, how did I do that except by behaving responsibly? But my answer didn't matter at all.

After the wedding and after Caroline and Paul had left, Jane and Cindy entertained the guests by telling them that Dad was an alcoholic and an abusive father.

It was a couple of years later that Cindy made the ultimate charge. I now see that it was inevitable. The Adult Child literature is full of repeated references to abuse, sexual abuse, and incest. She had been reading this mate-rial for several years. Her therapist had told her that she had the characteristics of an abused child. Then she had a dream. It is not surprising that she would have a dream that reflected the lurid ideas that she was immersed in. Her dream convinced her that sometime in her infancy, before her conscious memory, she had been sexually abused. She thought her father the most likely perpetrator.

A few months went by during which Maggie and my other daughters knew of this charge and I did not.

During this period I had nightmares. I had the same nightmare several times. I have travelled quite a bit in the western part of the United States. My nightmare was that I was a serial killer. In my nightmare, I found bloodstained clothes and other circumstantial evidence that made me realize that I had killed dozens of people everywhere I had travelled. I don't usually even remember my dreams, but on those occasions it took some minutes after waking for my pulse to return to normal. I clearly remember the growing terror I felt in the dream. Henry Lucas, the Texas serial killer, was much in the news. And, although I was unaware of it, my daughters had become convinced that I was something akin to a serial killer. When I found out about Cindy's latest charge, I understood the dream. My unconscious mind was dealing with the loathing that I felt from my daughters. My dream simply reflected the pain and horror that was my emotional life.

As soon as I learned of the newest development I called Cindy. She had found another 12-Step group to join. Cindy wouldn't speak to me, but the father of her baby told me a little bit about her new group. Todd explained that it is common for men like me to deny the charges. There was one story about a man who denied the charges for years, then thinking he was on his deathbed, admitted that they were true. He recovered and once again denied that he had raped his infant daughter. The other story that Todd shared from the INCEST SURVIVORS group was about a woman who told of having been raped the day she came home from the maternity ward as a newborn.

Both of these stories seem implausible to me. Deathbed confessions are found in melodramas, not in real life. In the second case, one would wonder how the victim found out about the crime. My guess is that it was with the assistance of a therapist.

The next weeks were painful. I made repeated phone calls. My daughters were distant or totally unavailable. They could not offer me reassurance. They didn't know what was true. All three were seeing therapists, going to meetings, and reading the literature. All three daughters had become Adult Children.

Painful Rejection

Being rejected by my children as an abusive father has been difficult. I was obsessed by it for months. During those early months I asked for an appointment with a minister at a church that we have been members of since we moved to Big City. The minister was a symbol of feminism for me and I thought that she might be able to help me understand what was happening between me and my feminist daughters.

As I write, there is a growing realization of how wonderfully understanding she was. She said, "Whether it's true or not, those girls will need a father the rest of their lives." I actually resented that statement at the time. But now I see it as a wise observation. And she hugged me and said, "You must be in a lot of pain." I went out to the car and cried.

A few weeks later, the minister preached a sermon entitled Beyond Codependence. Apparently, she had encountered a number of troubled people injured by the Adult Child program. She gave several examples in her sermon. Our situation with our kids was outlined without our names being used. A few friends recognized that we were being referred to, and were sympathetic. We live with this horror on a daily basis.

A Different Time

We will call my daughters Ann, Betty, and Carol. I had three daughters and now there are two.

In September of 1990 my middle daughter, Betty, age thirty-five, became pregnant. It was an unplanned and unwanted pregnancy. She has a ten-year-old son by her first husband. She and her second husband felt child rearing was a huge responsibility, and a second child was not in their plans.

By February of 1991, she was seeing a psychologist. She was feeling depressed, suffering with inadequacy, and feeling like a failure.

In April of 1991, she called crying and pleading with me. "Mom," she cried, "Will you still love me no matter what?" I replied, "Yes, of course. What's wrong, Betty?" She cried while telling me – daddy sexually abused her. I gave her all the reasons why this could not be. She accepts my answers. She continues to see her therapist.

The new baby arrived in June 1991. In August, my husband and I take our three daughters, their spouses, and our grandchildren on a seven-day vacation. Betty remained aloof from all of us. I explained it away as postpartum. Daughters Ann and Carol were annoyed at their sister for not being a part of the group. They feel she's up to her old tricks. She wants our attention. She's different from our oldest and youngest daughters, I tell myself. She was always rebellious, an attention seeker, a crusader.

The Accusation

Betty continues to see her therapist once a week. In November, one week prior to me and my husband going on a cruise, I receive a phone message on my machine. It is Betty. Would I call her back. I return her call at 10 p.m. that night. She asks me to do her a favor. I ask, "What can I do?" She replies, "Would you please go see a therapist?" I ask, "Why?" She says, "Because there is something I must tell you, and I feel you will need the support of a therapist." My heart stopped beating for the moment. The bomb had descended upon me. "Dad has violated me," she cries.

I begin to cry; I extend her my sympathy. My mind is racing. I can't believe she is saying this. I can't believe the gravity of her illness. I try to comfort her on the phone while my body is trembling. Our conversation ended about 12 a.m.

The next two days for me and my husband were like a death hovering over us.

I speak with Betty each day, trying to give her comfort and also trying to understand how this could be. I cry a lot while on the phone with her. She advises me to get a book called *The Courage to Heal*. She says it will help get me through this. She also gives me a phone number of a crisis center for incest survivors. It's a 24-hour hotline.

I call them. They reassure me that this incest has truly happened to our daughter. I ask could Betty be mistaken about who her abuser was. The woman on the other end of the phone replies, "Whomever your daughter has named as her abuser is a true fact." I feel sick and distraught. I'm shattered. I'm trapped in the nightmare of all nightmares.

My husband and I meet with our other two daughters. They confirm to us that this has not happened. Betty is again trying to get our attention. I say, "But why would she say such a thing? Why?" They tell us about their life in our home. It was, they tell us, a healthy upbringing, they never felt uncomfortable in their bra and panties with dad in the same room. They tell us we raised them with healthy attitudes about sex. Betty is lying, they say. "But Betty says dad has done this to all three of you. She claims you two are in denial," I cry out. Our two daughters again reaffirm this has never happened. December comes. Betty and I talk about Christmas. She says she will visit and exchange gifts when dad is not there. I tell her to come Christmas Eve. The whole family (35 of us), except dad, will be at my cousin's home. She can join me and her sisters there.

Going Public

She asks me if I'm ready to have everyone know that she has been sexually abused by her father. I say "No, I'm not." "Well," she replies, "I will tell them myself." I say, "Why do you want to say this?" She says, "I will tell anyone I want to tell." I reply, "Betty, stay where you are (125 miles away), and I will come see you and the children the day after Christmas."

I begin to see a therapist in early December. I am sick with grief. I speak with Betty's husband. I tell him Betty's stories are not true stories. The events she refers to are not events that occurred in our home or our lives. He impresses upon me that they are indeed true, and I must face the reality of it.

Daughter Ann calls her sister Betty. She asks her about the events, what were her experiences in our home. Betty has no answers. Again, Ann pursues the questioning. Betty can't give any facts. She becomes enraged; she screams at Ann, "Who are you, the jury? I say he sexually abused me and that's all you have to know."

In my talks on the phone to Betty, I ask her, "How old were you when this happened? How many times did this happen?" She says, "I was maybe three or four years old. It happened one, maybe three times, I don't know." I say, "But daddy was never home, he worked 16-hour nights, slept daytime. I was always at home. I didn't go to a job. Where was I when this was happening?" No reply. As weeks go by, the story and length of abuse increases. My son-in-law tells me that Betty has now recalled seven years of abuse!

Ann continues to call her sister. One night Ann dialed Betty's phone number 25 times. They were at each other's throats. Our daughters Ann and Carol begin to suffer as they watch their parents deteriorate. They are so very angry at Betty.

My visit on December 26th was horrible. I was so numb and so was she. I played with my two grandchildren, took some videos, and left after two hours. I drove 125 miles each way for a two-hour visit. I have not seen my daughter or grandchildren since.

The week between Christmas and New Year's Eve, Betty calls my mother and my husband's sister. Both women are in their 70s. She tells them of the alleged incest. My mom calls me; she tells me of Betty's conversation. I begin to cry hysterically. My husband takes the phone. He explains our situation to her.

I call Ann and Carol. I tell them to call Grandma; she needs to hear the truth. I can't go on. It is 6 p.m. Fully clothed, I go into my bed and pull the covers over my head. I am numb. How can a child do such a thing? Why is she doing this awful, terrible thing?

I say to myself she is truly ill. But not for the reason she claims. How can I help her?

Aftershocks
I send gifts and letters. She leaves a message of verbal

abuse on my answering machine. She calls twice to finish her message. She batters me verbally in her calls. She calls me "an enabler." She says I saw her father have sex with her and did nothing. I didn't protect her. That even the animals in the jungle protect their young. Her verbalization is horrifying.

After sending a gift to my grandson in January, she calls to tell me if I continue to send him gifts signed Grandma and Grandpa, she will return them to me. She tells me she has told her son he is not allowed to receive gifts from a child molester. (To backtrack a bit, she also told her 10-year-old son how grandpa sexually abused her.)

I'm in fear of her verbal battering. I stop writing her. I have no way to call her since she now has a new unlisted phone number. She also has changed her first name.

In late February, I send her a poem. I received a phone call again from Betty. She sounds fine. I ask how she is. She replies, "Wonderful." She asks me why I continue to write and send cards. I say because I love my grandchildren and my daughter. She hesitates. I ask if I can come see the children. She says, "You're not allowed." I ask, "Why?" She says, "Do you want a relationship with me? Because if you do, then you must admit that daddy is lying and I'm telling the truth." I say, "You *don't know* what I'm thinking." Again she replies, "Then you must be *telling* me you believe me." I say, "Don't put words in my mouth." With that, she begins again the verbal battering. I hang up. I have cried every day for two weeks since that last phone call.

The thought of never seeing our daughter and grandchildren ever again has become my realization. Our daughter has made her decree very clear! We are not wanted in her life.

I remember our years of turmoil in Betty's teenage years

and how my husband and I put all our time and energy into keeping her on a course of stability. Those years took away a lot of nurturing from our other two daughters. They have never complained. They always felt their sister to be a difficult person. They understood her need for us, and sacrificed themselves.

When Betty married, our relationship with each other became very close. We were best friends. I expressed and revealed my most inner feelings and most intimate chapters in my life. She has now turned all that against me. She has betrayed a love and friendship that can never be brought back.

All of this has occurred because my daughter was feeling depressed and stressed. She sought help from a mental health professional — one who has taken hold of her vulnerability, has given her a memory of things that have never occurred. He and many like him are as dangerous as Hitler was in the late '30s and early '40s. Many families like ours will be destroyed before society becomes aware of this holocaust.

So, I had three daughters and now there are two.

Another Try

> *Dear Betty:*
>
> *I pray you are all well. This letter was a long time in coming. You had been asking me about my life in months past. So here goes. It's a history lesson about what life was for me. It's a story I want to share with you now so you can store it away in your memory.*
>
> *As a little girl growing up in the 1930s, I learned how to take on responsibility. Children of that era had to share in family chores. I*

accepted this as a way of being, as a way of life. I handled things as they presented themselves. I never thought twice about it. I just did what I was told to do. I was raised with high morals and respect for family and God.

I went to church every Sunday and during the summer months, I and the other kids in the neighborhood went to what is now known as summer day camp. What I was actually doing was going to the convent area of the church where the nuns taught the girls how to do embroidery and other female crafts. During the early '40s, I joined the church choir and the church basketball team. So, I think you're getting the picture.

Given the background of love of family and church, to this day I find it very difficult to do, say, or act in any way that would hurt, offend, deprive, or destroy anyone. I tell fibs like anyone else, but I would choke rather than do an injustice to anyone.

My mother had her share of problems as a wife and mother, but she did only what she knew how to do. She told some really great bible stories and children's stories. She never read them from a book. They were tales she just knew. (She probably heard them in her childhood.)

Growing up in the '30s and '40s was an era when children were taught to obey and revere their elders. In my teen years, I went to the C.Y.O. dances, dances at our city park, rollerskating, hung out with the girls. We cut each other's hair. I also had rebellion in my teens. But didn't every generation?

In the '50s I was in my twenties. At that time I was a wife and mother. But I think I've been a mother all my life. I knew at an early age how to do problem-solving, how to cook, clean and care for children. (I babysat a lot.) I really loved the role of wife and mother. I always knew marriage would be my career. So I married early. I chose a man whose upbringing was similar to mine. Family and church and morals were steadfast in our minds.

My husband was also a man who took on responsibilities without question. He never said no to a parent or relative or even a friend who was in need of him. It was a way of life for us in the '50s. I stayed home and took care of our children. Dad went to work to meet our financial needs. I found my role as wife and mother a 24-hour job. Dad's job took up most of his day. More times than not, he worked 16-hour shifts for four and five days a week. So I again took the role of mother, nurse, comforter, teacher, cook, housekeeper, that I was trained for so early in life. And I didn't see anything wrong with having such an enormous task. This is what life was to me.

As I reached my 30's and 40's, I reveled in the blossoming of my three daughters. I wanted them to be popular, to do fun things, to know about sharing thoughts with girlfriends. I yearned for them to have happy teen years, not awkwardness, or unsureness that accompanies being a teen. I thought I would spare them all the hurts that come with being a teen, that I would love them and be an understanding mother. That I would be more lenient than my parents were and I would give them fewer responsibilities than I had. But I also felt my children would love me back. They would have high morals and respect for themselves and others. But unfortunately, I was not ready for the 1960s. The '60s was a society that was burning bras and flags. I was so unprepared. For all my training and wisdom of responsibility and love of family, this was something I was not ready for or knew how to handle.

In the '70s, as parents, we were facing challenges that were beyond parenting. The youths of the '70s presented problems that made even the experts throw their arms up in exasperation. But we, as a family, fared through it all. Some of us have scars. But it was a society that was not prepared to deal with the events of the time.

So we watched our daughters graduate from high school and college, saw them marry, shared in their joys, hurts, and their successes. We had our problems behind us in the '80s and found new joys in the adulthood of our children and the joy of a new grandchild. He brought many happy times to my life. Watching him grow was the highlight of my life. My heart was heavy also in those years; I had seen so much unrest and unhappiness in your twenties, Betty. But I also knew you would overcome your obstacles. You were strong, wise and so sensitive and compassionate about life. I sometimes wished I was as "together" as you. I wished I had the wisdom you had in raising your son. I thought you did such a spectacular and wonderful job of raising him.

So here I am in my fifties and the 1990s have brought me a new phase of life. I have lost a daughter and two grandchildren. I mourn for them every day. But the fact is they are not dead. They are still on this earth. But they are inaccessible to us. The '90s have brought new labels: incest and rape. Incest and rape are not new to society. But some professionals are using these labels as a healing tool.

This is a new phenomenon I did not expect to face in my lifetime or anyone else's. I did not expect a child of mine to have memories of incest. I believe my child does not have these memories. The memories my child lays claim to are not her memories; they are learned memories. I find society has taught a child of mine, a child who is bright, wise, sensitive, and compassionate to have a memory of something that has never happened.

I'm not a doctor, Betty, but I do know what events occurred in our lives. Incest was not one of them.

So if you feel this letter is a harassment to you and you need to call a lawyer, that is your right to feel how you feel.

But about how I feel, I will say this:

I feel society has torn my heart out and leaves it exposed for many hurts. It has cut my guts out and feeds upon them, and everyday it draws on *my blood. But the saddest blow life has dealt is it leaves my brain and thinking intact.*

So, Betty, there is nothing, absolutely nothing, a lawyer can do that has not already been done to me. I grieve every day for us all, and I pray every day for your recovery.

Love,
Mother

How Could This Happen?

When she was thirty-three, Susan had a revelation that she had been repeatedly sexually abused and raped for thirteen years by her father. I am Susan's mother, and I have been trying to cope with that revelation.[1]

> *We lied,* our son-in-law Steve said. *We're not at the doctor's office. We're at friends. We want you to leave the house and fly home. We've made reservations on the 3:30 airplane. The taxi will arrive in an hour and a half. Susan now remembers that she was seriously abused as a child by her father.*

Those were the words my husband Alex and me heard over the telephone at 9:30 in the morning on Friday, December 21, 1990. We had arrived in Any City on the previous afternoon after the six-hour flight from our home. This was our seventh holiday visit to Susan and Steve's home, a pattern begun before they had their first child. As in past years, the weeks before our flight had been bustling with happy conspiratorial coast-to-coast phone calls about secrets for presents and plans for our two grandsons. We arrived without a clue as to what was about to happen. An unusual winter storm had disrupted the ordinarily mild Any City winter with bitter cold and dangerous icy roads, in retrospect a fitting backdrop for our own chilling experience.

It was wonderful to hug and kiss everyone. Susan seemed thinner than when I had seen her in October and she seemed tense, but this was a very busy time for her. Emotions run high in most families at holiday times. I was soon alternating between the playroom where five-year-old Bobby was watching Sesame Street and the living room where I could be generally grandmother-foolish with two-year-old Paul and at the same time try to converse a little with Susan as she cooked dinner.

Small things that might ordinarily be dismissed can become significant with the vision of hindsight – a dinner a bit out-of-pattern. Usually Susan planned favorites for our arrival, but this time the rice was cooked with liver (which I really should learn to like) and the chicken was served so that Alex did not get a breast. Should we have been forewarned? Dinner-talk seemed normal and brought us up-to-date with news and gossip not important enough for phone calls.

After dinner, Alex helped Bobby put together a potato clock that we had brought, and I pretended to be a dog, a cat, and a sheep until Paul turned red with laughter. But Alex and I were tired and soon left to get ready for sleep. As she usually did, our daughter had left presents for us from the boys on our bed, drawings that they had made. Should we have been forewarned? I would have said that we were a close family in many ways.

Still on our usual sleep hours, I awoke in time to see Susan stumbling out of the house carrying Paul. *He was sick in the night. I'm taking him to the doctor*, she lied. The phone call from Steve came a few hours later. He delivered the terrible message unemotionally – no explanation, no justification, no details, no offer of joint counseling – just our exit visas.

Neither our daughter nor Steve have looked at me or spoken to me since those stinging words ordering us to leave their house and accusing Alex of serious abuse. That has been as painful as the expulsion and accusation because Susan and I shared so much of our ordinary day-to-day lives. We have continued to communicate using electronic mail (e-mail),[2] the communication mode of academics in the '90s, but our letters have all focused on abuse, her belief and my lack of belief in her revelation. She has cut off any contact by me with Bobby and Paul.

Alex and I have only just begun to overcome the heartache, the anxiety, the shame and the confusion enough to be able to share our story with a few people. "How do you cope?" we are inevitably asked. Every day has been hard and nothing has been resolved. Perhaps the most haunting question has been, "How could this have happened?" I have read and reread my letters with Susan, trying to understand something, anything, about how this could have happened.[3]

What Were We Supposed to Have Done? When?

Nothing else in my life has ever had so many "worst parts." So much that has happened seems so unnecessary. I don't suppose there is really any nice way to accuse your father of incest. But, the cruel dramatic gestapo-like techniques that included our trip across the continent, the surprise accusation, the ostracism, and the lack of details set in motion reactions that have made dealing with the revelation more difficult. *My therapist suggested that I ask you and dad not to come visit,* our daughter wrote later, *but I couldn't bring myself to do that.* What kind of professional advice had she been getting? I thought that therapists were supposed to help patients work to determine their own minds, not put them in conflict by suggesting that they do something contrary. Could a conflict between what she wanted and what her therapist expected have caused Susan to act in such an unnatural and cruel way?

Alex and I clung to each other to keep our hearts from breaking, too shocked to cry, and then we packed our bags and negotiated again the perils of the icy Any City roads, of holiday crowds and airline overbooking, to get to the safety of our home. Should we have left Any City? But who would want to stay where they were not wanted? What should we do next? After such humiliating treatment how could we ever speak to our daughter and Steve again?

Reason and love dictated that something was obviously deeply wrong with Susan and her husband. We had had thirty-three years of love and affection from Susan, too much love to let pride shut us off after a single incident. We had too much concern for her well-being at a time when a complete and sudden switch in her behavior seemed to reflect some kind of nervous breakdown, a fact recognized in a letter from Steve weeks later. We didn't even know what we were supposed to have done. Serious abuse must certainly mean sexual abuse.

Susan had been really stressed by the earthquake last year while living in Any City. She was struggling between the pressures of career and motherhood, and I knew she had some fundamental problems in her marriage because she had confided in me a year earlier. Steve was very unhappy in his job and resented Susan's impulsive decision to make the move to Any City in order to get her early tenure. Perhaps Steve was so quick to accept something as horrible as this because for him it could explain his dislocation from the job he loved and the town where he had family. Surely this confusion would be corrected quickly. I sent Susan an e-mail message and she responded.

Following are some excerpts of our communications during the Christmas season.

December 22
Dear Susan,
I love you. I hope that we can keep some communication going.

December 23
Dear Susan,
I'm glad that we can write. I love you. I cannot deal with your memories — because I don't know what they are. We have been accused of something, but I could hardly go to a therapist, as you ask, without knowing what the details are. What is supposed to have happened? You asked me to tell you about your teachers in elementary school. . . .

December 24
Dear Susan,
You have made serious charges against us. I don't have the slightest idea of what you are upset enough about to have initiated this crisis. I don't know where to begin to do what you ask and see a therapist like yours who is a young clinical psychologist, a female and a specialist in sex abuse. I don't know if your memories are from the time of nursery school or later. You are going to have to tell us specifically what you remember. We are devastated by the accusations and by being thrown out of your house. You asked about our trip to India and the six months we spent living abroad when you were in ninth-grade. . . .

We went through Christmas in a surreal holding pattern. There seemed nowhere to turn. The library was closed. Doctors were away on vacation. A wonderful friend came when we called and we survived. We didn't even know what we were supposed to have done. Could there be anything worse than having a child you have loved and cared for accuse you of abusing her? Her death perhaps. Her suicide certainly. Our daughter wasn't dead. There was hope. I still felt in my heart that this had to be some kind of horrible mistake. We made arrangements to change the locks on the doors of our house.

December 27
Dear Susan,

I do not doubt that you have painful memories, but I do not remember you ever being abused by Alex. What do you remember? I have no desire to deny any truth as you claim. You asked me to write about my own childhood....

December 28
Dear Susan

I thought that you should know that we finally have heard some specifics of the charges. Your grandmother told me. You think you were sexually abused by Alex. Why could you tell her and not us? Perhaps by analogy you can understand where I am. It is as inconceivable to me that this could be true as it would be to you that Steve would do such a thing with Bobby and Paul.

We do love you deeply. Please understand that. We understand that you are hurting terri-

bly. The depth of your pain can be judged by the
fact that you were willing to throw away our
relationship on the basis of a vague memory
that occurred after a suggestive probe by your
therapist, rather than act in any way that left
doors open.
   Our hearts are heavy because we feel that
there is nothing that we can do or say that is
going to make any difference. You asked about
the summer in Detroit....

Doubt finds fertile soil in confusion and ignorance, and
so doubts sprouted in my mind. Maybe something did
happen to Susan and she had transferred that memory to
Alex. Susan had done lots of experimenting with drugs
when she was a teenager. Could that have caused memory
confusion? Could Alex have a side to him that I didn't
know about? No, that wasn't possible. I've known him
since he was nine years old. But would anyone make up
such a horrible accusation? How could I have been unaware of sexual abuse? What had really happened? What
was Alex supposed to have done?

December 29
Dear Susan,
   We are struggling to understand. As you asked
us to do, we are reading Courage to Heal.[4] *We*
have been searching our souls and our pasts.
We have an appointment with a therapist next
week. But we don't know what we have done.
   You may be right, perhaps my last message
sounded as though I were closing doors. I don't
want to do that. But I could not bear to see my

grandchildren as I last saw them with their mother secreting them out so that there could be no goodbye.

You asked about what I remember of the years when you were in nursery school and we lived in New York City . . . .

December 30
Dear Susan,

All we have wanted to do is help. We have felt so cut off and in the dark and hurt. Alex said on the plane coming home, "If I take sodium pent will that get at the truth, will that help?" We haven't had a clue of where to begin. You have given us some information in your last letter. Maybe something happened in our family that we have repressed. I hope not but we will certainly try to find out.

I don't happen to agree with you that the past is an enormous tragedy. I have found joy in most of my life and am proud of overcoming the problems. I count myself unbelievably fortunate that I have had Alex and you to accept my love. I count myself fortunate that you have been an intelligent, kind and beautiful person. I hardly know anyone who has not been thrown some curve balls.

You don't have a history of inflicting pain. You have been wonderfully supportive to us. We love you. That is why what has been happening has been such a confusing mystery to us. From my perspective there are so many things that do not add up yet. There are some things that seem so very inconsistent to me. When you share with us what you know, perhaps we will be better able to help you.

Susan, you asked why Alex has not contacted you after you evicted him and accused him of abuse. Why do you think that Alex should be the one to initiate contact with you?

I am working on fleshing out some of the details of the incidents about which you last wrote. . . .

Susan did initiate contact with Alex and they wrote many letters to each other. She reported that she felt confused by the contrast of her memories and her feelings of love for Alex. She complained that she didn't think he was proud of her. As she had for me, she delved into details of his childhood. Why this fascination with our childhoods? It was months before I understood that "the notion of an intergenerational transmission of violence has become the premier developmental hypothesis in the field of abuse and neglect," even though longitudinal research has shown that the vast majority of children who are abused do not go on to repeat the offenses (Widom, 1989, p. 160).[5] Our daughter decided that Alex and I had been abused and that therefore her abuse must have happened.

New Year's Eve brought with it our thirty-third wedding anniversary. We kept our long planned dinner engagement. We did not tell our young companions. They would hate us, I thought. We could not tell them. Exercising the human spirit to endure, we put aside the madness and chatted about other things. It was a joy to be distracted for a few hours. Clearly, it was going to be important to maintain some part of life that didn't involve this insanity that could become so consuming.

Who Would Believe Us?

The problem, of course, with accusations of sexual abuse is that the accused person is assumed to be guilty. It's like the old "When did you stop beating your wife" problem. How do you prove a negative?[6] We live in a country in which people are supposed to be assumed innocent until proven guilty, but that is not the case with sex abuse. Even the legal system has changed on this highly charged subject – changed but at the same time neglecting to provide any mechanisms for the change. Many people find these changes dangerous and alarming. That's why groups like Victims of Child Abuse Laws (VOCAL) have formed. I was lucky, I thought, that I had a previous relationship with a wise and respected psychiatrist who already knew much about me. It wouldn't seem so shameful to talk to him. I was lucky, I thought, that we had the financial and educational resources to find qualified support.

As I have since learned, however, revelations of sexual abuse made many years after the fact are considered by some sex abuse therapists to be found in just such successful families. "He or she is likely to have pursued a higher education and to be successful in the professional or business world, often holding a very responsible job. Frequently, the person will be married and have children who may also appear to be well adjusted and asymptomatic" (Sgroi, 1988, p. 151).[7] Isn't there something inherently puzzling in this? Doesn't sex abuse cut across class, economic and professional distinctions? If abuse is more frequent in successful families, why do the data show increased abuse in times of economic down trends? Perhaps only people from successful families have "revelations." Are revelations of past sexual abuse only for the privileged and the educated? That seems hard to believe.

Alex and I had had our share of problems in the past. Alex's drinking had increased over the years, but at my pressure, he stopped a decade ago. That history didn't lessen the anxiety before we went to our early morning appointment. We were well aware of the connections between alcoholism and abuse. *Will the therapist believe me?* Alex asked. *When I met with him ten years ago, I assured him that there was no abuse of any kind,* I replied. But what did our story look like? We couldn't give any details. All we could say was that we had been expelled from Any City and that Alex had been accused of some sort of sexual abuse but we didn't know what. The fact that such an accusation was actually made, even if false, must be evidence of some terrible family trouble.

January 3
Dear Susan,

As a child you were one of the most adventurous and exploratory and energetic human beings I have ever met. You were also one of the most trusting. Our guiding philosophy, if you can call it that, was to try to provide environments in which those qualities could be nurtured, but environments in which you would be safe. Raising a child who was a teenager in the culture of the '60s was not the easiest of tasks. I worried more than you can ever understand and I had so many conflicts between my own conservative beliefs and the ambient culture or counter-culture pressures about what probably led to future happiness. You know how I disapproved of your taking drugs and you told me how old-fashioned I was when you embarked

upon your sexual explorations with a variety of
partners. Yet, all in all, we felt we had an easier
time than most of our peers. Valedictorian of
your class in addition to completing high school
in three years — your explorations seemed within
the bounds of the time and did not seem to hurt you.

The therapist listened. He probed. He empathized. He was obviously distressed by our situation. He was supportive. We should come back in a week. He would do some checking and he encouraged us to continue writing to Susan. He seemed surprised that we had not asked Susan to tell us who her therapist was since it was our understanding that the therapist had brought up the subject of incest, recommended that she read *The Courage to Heal*, and was the one who had made the diagnosis. We were still in emotional limbo as we received more painful details from Susan.

January 4
Dear Susan,
The letter that you wrote to Ralph when you
were living with him as a freshman in college is
terribly painful. It is heart wrenching to feel the
depths of your despair because of your hunger
and extreme desire to be thin, your anorexia. Is
that the evidence of abuse? You told me at the
time that Ralph wanted you thin. Why isn't your
relation with him a partial explanation for
your anorexia? What about your headstrong
decision to marry him when you were a senior
only to get divorced nine months later?
You asked me to respond to a story that you
wrote in the fifth grade. Is this your evidence

of sexual abuse? I must ask, "What was the assignment? What books had you been reading at the time?" Your story does not seem unusual to me given the lifetime I have spent reading children's stories.

Is the evidence of sexual abuse you think I missed your anorexia in freshman year at college? Your stories from the fifth grade? Your teenage journal entries?

January 6
Dear Susan,

Thank you for the information about calling a social service agency to find a therapist who is female, young, a clinical psychologist, and an expert with issues of sexual abuse — a therapist like yours. Thank you also for the reference in Courage to Heal *about what the "mother" is supposed to do and feel. I cannot lay all the blame on your father. I cannot blame anyone but myself for failing to see your pain and for being unaware of the terrible circumstances, the hell, you must have been living through. And the hell you are living through now. I am so sorry. I love you.*

I have had the feeling that ever since this sad business began, my daughter has been trying to fit me into the paradigm of the wife of a child abuser and I have found it insulting. Financial independence, academic and professional achievement, political activism are mine. What does Susan really know about the challenges to achieving these for women who came of age during the '50s? How much of the changed cultural expectations for women has she mapped on to me personally? Has she mistaken the fact that I viewed my professional options less broadly than she did hers as evidence that I am subjugated? So much does she try to put me in her image of the mother of an abused child that she even made the suggestion that I did not write my own letters.

The pain of her degradation of me has been profound. The insults in her letters, the accusations of my incompetence not only as a mother but also as a woman have created wounds that will be difficult to heal. But I have also understood that from her perspective it was necessary to dismiss me. Then it would be just her word against Alex's word. By thinking of Susan as temporarily deranged, I have been able to keep feelings of love alive, but I have not been able to find the same excuse for Steve.

On January 6, a full seventeen days after our eviction, we finally received the letter containing Susan's alleged details of her abuse. It was horrible. I responded.

> *January 7, 1991*
> *Dear Susan,*
>
> *My poor dear Susan. No one should have to have such secrets locked away. How horrible. My poor child. You have memories of being abused starting at age three, of being forced into sexual intercourse between ages fourteen and sixteen, of being raped at age sixteen a few days before you left for college. I struggle for understanding. My heart weeps for you. I am so sorry for you. Alex has no memories of all this. I have no memories of all this. In our small house, for so many years, how could all this have hap-*

*pened without my awareness? Finally you have
given us the details that you remember.
      I write my own letters. I'll tell you what I
remember about our early years. . . .
          I love you. I am struggling.*

It was crazy. None of this made any sense to me. Where
was I when all this was supposed to have taken place? How
could someone blot out thirteen years of incest going on in
a little house where every sound can be heard? How could
two people blot out the same thirteen years? No, this was
bizarre. This just didn't make any sense.

We had more to deal with at the next visit with our
therapist. We had the details of the accusation. During this
period our therapist had spoken to an expert on memory
who felt that it was highly unlikely that a sixteen-year-old
would repress memories such as Susan claimed. The expert had said he had recently been getting many other
such calls about accusations of sexual abuse from families
with a child claiming repressed memories and dissociation.
There is some comfort in learning that you are not the only
one to suffer the same situation, I guess. It occurred to me
that if this could happen to us, then our problem may
represent just the tip of an iceberg. *How many people
who are accused of sex abuse have either the resources
or the resolve to get even as far as a therapist?* I asked
Alex. The shame that comes with being accused of sexual
abuse is so intense that every inclination is to keep quiet
about it. Even if you know that it didn't happen, the pain
and the shame that your very own child is making such a
claim is so great that most parents we have heard about in
similar situations quickly disown and disinherit. It becomes
a way to survive.

At this point our therapist and the expert had no more than our word against Susan's word. *Would you be willing to take a lie detector test?* he asked. *The expert could arrange it.* Would Alex do it? You bet. Alex is a kind and a loving person. Whatever his faults, lack of courage to face the truth was not one. It was six very long weeks, however, until the test actually took place and his memories — or lack of the critical memories were confirmed. But what is the value of a lie detector test? We were still discussing it months later because our daughter felt it was irrelevant.

> *June 20, 1991*
> *Dear Susan,*
>
> *I know that such tests are not admitted into court as evidence and that they can be unreliable. I know that their reliability depends greatly on the administrator of the test and that they are more an art than a science. That is why we went to the effort and expense of paying for someone to come from Big City to do the test. The administrator has about as high a reputation for reliability in this field as anyone could have. The results of his tests are taken seriously by people in the field and by psychiatrists and lawyers.*
>
> *If you were to take a lie detector test on these issues, I would fully expect you to pass. You believe what you say about abuse. Whether accurate or delusions, you would pass a lie detector test. A lie detector test for you would give us no information. We agree that you believe what you say about your memories of abuse. It is, however, effective to administer such a lie detector test to the father in these cases.*

A lie detector test can give some determination as to what a person believes. Alex was being tested against what he said he believed. Alex said that he did not sexually abuse you. The lie detector test showed that he believes what he said and is not lying. Thus, for him to have abused you means that he would have had to repress all the memories. He has no history of blackouts, memory loss, or physical aggression.

We are left then with the following: the situation that Alex is lying (less probable given the lie detector test) or that two people repressed exactly the same memories that extend over a period of thirteen years. What do you think is the probability for that — memories that would have been highly charged for both. What is that probability when coupled with the fact that no one else seems to have had a clue that all this was going on?

Until the lie detector test we remained in limbo. We were relieved when Susan's twenty-seven-year-old sister, Sandra, whose bedroom had been next to Susan's, told us that she personally had no memories of Susan's sexual abuse. She certainly had told none of her friends at the time. But we were heartbroken to hear her say, *in my experience, people don't make up stories like that. Susan must be telling the truth.* Sandra's "experience" was from hearing the stories of other women in the 12-Step self-help groups in which she participates and from reading *The Courage to Heal* which someone in one of her groups had recommended to her. Until the lie detector test, we had only our story, but our friends believed us. Alex had a reputation for telling the truth. In fact colleagues frequently complained that Alex told the truth even when others did not want to hear it.

Imagine, just a few months earlier, I would probably have assumed that if someone were accused of such a crime, he would in all likelihood be guilty. We were not especially happy to learn that under the law of our state, Susan had two years in which she could bring legal charges after her mid-life revelation. Legal charges! Had Susan's therapist made a formal report of her diagnosis because of mandatory reporting laws on sexual abuse? We still do not know the answer to that question. Do we have any rights at all in all of this?

To the Library

I had a need to know more and I desperately wanted to keep contact with Susan. I found security in the familiar stacks of the library. Article by article, book by book, shelf by shelf I went trying to grasp some larger picture.

January 10

Dear Susan,

I am curious about your therapist for a number of reasons. I love you and want you to have the very best care. My concern was first raised by being informed that (a) the therapist had raised the subject of incest rather than taking it from you and (b) that you have been using hypnosis. There is much debate about the reliability of memories recalled under those circumstances. Also, I am aware that there is a Clinical Incest Group in Any City whose members enter the

therapeutic situation with the bias that 50% of
their patients will not remember sexual abuse
and incest and so the therapist has to draw it
out. This is outlined in a book by Maltz and
Holman[8] who have many followers in Any City.
Don't you think that there might be some dan-
gers in such preconceived assumptions?
I am puzzled by your desire not to let us know
who your therapist is. What are you trying to
hide? I do hear you. I love you. I can feel your
pain and hurt.

In the library I awakened to the social and political
dangers of the current crusade to wipe out sexual abuse.
Belief that the "rightness" of one's cause justifies any means
is an eternal danger. It goes without saying that human
beings should not abuse each other, sexually or any other
way. Zealots who lead crusades based on their belief of
their own moral virtue and superiority have a history of
bringing much repression to the world.

I found an overabundance of "slop," articles and books
in which the authors lack respect for the bounds between
therapy and politics and in which they pander to emotions. *The Courage to Heal*, which Susan referred to as a
bible, on page 22 tells the reader, "If you think you were
abused and your life shows the symptoms, then you were."
This is a political statement, not a scientific one. There
does not exist empirical evidence to support such an assumption. In fact, there is actually much dispute in the
literature on just what signs actually are related to sexual
abuse. These signs were so broadly defined in most of the
sex abuse articles, however, that some of them could
certainly be found at various times in most people.

Due to memory loss, only about half of female incest survivors in your practice may be able to identify themselves as victims during your initial inquiry. . . . If you suspect the possibility of childhood sexual abuse based on physical symptoms and other clues, even when the patient has no conscious memory of sexual violation, share this information with your patient. . . .set the stage for hidden memories of incest to surface. . . . (some of the signs) Physical problems: chronic pelvic pain, spastic colon, stomach pain, headache, dizziness, fainting, chronic gynecologic complaints, sleep disturbances, depression, asthma, heart palpitations.

(Maltz, 1990, p. 45).[9]

Belief in these signs of sexual abuse represents very muddled thinking on the part of therapists. I learned that the signs referred to are based on symptoms described in "post-traumatic stress disorders." Writers like the authors of *The Courage to Heal* have taken these signs and reinterpreted them to predict that sexual abuse had actually occurred if any of the signs are evident in a patient. Just because known victims of sexual abuse may suffer from anorexia, obesity, or sexual problems, it does not follow that having anorexia,[10] obesity, or sexual problems implies that a person was sexually abused as they assume. There are too many other circumstances in life in which people display these symptoms.

Fortunately, I also found some literature that did not seem to pander and which attempted to document arguments with research. It was a great relief to find "Accusations of Child Sexual Abuse"[11] and "Witness for the Defense"[12] for example. The problem, however, was that this body of work pertained only to accusations made by young children. There was a void when it came to current research articles about women claiming to have had revelations of long past sexual abuse even though the manuals for treatment of this condition have proliferated. Even so, if the evidence of recent research showed that adult eye-witness testimony is not always reliable and if the evidence of recent research showed that children's memories were not always reliable, how could therapists, trained and certified, be so sure that women who had gone for years without remembering could suddenly have memories that were always accurate?

Gaining some sense of perspective and security from the reading, Alex and I finally broke our silence and began to tell a few of our friends, our older friends. One couple in particular provided the love and emotional support that we needed to keep up our fight to love our daughter and not take shelter by disowning or disinheriting her. The wife, an outspoken feminist, was deeply concerned about the effects on the women's movement if many false accusations such as ours began to take place. She gave me a recommendation of a young therapist, a social worker, who specialized in sexual abuse matters. The social worker was described as a very fair person and sounded like the kind of person Susan had been asking me to see. Perhaps if I spoke with this woman, Susan would know that I was trying to understand.

I was excited and hopeful on the drab February afternoon before the appointment. I certainly did not expect this young therapist's absolute belief that Susan's story must be true. *Children don't lie about these things,* she said. But, Susan was not a child. She was a thirty-three-year-old woman entering mid-life. Is a thirty-three-year-old woman incapable of delusions? "It is so painful for a person to remember these things that she would never invent them. It is just too painful." I asked, "What is the research evidence for all this?" She replied, "It's all so new. We're just getting to the point where women are not afraid to talk about these secrets." She was anti-Freud but seemed not to know Freud's work, and she gave me a publication from *Women Organized Against Rape* from 1980 that stated the feminist position that family-oriented therapy in incest put the responsibility on a faulty family rather than on the offender.[13] The feminist position is that only the adult male offender is at fault. Then I began to wonder if one side effect of Masson's critique of Freud (1984)[14] was to give feminists the additional idea that anyone making a claim of long repressed memories of childhood sexual abuse is to be believed? *Hey! I'm against rape and incest too,* I screamed silently. Didn't she see the irony in her argument that if some memories are too painful for people to invent and thus must be true, then it had to follow that these very same actions would surely be too horrible for someone to actually do and thus are to be disbelieved. Unless, that is, she actually believed that men were capable of thinking and doing these things but that women were not. Both points are unsupportable.

I was crushed. It was hard to get out of the office fast enough to get away from this woman whose melodious voice was overflowing with patronizing sympathy for my plight. She was pitying *me* because I was a victim! I was so crushed at this woman's total disbelief in my own recollections that for the first time I thought that life was not going to be worth living if this was the kind of reaction I was going to get. I lost all hope. I cried. I thought of suicide. I felt profoundly insulted. *I can deal with rape or incest,* I thought, *but I cannot deal with being a non-person.* Neither my daughter nor this therapist seemed to feel that

I was a conscious conspirator in all that was supposed to have happened. Instead there was the assumption that I was "out of it," was somehow absent as a sentient human being and was pitiful and of no account. Young women seeking therapy claiming – after explicit probing and perhaps even hypnosis – to have long repressed memories of sex abuse were to be believed, while older women whose lives have attained some balance and a semblance of order were not to be trusted to have reliable memories or judgment. Is this what the feminist movement had come to? My despair turned to anger and the anger to action. I set as a goal to change this one young woman's view of the situation. I returned after the lie detector test. She spent a long time reading every word of the copy that I brought with me. Like me, she had never seen the results of a lie detector test before. She admitted doubt. Surely, now our daughter and her husband would come to their senses too. But that was not to be.

April 12

Dear Steve,

You feel that the e-mail interaction is driving Susan and me apart. I would support alternative interaction that would help to resolve this. I would have stayed and had joint counseling at Christmas. I would talk on the phone. Once Susan, as she herself wrote, finally got "bored" with keeping the name of her therapist from us, we tried to get her therapist to talk to ours. You and Susan have set the limits on the conditions of communication, not me.

I never said anything about a "conspiracy." I know of no conspiracy. Maltz, in her book, thanks and lists the members of the group who have been working with "adult survivors." I have tried to make the point that the general climate around the issue of sexual abuse is highly charged and political. For a number of years, for example, therapists have insisted that children don't lie about these things. Yet there have been many false accusations of sexual abuse. In fact, in the March 4 issue of TIME *there is a short rehash of the subject with the information that the "controversy is sure to escalate this spring, when the American Psychological Association publishes a book called* The Suggestibility of Children's Recollections." *There is even more controversy about the validity of repressed memories and dissociation.*

Steve, it seems that there is nothing that we can do. You are convinced by the "gestalt of symptoms." I just am not impressed by your list of symptoms:

● *Anorexia: That could have many different underlying causes.*

● *Susan uses a fan at night to sleep: Some people take sleeping pills.*

● *She has difficulty dealing with your family: Until this, she got along just fine with us. I can't follow your logic here.*

● *Childhood stories: These were reinterpreted by people looking for evidence, not given blind evaluation.*

● *Susan chose to leave your former town when she was not given tenure: That is the usual response to not getting tenure. Frankly, I think you are having difficulty accepting the fact that she chose her career over your stated preferences.*

Are We the Only Ones?

As I have asked and asked myself how this could have happened to us, a family that was loving for so many years, a family that shared so much of life even after the children had grown and the responsibilities shifted, I have made lots of lists of possible reasons. Of course the truth will be somewhere in the shuffle of a whole context of interacting factors. Nevertheless, my explanations seem to fall into four general categories: our faults as parents, some physical problem, stresses my daughter and her husband have been under, cultural context.

● Have Alex and I failed as a parents? I can't help but ask this question. I can think of a million things that I would do better a second time around if life let me sign on again. But in spite of this terrible mess, I really don't think that Alex or I did fail. We can all only do our best as we muddle through life. We did our best with what we knew at the time, and until the "revelation" that was better than OK. Agonizing over whether I should have interfered more or interfered less or done this or done that is not going to get anywhere now. We simply don't know what the result of other decisions might have been. Agonizing after the fact in a situation not to be replayed is a waste of effort. Who could it help?

● We have learned a tremendous amount in recent decades about the biological bases of many behaviors. The chemistry of a host of behaviors such as depression is beginning to be laid bare. Our culture approaches so many problems from this perspective – "Take a pill. Feel better." I can't assume that Susan's problem is chemical any more than I can assume it is emotional. I would feel better, though, if I knew that she had had a complete physical examination.

● I know that Susan has been under tremendous stress on many fronts. She has cried out in her letters her feelings of having been violated and her feelings of inadequacy. She begged for our belief and approval. She accused me of not hearing. But I have heard and as her mother been privy to so many shared confidences, I happen to see other more immediate reasons for her stress. Some of the thoughts that have gone through my head:

About Her Feelings of Inadequacy:

We did have very high standards and expectations about her achievement, but our love and respect did not depend on grades or honors. Intellectual families tend to be achievement oriented. We have been tremendously proud of her achievements, but our pride is greater because we have seen Susan make the world a little bit better than she has found it. But, yes, I think that some of her stress was because she wanted us to be proud of her work.

Academics are expected to publish. When one college did not give her tenure, lack of major publications was cited. Susan had a grant last year to write but no major work appeared. Could she feel inadequate because of that?

Steve wrote to us this spring that he had *"begged Susan not to bully me into moving to Any City"* when she had an offer of tenure there. How much of the stress that she was under was because she felt responsible for the move and responsible for the fact that Steve was so very unhappy in his job? Steve always seems so dependent on Susan for everything.

Could Susan be feeling inadequate because Steve's un-happiness had translated into lack of sexual interest?

When Paul was a year and a half, Susan confided to me that she didn't know how to stop nursing. There was the move and all . . . A year later she was still nursing Paul. Could this be related to the issue of incest? Could the nursing be a substitute for something missing with Steve?

Could Susan be exhausted and frustrated from the problems of trying to find adequate day care for the past seven years? I know, because she told me, that she sometimes wished that she could just stay home and be with her children. Could she be under stress because she felt torn between her work and her children?

Four women my age have independently suggested to me that perhaps Susan felt extra stress and inadequacy because I had recently had tremendous professional success. They suggested that she had an image of me that did not include serious, visible success and that this might have been a trigger for the timing of her revelation. No man has suggested this. No younger woman has suggested this. I don't know.

About Her Feelings of Having Been Violated:

The earthquake severely damaged the house in which Susan was living last year. One whole section had to be blocked off. The traumatic effects of the earthquake were obvious to many people who were with Susan. Even before her revelation, I felt that she was especially upset because the bed in which I had been sleeping while visiting her, less than 24 hours before the quake, was virtually destroyed by the hundreds of books and four huge bookcases that had fallen on it. Earthquakes violate.

Susan told me that in October a student who was supposed to have completed work for a joint conference presentation had not done so. Would she feel betrayed by this person? Is there a connection in this to the fact that the student's excuse was that she had been sexually abused by a professor?

Susan came to visit me for three days with the children in October on her way to a wedding. It was during the week. I had thought that I would have more time to be with her than it turned out that I had. The obligations that came with the recent changes in my work had surprised and overwhelmed me. Susan told me that she was hurt because I didn't have more time for her.

Is "violation" a feeling that comes when tenure doesn't? But she got tenure at a better place. Yet, it is well known that issues involving tenure are exacerbated for women.

However we may have initially shaped it, Susan has ultimately created her own adult life and she is responsible for it. I can understand latching onto an explanation that gets both Susan and Steve "off the hook" as it were. One person even suggested to me that Susan felt so close and secure in her relationship to Alex and me that she knew at some level that even with the horrid accusation we would still be there. It is a thought that had occurred to me but seemed too self-serving to maintain. I would feel so much better if I knew that Susan had had a second consultation with a politically neutral older therapist of either gender. For any other serious medical problem, a second opinion is recommended. Why not for therapy if the diagnosis is as serious and devastating to all involved as incest?

● I suspect that the contemporary cultural and social climate has set the scene for what has happened to us. Susan went to a therapist when she was vulnerable. Could she have been especially susceptible to suggestion in those circumstances? Research is full of examples of how people are influenced by the expectations of the people they are with and by the way that questions are posed. To be against child sexual abuse is a "politically correct" position, especially for activist women. To be a "victim" of something is almost a social necessity on college campuses. So much support and so much zeal abound for such accusations that more and more unjust ones, such as in our case, are being made.[15] The current climate surrounding child sexual abuse is so politically charged that it has even been referred to as a "witch hunt."[16] I have come to believe that our very sad situation happened because my daughter's mental stress happened at this particular time and place in history.

June 29
Dear Susan,
We really do seem to have reached a stalemate of your memory vs Alex's and my memory. I am sure that is why you have to keep trying to put me in the position of being a "dodo," a nonsentient, pathetic being, who was unaware of all that was happening to you and thus did not save you. If I won't support your belief that you were abused, and if you dismiss me, it is just your word against Alex's and the climate is such that most people will probably believe you — at least for a while.

But think of what you know about memory. Memory is reconstruction. Memories can be altered. Memories recalled in a time of present personal depression are known to be reinterpreted in a highly negative fashion. Memories recalled in a time of happiness are likewise positively interpreted. This is the way human memories work. Memories are reconstructed in

terms of the facts and they are re-interpreted in
terms of their emotional impact.
I love you Susan.

Getting on with Life

How have I coped? In November, Susan lovingly sent us boxes of pears from the tree in her yard so we could share. In December, Alex spent days turning the pears into candy for Susan. A few weeks later, a phone call from her husband, Steve, took all the sweetness from our lives. I really don't know how I have coped, but somehow I have, better than I would have predicted. Certainly the love and respect that Alex and I share for each other is the foundation. I have gained a new understanding of the depth of our relationship. My sense of humor affords perspective and most of the time a positive view of life. Our friends, therapists, and the caring people I have met both in person and through the literature in my quest for understanding have made living through the past six months possible.

Turning my anger to action has surely helped. That has translated into writing this article. I don't really want the world to know what a rotten mess has taken place in my life but perhaps, by sharing my story, others will become alerted to the fact that false accusations of sexual abuse are being made and that the results of such accusations result in major tragedies for all the people involved but especially for the person making the charge. I write this because I am disturbed at the lack of critical thinking that seems to abound in the area of sexual abuse in people who are otherwise very rational. I write this because I am concerned about how ready the population is to accuse people of sexual abuse. The media has whipped people into a frenzy on the subject. I write this anonymously only because with all my heart I hope that we will be reunited with Susan and I don't want to embarrass her.

I don't feel angry at Susan, although sometimes I just want to shake her to get some sense in her head. I am, however, very angry with her young therapist whom I know only through the few defensive comments that Susan has shared. I suppose it is to be expected that I would want to blame the therapist instead of my daughter. Susan may have been vulnerable when she went to this person, but she deliberately chose a therapist who represented a strong feminist political perspective rather than a therapist who was family oriented on issues of sexual abuse. I feel that something is terribly amiss, even so. From my perspective the therapist seems to lack wisdom, compassion, understanding, and basic scientific knowledge of memory and mind that should be a prerequisite for a license to practice psychology. Probably, in fact, she is just young (thirty-two), inexperienced, and full of righteous anger at all the sexual abuse of women in the world.

Concerns

To me it seems immoral, even so, that this woman has been willing to label Alex as a criminal, but unwilling to make a phone call to talk to us. Is that how it is supposed to be in therapy? I have noticed in the magazine and newspaper accounts that many revelations involve accusations of abuse by fathers who are dead. Is that why the therapist and Susan will not talk to us? Is cowardice in a new wrapper? Do therapists not have the courage to face the people they hastily accuse and whose lives they destroy?

To me, it seems cruel that the therapist advised Susan to tell our grandsons that Alex had done terrible things to her and that Alex and I had been keeping terrible secrets about it for many years. Can it possibly be good for a two- or five-year-old to be told that a grandparent that he has loved is really a monster? How can a young child digest information like that? Wouldn't it have been better to tell the children that we were dead? We live six hours away by plane and saw the children at most three times a year in their parents' home. Where is the rational thinking in believing there was danger to warrant giving such information to children – even believing in the alleged events of thirty years past? What was the reason for such advice? It seems so unnecessarily cruel to my grandsons.

To me, it seems slanderous that the therapist advised Susan to tell the children's teachers that we had been abusers. Never even a phone call to us? Never a check about a distraught young woman's dramatic revelations? Such arrogance in her own diagnostic ability!

To me, it is irresponsible to have made such a serious diagnosis on the limited information that was available.

To me it seems unethical to give a patient a book as suggestive as *The Courage to Heal* before a client has had a clear revelation of her own abuse.

To me it seems incompetent to have made such a diagnosis given what is known about the vagaries of human memory. It seems incompetent that a psychologist whose training is supposed to be "scientific" would recommend a book to clients whose premise is without empirical foundation: "If you think you were abused, then you were."

To me this whole episode seems cruel and unnatural and unnecessary. For the last four months material to be used in filing complaints against this therapist has taken space on the right hand corner of my desk. My inaction is only because people I respect warned that it might jeopardize an eventual reconciliation with Susan.

I am very angry with Steve although Alex says, *Don't be. He can't help it.* I am angry that Steve did not provide the kind of buffer that I think Susan needed. I am angry that the best reasons he can come up with for believing the memories are: (1) *because of circumstantial evidence and parsimony*, (2) *all of a sudden I had a single explanation that neatly predicted most of the neuroses*, and (3) *I have been unable to come up with any alternative explanation for the memories she reports.* It's hard to argue with reasons like that. The fact that Susan's "explicit" memories are full of contradictions, that the timing of the alleged rape makes it impossible to have happened, for example, mean nothing to Steve. He believes.

I am angry with the establishment that has been responsible for the training and certification of my daughter's therapist — training that has resulted in Susan being in the terrible position that she is now, rather than having been guided in a more gentle way through her disturbance. It seems wrong to me that clinical training programs and certifications boards license therapists to deal with issues of the human mind without assuring that they have an understanding of the reasonable limits of what they might legitimately know. That is giving license to incompetence. It seems wrong to me that programs do not ensure that therapists grasp the ethics involved in imposing their opinions on patients. That is giving license to unethical behavior. I am going to work to change that.

I am going to get on with my life because I think that will be the best for my daughter. I will wait for her. I cannot change what has happened and I am not going to let it destroy the good things in my life. If Susan makes a sincere opening, I will accept it. A few weeks ago she asked if I would go to Any City for joint therapy. She gave me a list of conditions for this "test": I was to come alone and stay in a hotel, I could not go to her house, I could not be alone with my grandsons, I would meet her with her therapist, I would be free to leave if I wished, I might not see her again after one session. I offered to meet her in some neutral place of her choice with no conditions. She could not accept that. I offered to stay with friends in Any City. Then, Susan said she did not think the time was yet right for me to come.

I am about to put this story in the mail. In the same mail I will post a letter to Susan's therapist inviting her to talk to us and offering to pay for her air fare and time to come to our city under any conditions with which she feels comfortable to see for herself the little house in which the alleged abuse was supposed to have taken place, to meet the people who knew Susan as she was growing up, to see three hours of tapes from the lie detector test. Wouldn't Susan be the beneficiary from the insights we gain from each other? Isn't it appropriate that we speak inasmuch as the diagnosis of incest has so totally devastated our lives?

July 12
Dear Susan,

    I will come when you want me to. I have deep sadness for the lovely, kind, brilliant 33-year-old woman who now has such terrible memories and who sees her parents as people to fear.

                             Love, Mom

For citations to this story, see p. 335.

A Personal Account of "The Accusation"

The Background

My husband, Fred, came out of Germany – a child of the Holocaust – in 1939. I was born in New York and raised in a poor but upwardly-mobile environment with an emphasis on education and the arts. My husband and I are in our late fifties. We have been friends since we attended the same high school. We had a family – three daughters who are bright, artistic, and musically talented. They traveled to Europe and across America and were very involved in academic and cultural activities.

Our children were supported in all their endeavors. They were enlightened and enjoyed our many intellectual soirees with members of the academic and art worlds. My husband works as a designer. I have taught art, special education, kindergarten, and Chinese cooking. My eldest daughter, Carol, thirty-nine, majored in history, Phi Beta Kappa at Berkeley and then went on to become a lawyer. She was a proficient classical guitarist. My middle daughter, Dierdre, thirty-five, was a good student with an art degree. My youngest, Penny, twenty-six, was a musical prodigy, gave concerts at Lincoln Center and went to law school. She is presently a lawyer; her sister Carol was her mentor.

We had our holiday gatherings, our loving moments and our blowups. Six years ago my husband started drinking in the evening. (The children no longer lived at home.) My intentions were good when I asked Fred to go to Alcoholics Anonymous. He did go and told the children and so they went to Adult Children of Alcoholics meetings. It was there that they heard stories of beatings, incest and that one does not have to drink to display alcoholic behavior — a "dry alcoholic." They equated their father's occasional temper tantrums with his being a "dry alcoholic" and labeled me an "enabler." They learned about dysfunctional families and "toxic parents."

Carol, the oldest, was attracted to this group of many young people who were seeking revenge because of their havoc-ridden childhood due to alcohol. Her imagination soared and she began to see herself in many of the stories. She identified! She had just adopted a little girl and was feeling many strange emotions. Carol already had a six-year-old natural son. A member of AA suggested that Carol see a social worker who *specialized* in hypnosis and regression therapy. The member also suggested that Carol may have been molested as a child. After several sessions with this therapist, the revelation that my daughter was sexually abused by her parents was established. The book *The Courage to Heal* was suggested as a reading to understand the issue. My daughter now became a regular member at *incest* support groups.

The Confrontation

In November of 1988, I was told not to visit for Thanksgiving or to call my daughter's (Carol's) home. She would be in Big City on May 15, 1989 (Mother's Day) with her husband and therapist. I could have a therapist and/or friend present at a meeting that we would have at that time. This affected our relationship with our other daughters. My middle daughter refused to see us. (She was married with a young daughter.) We agonized over the shut-door policy and were stunned. The day arrived with my husband and me holding on to one bit of information offered us by my youngest child. We were told it was a sexual issue and that we were both involved. The therapist, Carol and her husband came to my home. Carol and her husband greeted us with the normal hugs and kisses, though somewhat restrained. I had two childhood friends (one a psychologist) present.

Carol was soon on the verge of hysterics. I served tea to the assembled guests. Carol was tense but managed to deliver a well-rehearsed speech . . . pausing appropriately to make her accusations, pointing a finger at her father and me.

She said that through hypnosis she was able to remember that she was molested by a stranger in the backyard when she was eight. She said she didn't tell us back then because she knew that we wouldn't care. Then she regressed further and claimed to remember that her mother inserted objects into every aperture of her body while her father held her down on the kitchen table under the lights. "You continued to do that to me for years," she cried, "my father always loved you better than me and did whatever you wanted him to do."

She claimed that I was a "codependent" and that, therefore, she had acted as the mother to me and her little sisters. I recovered my voice and said that I revered and respected her all her life. "Why would I do such brutal things to harm you?" I asked. "Because you were such a prude, you wanted me not to turn out like you," she answered. "You made me promiscuous . . . you made me want sex all the time." I almost passed out. (I held off until they left and then I did something I have never done in my life . . . I fainted!) My friends made me promise that I would not be emotional . . . I would maintain my cool . . . no matter what was said. However, as the ugly accusations continued, I began to cry. Carol said later I cried because of my guilt. She never understood that I cried for my sick daughter. She continued . . . her father always wanted to rape her but that he only started when she was thirteen. My husband was livid. I asked if she had seen the movie *Sybil* since much of her story was so similar to what happened in that film. The social worker, Karen Brown, intervened. "I helped her remember the past," she stated. I was furious at the lies Karen accepted as true and perhaps had helped implant in my daughter's mind through her therapy.

My husband expressed his feelings when he could regain his composure, after the shock of the terrible accusations. He said he may not have been a perfect father. He was very young to be a father. "As you grew up and we discussed social and political issues, I loved your mind and we became close. I was not a child-oriented parent like your mother but I respected my children, albeit from a distance. I worked hard to give you kids everything I could. How can you do this to your mother? She was devoted to all of you. You were her whole world. How can you do this to her?" Carol jumped up and cried, "You always loved her more than me! You always stuck up for her." I rushed to my daughter's side. Her husband had his arm around her, rubbing her back. "Carol, this is all a fantasy," I said. "Like from a bad dream." I asked her husband if he remembered saying when my grandson was born that I was the quintessential grandmother? He looked down. "For God's sake, be rational," I said.

My friend, the psychologist, told Karen and Carol that their truth is not necessarily the ultimate truth and he began to tell what he knew about my husband and me as people and parents. My girlfriend did the same. I went on to explain that our house was an open house to all the friends and family. . . an open door to everyone. We were not perverts. We respected and adored our children. Carol's husband sat with his arms around her. I suddenly felt angry – I wanted to shake her, even smack her (which I never, ever did) for this was my reward for all the years of making her the center of our household. Everyone looked up to her. Her brains, her talent, her beauty were admired by the whole family. Her joyousness, her bubbliness was a trademark.

Further along in the conversation, she blurted out, "I couldn't sleep with my husband anymore. Now I keep getting pains in my insides and I couldn't have a second child because you destroyed me." "That's enough," I said. "You had tumors on your ovaries and your scar tissue from the operations prevented you from conceiving a second child. How did you ever have a first child if your insides were destroyed?" I asked. Hit with logic, she cried, "Confess . . . confess! You are in denial and have buried what you did to me!" she yelled. She held her hands to her chest and threw them in a grand gesture towards me. "I TAKE MY SHAME AND GIVE IT ALL BACK TO YOU." Karen looked on supportively. My girlfriend said, "Carol, your mother idolized you. You were the apple of her eye. I have known you since you were an infant." Carol jumped up and screamed, running to the door. "LIARS . . . LIARS, all of you." She grabbed a vase and smashed it to the floor, saying, "That's for all you have done to me." She walked out and her husband followed but I stopped Karen. I asked, "Did this begin when she adopted a baby?" "Why, yes, it did," she replied. Looking a little surprised. "You know," I said, "when she was four, Carol was bitten by many green sand bugs and her buttocks were covered by infected bites. My friend, who was a registered nurse, said that rather than scaring her at the doctor's office she would lance the boils and medicate them at home. We agreed and my husband and I comforted her and held her gently while the boils were lanced. She cried quite a bit but she healed. I knew it was traumatic. Could she be translating that incident to this mess?" No answer. Karen Brown walked out the door. When they left I fainted for the first time in my life.

The Whole Family Suffers

Carol's grandmother escaped the Holocaust. Because she stands by her son, Carol will not speak to her. She is eighty-five years old and is heartbroken.

Fred and I went through many stages . . . pity . . . anger . . . fury. I wrote letters. I went to the library to read about molested children. She never fitted any profile. I explained . . . I sent her happy childhood pictures. She closed all avenues and got an unpublished number . . . told us all correspondence will go into the garbage . . . When we were ready to confess, to call Karen. The hold this woman had on my daughter was incredible. My daughter became completely dependent on her. Karen could never understand that those lies were causing us such torment. I tried to call Karen several weeks later. I spoke to her answering machine. I had bronchitis and laryngitis and I feebly tried to speak, telling this woman about Carol's childhood. I heard she told my daughter that I sounded like a crazy person. So much for professional compassion on her part. She never returned my call.

At first, my other two children were caught up in this madness.

My youngest daughter swayed back and forth until she recently came home to live with us. Now she believes us completely and is very troubled due to years of her sister rationalizing how we were truly molesters. People tell me Carol uses her excellent skills as an attorney to accuse us of vile things. My very own younger sister who has lived through trying times (we lost our parents and sister to terrible deaths) has gone to Carol's aid. She was threatened, as were my other children, that any contact with us automatically puts her out of the picture.

People tell us that Carol has completely flipped. Carol now accuses us of Satanism. She claims that when the girls were little, we did things with animals, and we put their hands in blood . . . that my husband is not the father of our youngest daughter, that my husband tried to rape the middle daughter and knocked Carol unconscious when she tried to stop him. This is material all gathered by a team of therapists she is presently "recovering" under. Carol is no longer speaking to her two sisters for having contact with us. Carol was told by the therapists to discard anyone in the family who does not believe her.

My son-in-law is caught up with what textbooks call *folie a deux* (folly for two). He will not speak to us. He yelled at my middle daughter for inviting us to Florida where the two sisters live a mile from each other. "I needed to hide the children from your parents," he reprimanded. What kind of therapists try to separate families with hate and anger? My grandson is also affected. He used to be a bright, healthy youngster who adored us. Now he hates us and is kept away from us.

In these last years I have become a diabetic, have high blood pressure and am suffering from heart and stress problems. The therapists have destroyed our lives with age-regression hypnosis that recalls so-called memories that are *not true.*

Fortunately, two of our daughters now understand what has happened, but their lives, too, have been affected. They bear the scars of this tragedy that has happened to our family.

From Somewhere in Oregon . . . We Lost Our Daughter Through Psychological Counseling

We have lost our wonderful daughter through psychological counseling. Until two-and-a-half years ago, my daughter, age twenty-eight, and I were very close. In fact, she was close to our whole family. She was an easy child to raise and later worked diligently for her nursing degree.

She went to a marriage and family therapist for counseling two-and-a-half years ago. Our daughter had felt very depressed. She may have experienced burnout, or it may be some form of mental illness. She was depressed on and off during her teens, but not as badly. She was wrongly diagnosed. We think that her therapist was over-zealous, and induced memories that our daughter had been sexually molested as a child.

Our daughter told me that, when she went to therapy, the counselor told her right away, "I know just what's wrong with you. You were sexually molested as a child." Our daughter said, "Oh, no. I'm sure I wasn't." But after more "therapy" from this woman, our daughter began believing it, and she thought it was so neat that her therapist knew right from the start what was wrong with her. Our daughter said that her therapist said, "It's usually done by the father in the family." She was trying to get our daughter to "remember." *She was beginning to have what she called "memories."* I questioned my husband, and he said absolutely not. He had never ever sexually molested her or any of our children. I believed him completely.

The therapist took our little girl to a private sex abuse center in Big City. They believed her so-called "memories" and carried on from there with therapy making her punch punching bags to get her hate out at her perpetrators. They developed an awful anger in her. *She will not see us anymore.*

The tragedy is that none of these "memories" happened. Those aren't "memories" she's having. *Then she began having "memories" that we were cult members and devil worshipers and that we cut up babies and sacrificed them.* She is being driven out of her mind. Last Christmas I sent her some shoes and she cut them all up, carved into the soles and sent them home. She thought she had to do that to keep from getting a demon. She thought we were putting a curse on her. At Christmas, when we saw her, *she had to have the therapist at her side* who, after our daughter's accusations, kept telling us, "that's right, you did molest your daughter, and that's right, you did, you did, cut up those babies. You're just repressing it."

We are Christians from many generations back. We have never had anything to do with devil worship.

We wanted to go down there when our little girl was at the sex abuse center, but we were told it would be better if we didn't. We were not included in therapy even though they claim to practice family therapy. The therapist will not see us or answer our phone calls. We've tried for a year. If she's a family therapist, it seems she would include us.

Our daughter is very suggestible, trusting, and believing. We feel she was talked into those things easily, at a time when she was already burned out and depressed. Those "memories" seem so real to our daughter, but we know for sure they aren't memories.

After the Divorce

My story began as a seventeen-year-old junior in high school with a pregnant girlfriend. We married on March 8, 1952, and I continued on in school the following year to graduate. My wife quit school and did not graduate. Only within the last ten years did she obtain her G.E.D.

We did not have a happy marriage but I did stay married until all of our three daughters married. After their marriages, two of my daughters had very little to do with my ex-wife. She had been a very demanding person and showed little respect for their ideas. She wouldn't even let them in the kitchen to cook as she felt they could do nothing right.

In fact, when I divorced my wife, the kids questioned me why I took so much abuse and remained married for so many years (twenty-eight). I told them I felt it was my obligation to stay married to keep the family together. I remarried a younger woman soon after my divorce, whom all the kids got along with—even though she was younger than my two oldest daughters.

My second oldest daughter, Lucy, had problems with her marriage and divorced. She is also a graduate in psychology from the University of Wisconsin in Madison, where she continues to live.

In the fall of 1989, she called me down to Madison as she was having a problem coping with her divorced life. (She and I have always been very close and I'd always drop everything to go down to help her.) We went back to her apartment where she discussed the abuse her mother had given her and her other two sisters. I told her I was not aware of abuse and I should have been told. She related how her hair had been pulled and she'd been hit on numerous occasions. The hair-pulling related to when she had her ponytail done. It was held with a rubber band.

She also felt her mother had tried to drown her while washing her hair. I was there most times and know this is untrue. She seemed assured after I told her to forget the past and if she still had a problem with "Mother" to just visit her less or not at all.

It was not until my second wife left me that I received a letter from Lucy in November 1990 in which incest was mentioned. I didn't even finish reading the letter before I called her. My question was basically this: Who in our family was responsible for this? Was it mother, sisters, either grandmother or grandfather, or which other relative? I told her it surely wasn't me, so who?

Her reply was, "Think about it, if it wasn't you, who else was there?" She then hung up on me. I called Children's Protection Agency to find out what to do, because if it was my ex-wife, I wanted to go after her and have her seek counseling.

It took me a couple of days to think about how to approach my ex-wife to discuss this with her. She had been abused by her mother, a person who drank heavily. So I took her to lunch to discuss the possibility of her being sexually abused by her folks. She claimed not and I believe her. I then received a letter from Lucy in which she claimed I was the person who raped her since age three. I showed this letter to my oldest daughter, Vicki, and she was dumb-founded. She said someone was always there, either mother or other sisters, so she felt this was wrong. In her letter, Lucy said she didn't want me to contact her ever again and so far I haven't.

Until today. And all I did was to ask for the name and address of her therapist. I had asked previously but was not given this information.

I want to have a family discussion with all members of my family to discuss what is going on. If someone is to blame for actual incest, it has to come out and be discussed. My daughter needs help, and I have neither the time or finances to follow through.

I personally feel that no incest took place but was instead manufactured by her therapist. One reason for my thinking is this: The therapist moved from Madison to Milwaukee some 100 miles away. Lucy wouldn't even consider another therapist. She evidently is hooked as she goes to him (or her) several times a month.

A Mother in Deep Sorrow

It was two days before Thanksgiving and it was a warm day for this time of year. I was grateful because I had a lot to do to get ready for the big day, and I did not want snow interfering with all I had planned. I was also grateful that I lived near my job so I could dash home for lunch. I had planned "lunch on the run," because I wanted to get to the bank and also pick up the turkey. After work, all I had to do was get a few more items from the store. My head was filled with pumpkin pies, dressing, and cranberry sauce. My husband always wanted the traditional dinner. I made a big mistake – one of many that day – when I looked in the mailbox. I usually don't when I am in a hurry. I never made it back to work that day or for several thereafter. What was worse was I could not tell anyone why I was not there.

The Letter

My heart began to pound when I saw the envelope. It was from our youngest daughter and sent overnight-express mail. "I am going to see her in a few days," I thought, "What is this all about?" I had been having many worries about our daughter, Sandy, the last few months, or was it years? No, months, it only seemed like years. She was a lovely person, beautiful and bright (graduated magna cum laude from college only a year ago.) We were so proud of her.

Before all the trouble started I had been feeling like the luckiest person alive. My husband and I are at the top of our careers and both enjoy our jobs thoroughly. We have a strong faith, a wonderful church, supportive family, and the most wonderful set of friends a person could ever ask for. God has given us three beautiful children; all are attractive and smart. They have all graduated at the top of their high school and college classes. The two older ones are married and have given us five beautiful grandchildren; all take after their parents. (Do I sound like a bragging mother? Well, I have a lot to brag about.) In addition, we had raised two foster children. Both are doing well. Our foster daughter is married to a great guy and we have two wonderful foster grandchildren, who are really like our own.

Then about a year ago things started to go awry. Sandy was not coming home as often as she did. Weddings of friends would come and go. She declined to become a bridesmaid at another friend's wedding. Conversations were becoming very strange.

On her father's birthday the previous January, she had called to say — for his birthday present she was going to AA. We were stunned, because we did not know she had a drinking problem. Well, that's the place to go, we thought. She went with a vengeance — every night, twice on Saturday and Sunday, and even during her lunch hour. She started going to a therapist and then the real trouble started. I got *The Courage to Heal* for Mother's Day. This is a book for incest survivors. We were baffled. I read the book but did not understand why she sent it. On Father's Day, my husband was told the book was his present also.

The last time we saw her was on her birthday in September 1990. We took her a color TV set to replace the tiny black and white one her sister had given her for a college graduation present. She was very cold and sat cross-legged in the corner. She would not tell us why she had been acting this way. She didn't say much of anything, except a very polite thank you. She lives two hours from us, so I said teasing, maybe we will camp out on your couch. (It was a loveseat and no way would fit us, so it was an obvious joke.) She said "NO" very loudly. We were baffled.

Well, I opened the letter and it was worse than even my imagination had conjured up. She accused us both of some kind of vague sex abuse. She said she did not want to have any more contact with us, her grandparents, aunts, cousins, uncle, or any of our friends. It went on and on. The only thing I can compare it to was the day I heard that my father had died. At least for that news I was prepared. He had been sick for a couple of years. I felt as though my daughter had a knife and was stabbing at my heart. I was totally devastated.

I called work, and then my husband, and then my mother. Mistake number two. I nearly gave my eighty-year-old mother a heart attack. I could barely talk but told her I was coming over. My husband met me there. We cried, sobbed, hugged, and cried some more. We were beside ourselves. We did not know our nightmare was just beginning.

Cut Off

We called her — her number was changed. We called work — they would not put us through. We called her boss — nothing. We called the therapist. She would not return our calls. We wrote letters, our relatives wrote letters, our friends wrote letters. Nothing! We went to therapist after therapist of our own. One said, "Why are you sacrificing yourself for your daughter?"

One stared at us as if to say, "Well, didn't you do it? Women do not lie about such things." Another said, "You must accept this. You can do nothing about it. Your daughter is gone." We could not accept this, nor will we ever.

We love our daughter and refuse to believe she would do such a thing in her right mind. We were a loving family. We go to church; I sing in the choir; and both of us teach Sunday School. We love God. We love our children more than anything in the world. We made mistakes to be sure, but only did what we thought was best for them. We would never hurt them. If anybody ever did anything to them, especially sexual abuse, we would go after that person with everything we had.

Blow number two hit a day later. Sandy sent a copy of the letter to her brother and sister along with another letter to them saying they should not let us see the grand-children. Will my heart ever heal? I doubt it. I cried all day for several days. For weeks I woke up crying and went to bed crying. I cried in the shower, while cleaning house, while washing clothes, when I went shopping or walking the dog. My head and heart hurt from crying.

That Thanksgiving was the worst day of all. My mother would cry; then my sister would cry; then I would cry; then, just before we ate, my husband demolished us all with a tender prayer "to watch over Sandy." We tried to watch comedy movies my sister brought over and at least we could stop crying for a minute. Christmas was better. All the children, except Sandy, came home. We were so busy cooking and opening presents we almost appeared normal. The grandchildren were wonderful and such a blessing and joy.

Everything got worse. We could make no contact what-soever to find out what was going on. Where were these weird things coming from? One night I felt the presence of something loving and wonderful; I called it my Guardian Angel. I finally stopped crying. I was so touched I bought a little Guardian Angel pin for Sandy and had her brother send it. It made her furious and she called up our son and reamed him out. Previously, this sweet little girl would have been touched. I found out months later that the head had come off and she thought we had done it on purpose.

With no communications there was no way to explain anything.

Nine months later the worst blow of all came in the form of another letter. It seems she was mistaken about my abuse. (Thanks a lot! Where is the apology?) But it was her father who had sexually abused her. Graphic details — straight from a porno magazine — followed. I immediately threw up. My husband took over. First he took a lie detector test, which proved without a shadow of a doubt that he had not done anything so terrible. Not one of our friends, relatives, or anyone who knew him, believed it, but others may not know what a wonderful, kind, Christian man he is.

Taking Initiative

We contacted the Cult Awareness Network (CAN). We went to their national convention and learned a great deal. We contacted other families who had also been falsely accused and found loving support all over the country. We also felt sad that so many families were going through the sorrow that we were experiencing. Several groups have been formed from these families. It seems to be hitting epidemic proportions. Men and women going to therapists and all of a sudden recovering repressed memories of abuse they did not have before. It seems the younger, less experienced, and less degreed the therapist was — the sooner they found the abuse. Some on the first, second, or third visit.

These are not remembered memories, but memories that come after hypnotism, trances, meditation and just plain suggestions. It is awful, such a terrible abuse by therapists and a terrible disservice to those who have *really been* abused. If a person abuses or rapes another, he or she deserves to be punished. If a therapist makes a person believe this has happened, when it has not, doesn't that therapist deserve to be punished? I believe so, because that client suffers all the trauma of a real abuse victim.

So far we are trying several things: A letter via our daughter's lawyer suggesting a contact—the lawyer is a friend with whom she still has contact. Prosecuting the therapist—so far nothing is working, but we continue to try. We are trying to take back our life. We thank God for what we still have. Some families have lost several daughters. One man lost two daughters and his wife, who believed the daughters. The two sons were wavering until the daughters said the man had raped them, too. The sons knew that wasn't true, so they realized all of it was false.

We will continue to try everything and pray continually that we will someday have our daughter back intact.

We still love her with all our might.

Profile of Jeanette

Physical information

Date of birth — 9-4-54   **Ht.** 5 feet 4 inches   **Wt.** 115

Fifth of six children — 3 older sisters, 1 older brother, 1 younger brother,

Father — M.D. — Surgeon   **Date of birth** — 9-4-20

Mother — full time homemaker   **Date of birth** — 9-8-23

Siblings say above parents were moderately strict yet very fair.

Parents were married 11-27-42 — 12 years before Jeanette was born. She was the fifth child in 6 ½ years. Grandparents of 12 grandchildren — ages 21 years to 9 months.

Jeanette was born in a small town — "Anytown," California.

Her father was called back into military service — 12-56.

Between 1956 and 1962 family lived in Calif., Wash., Mass., Ariz., and back to Calif. By this time Jeanette was almost eight.

Jeanette was married in Southern California in 1977. They have two boys — ages 13 and 8.

Physically she was very active – she had to be to keep up with four older, very active, siblings. Her family took regular annual vacations together at the Colorado River where they enjoyed their mobile home and ski boat for eighteen years. Her family lived in a large home on a 1½-acre lot for twenty years and Jeanette enjoyed horses and quarter horse shows from age eight to age seventeen. She was head cheerleader during her four years of high school and was very active in school drama and musical events.

Jeanette did have a bout with colitis during her first year of college but was healed during a spiritual healing service. The only other problem she had was a broken collarbone

— a result of a fall from a horse. She had one or two very rare nightmares that we, her parents, were aware of. We never noticed any eating disorders.

General information

Jeanette is very intelligent — strong in abstract reasoning, is a great organizer, excellent (self-taught) on computers, writes beautiful letters and lyrics — has a lovely voice. She entertains beautifully for large church groups and small social events. She's an excellent cook.

Religious background

Jeanette was born into a Catholic family — father was Baptist, mother was Catholic. Parents joined the Lutheran Church in 1958. She attended church and Sunday school weekly with her family, and was confirmed in the Lutheran Church in 1967 at the age of thirteen. She made a personal decision and was "born again" in 1971 at the age of seventeen. The family had grace before meals, good night prayer and her mother read briefly from the Bible at breakfast time. Jeanette and her husband were and still are very active in their church after their marriage. The family changed from a Lutheran church to a Baptist church, then to an extremely charismatic Christian (?) church. Jeanette organized a small ladies choral group which became part of the worship service.

Educational information

Jeanette attended public schools from kindergarten through grade 12. She earned a B.A. degree in drama from a major Southern California university. She had several voice teachers and writes and sings lovely religious lyrics. In 1991 she enrolled in a "Littauer" seminar for training to help others to "recall" their "memories" as she had.

Work information

During her school years Jeanette received an average allowance for chores done at home – set table for eight twice a day and clear table twice a day – clean own bedroom and one other room weekly. She earned extra money baby sitting, and doing family ironing. In high school she baby sat, washed dogs, etc. In college she was a waitress to earn her spending money. As long as she was a full-time student her parents paid for her room, board, tuition and books.

Emotional information

When compared with her siblings and friends Jeanette was very normal – typical teen age rebellion, tantrums stopped at age three to four. She had three sisters to whom she could ventilate her anger regarding her parents. She was very close to one sister who was twenty-two months older – they shared confidences and lived together for two years during college.

Neither three sisters, two brothers, nor either parent have one trace of a memory or evidence that Jeanette was ever molested physically or sexually by parents or grandparents. Also, none of the other children nor I, Jeanette's mother, have any memory of being molested in any way. See copy of the letter Jeanette wrote to her father sometime between the age of nineteen to twenty-one.

Also, the claim of her grandparents being involved in Satanic worship and ritual is ridiculous. As an only daughter I, Jeanette's mother, cleared out my parent's entire apartment after their deaths and there was not a single trace of any demonic activity. I knew my parents for fifty-four years and never saw any indication of Satanic worship. Until I married, we attended, as a family, a Catholic mass every Sunday morning (even when vacationing) – confession and communion monthly – Catholic school seven years – and confirmation at age thirteen.

Jeanette's husband is a very well educated, very calm and gentle man who is very active in Christian work and apparently believes his wife implicitly and is very supportive.

Beginning of the Problem

In 1979 Jeanette began to show physical problems. Her husband's mother was very critical and disliked Jeanette intensely because she was not the daughter-in-law his mother had chosen. Jeanette's husband's family had been thoroughly trained to be totally supportive of their mother, and Jeanette, having grown up with three sisters and two brothers, was well able to stand her ground with her mother-in-law. This may have been the cause of the physical problems.

We began to notice Jeanette becoming obsessed with her minor physical problems and decided she was becoming a hypochondriac and she was financially able to afford any and all types of treatments, which she utilized well over the next ten years.

Jeanette also showed signs of a great interest in books with mystical themes – "Lion, Witch and Wardrobe" series, "This Present Darkness," "Piercing the Darkness," etc. – all of these books with a Christian basis.

About 1987 Jeanette began to dream (or see) demons, robed and hooded, surrounding her bed during the night – she and her husband shared a king-sized bed – and upon one occasion was levitated.

Sometime during 1990 and 1991 she began reading

some of the Littauer's books (Christian authors) — "Freeing Your Mind from Memories That Bind" and "The Promise of Restoration" — also "Door of Hope," by Jan Frank. She then began seeing a Christian psychologist and a Christian marriage, family and child counselor, at which point Jeanette began to recall very strange memories. See attached list, titled "Scenarios." These memories gradually expanded and became more detailed during this period.

In 1991 Jeanette received a "Word of Knowledge" from a woman (a total stranger) at a Christian retreat that they should sell their lovely home as soon as possible and move out of the state as her family and home were in great danger. This they did.

In 1991 Jeanette became convinced that her mainstream Baptist church was deeply involved in Satanic worship (one of the ministers and others from the congregation). She and her family left this church.

In May of 1991 Jeanette began making accusations about her parents and grandparents. These are shown on "scenario" list, attached.

In 1991, Jeanette requested that her parents not telephone her. We could write a letter if we wished. She also warned her sister not to leave her two small children with their grandparents. If any of her siblings do not support her "memories," her relationship with them is terminated. She indicated that she has been advised by her counselor that this separation is necessary but, hopefully, not a permanent one.

In 1992 Jeanette now claims that she is greatly recovered from the trauma and her physical problems, and spiritually is "closer to God" than she has ever been.

To her family this is similar to the explosion of a nuclear bomb and all seven of us are experiencing the effects of the fallout.

Is Jeanette the victim of mental illness or of demonic activity? As Christians we are praying for mental healing and/or a termination of possible demonic activity – also a miraculous restoration of the wonderful, happy, united family (twenty-five of us) we once had.

This story of abuse by grandparents and parents, and her belief in Satanic worship and rituals by maternal grandparents is pure delusion and is very repugnant to us, her parents. Her father is so incensed that he has broken off the father-daughter relationship for the time being. Her mother still has a faint hope of keeping the door of the relationship open, but is in a quandary as to how this can be done.

Jeanette's Letter to Her Father

Dear Dad,

Often I find myself thinking about how lucky I am to have been born into the family that I was and how much God has blessed me with the parents He gave me. Unfortunately, I realize that I have never told you how much having you for a father has meant to me.

Thank you Dad for being a father that I could always look up to and respect. I often praise God that He gave me a father that loved me enough to discipline and yet was fair with me. I never once was ashamed to bring my friends home and introduce them to my Dad. On the contrary, I am very proud of you.

I realize Dad, that over the years you have worked very hard to provide your family with so many extra things that we could all share in and enjoy together, all those extras above and beyond providing very well for us in the basics. I want you to know that I really appreciate how hard you've worked to do this.

When talking to other people and hearing about their parents and family life, I come to a true realization of how blessed I am to have the parents and upbringing that I have and feel sorry that others weren't so lucky. Well, anyway Dad, thank you for being the father you are. Thank you for being you. I love you very much and am proud to be your daughter.

Scenarios

Scene one – Jeanette was sexually molested by both of her grandparents – probably about the age of twenty-eight months.

Scene two – Jeanette accuses both her grandparents of Satanic worship, even to the point of infant sacrifices. These activities occurred in Vallejo, California. She says her grandparents moved to Yucaipa because they wished to be near Redlands in order to be near a witches' coven.

Scene three – Jeanette accuses one parent of sexually molesting her and accuses the other of being completely aware that Jeanette was being molested and did nothing to prevent this. Jeanette also states that her siblings knew she was being molested yet all seven people involved are refusing to admit this situation existed and are banding together to cover up in order to protect the family reputation.

Scene four – Jeanette feels it is her duty to warn her siblings that they should never leave their children with their parents, as neither of their parents is to be trusted.

A Father Speaks

Our daughter is the victim of a "Great Cosmic Con." Her mind has been kidnapped and raped!

Unfortunately people often conclude that mind-control victims must be "sick," "stupid," or "crazy." Our daughter was none of these. Most people do not understand the subtlety, complexity, and insidiousness of psychological manipulation. The victim's history is rewritten.

We had a very normal, middle class family! Mom fifty-one, Dad fifty-four, son twenty-eight, daughter twenty-three. Non-practicing Catholics.

Our daughter, Margaret, graduated with honors from high school, was vice president of her senior class, lettered varsity swimming four years. She was very excited about going to U. of Wisconsin at Madison. No drugs, no problems. Great kid.

College

Freshman Year: She got a 3.00 GPA and seemed happy. When she was home for Christmas she *very* seriously asked all of us at dinner: "What traumatic thing happened to me as a child? There must be something because I don't remember my childhood." She lived and worked at home that summer – seemed happy – was dating.

Sophomore Year: Big personality changes. Not getting along with Mom. We found out later LSD was used often (ten times) and pot smoked every day. Taking some courses in *Women's Studies* and is thinking of that as a major. We start to hear words like DNA, right brain left brain, eating lower on the food chain, and holistic healing. She tells Dad she can't live at home in the summer because Mom is too controlling. Grades start to fall to a C. She is not happy about that. She gets a job in Skagway, Alaska. Meets a woman (lesbian) who is very influential. Still dating. Arrives home from Alaska, says almost nothing about people or work place.

Junior Year: Huge mood swings. Roommates have told us drugs were used (LSD and pot) a lot. She would study nonstop for two or three weeks and then no studies and only social life for two or three weeks. Starts to hang out at a *New Age* Bookstore. Decides to major in Political Science — fails. We hear words like yoga, astrology, and reflexology. She drops out of school second semester and takes care of her sick Grandma for two months. She returns to Madison and works at Bookstore and *loves* it. She tells parents she has a sexual problem and goes to a hypno-therapist. She stays in Madison for the summer and seldom comes home. Ends some long-time friendships.

Senior Year: She takes only two courses and then doesn't really go — flunks out. Comes home at Christmas and greets us with "Happy Solstice"! She tells us she only needs two hours sleep and how good she feels. Talks a lot about *Goddesses.* We see her go in and out of what we now know to be cult personality. She is very difficult to be with.

March 15, 1990: Dad calls — she won't speak to him, tells him to have Mom call her. Mom calls and she tells her "either stop your pattern of denial or divorce your husband or I will never see or speak to you again." Parents get in car and drive one-and-a-half hours to Madison. She is hysterical and calls police to make parents leave. Parents leave before police come. Tells brother next day she has been sexually abused by Dad her whole life and had a flashback when reading *The Courage to Heal.* Mom knew and did nothing to stop abuse.

She uses *The Courage to Heal* like a Bible. She is now

living in Homer, Alaska, we do not know with whom but we do have a phone number of a woman she used to live with in Madison who is now in Homer and says she can get messages to our daughter on a "Bush Radio." She will not return phone calls or answer letters. Mother received one letter and had one visit. Conversation and letter are right out of the books she is reading. She told her mother she is now a lesbian.

A Letter to Mom

Mom,

I was composing a letter in my head to you the day I received your card. I'm glad you wrote a note to me alone. I've been thinking about you a lot recently and hoping you are feeling strong and healthy. I've tried very hard to understand how you could abandon me . . . twice. I think of how scary and dehumanizing it must have been for you. At my age you were married and ready to have a baby. Raised in Catholic schools, married to a sexist pig, scared to define yourself outside of a relationship with a man. I try to imagine what it must feel like to be fifty years old and have your daughter tell you that your husband sexually abused her. What are your options? To leave the relationship in your life that gives you your only major source and sense of emotional security, of financial security, of social standing and respect among your peers? Quite honestly I don't know if I would have the courage and strength to believe and support my daughter any more than you have. In fact I might get so scared that I would search for ways *to explain her accusations. I might imagine that she had been influenced by someone and convinced that things that never really happened, did in fact occur.*

So right now what do I ask of you? I ask that you feel strong and be loving and kind to yourself. I ask that you deal seriously with your addiction to prescription pills. I ask that you encourage Dad to stop harassing me through the mail. I will not call or visit you until you are believing and supportive of me. I would like a letter if you feel like responding on your own, and not for Dad. If you write I would like to know: What do you see as unhealthy in our family relationships? (prior to my confrontation) Why didn't anybody take me seriously when I repeatedly asked for psychological support outside the family for feelings of suicidal depression? (especially during high school) I haven't felt suicidal for the first time in my life since I remembered the abuse; I've stopped directing the anger inward. Please don't continue to dodge these questions; I'm open to hearing your most honest responses.

A Mother's Diary from the Twilight Zone

The woman whose diary is excerpted below feels she has entered a "Twilight Zone" conjured up and conspired in by so-called "Satanic cult experts." The diary recounts her anguished, frantic efforts, first to heal her bulimic daughter and then to find her after she disappears. Everywhere she and her cancer-stricken husband turn for help — mental health therapists, private investigators, law enforcement officials in four states — they are met with incredulity and suspicion.

Our daughter Amy came home from college one weekend in late January of 1990. My husband Dan was on his way home from being out-of-state on business, so it was "just us girls." Amy asked me if she could have a serious discussion. I said, "Oh, shit — not one of those!" and chuckled. We sat down and she began to cry and told me that she had been bulimic since her sophomore/junior year in high school. I hugged her and said that it was a surprise, but not really a great shock. People had sometimes asked me if Amy was anorexic, and I would always adamantly say, "NO."

Then Amy said that was not all she had to tell. She said that she had been having flashbacks for about a month of being sexually abused when she was in kindergarten. She was almost 100 percent certain that it was her school principal. She began to cry almost hysterically and asked if I believed her.

"Of course I do. You would never make up anything as horrible as that!" I said. "I don't know where to take you that is good. So, first thing tomorrow morning we will go see our family doctor for his advice on where to turn." And we did.

The doctor was very kind and understanding. He listened to Amy describe some of her flashbacks and agreed that something might have happened. He said he would find someone to refer us to. We said okay.

The weekend passed and Amy decided to go back to college on Sunday evening. On the following Friday, I received a frantic and hysterical call from her while I was at work. She said that she couldn't go on and could we please pick her up on Saturday. I said, "Sweetie, calm down and hang on. Your daddy and I are leaving right now, this very minute, and we will be up to get you."

Getting Help

Before we left town to get Amy, I stopped by our family doctor's office to let him know Amy's condition and to tell him she needed help NOW. He said for us to go and get Amy and then call his office — he would set up an appointment for us with a psychiatrist. And that is what we did. We went straight from Small City to College Town to a psychiatrist who was nice enough to take time to see to it that Amy was calmed down. At that time we made some future appointments for not only Amy, but also for Dan and me to talk with the psychiatrist after she had seen Amy again. Amy went for approximately five sessions.

Home life was a constant turmoil, as poor Amy was being besieged with more and more memories, most of which were very shocking and horrifying. She continued to see this psychiatrist for a while, and then Amy decided that she and the doctor had a personality conflict. Well, you read and hear from time-to-time that finding a good counselor you can relate to is sometimes like going shopping. So, when Amy told us that, we said, no problem, we will find someone else. Looking back on it, we didn't consult with the psychiatrist at all prior to making this change. And I believe that this was a grave error on our part. We should have at least heard the other side of the story, and then perhaps this whole ordeal would have been avoided. Part of the problem was that Amy felt that, for her to get better, she needed to relive every minute of her abuse. And the psychiatrist, I believe, felt that Amy needed to learn how to deal with the abuse and go on with her life.

Dan first became aware of Ms. G. when she was a guest speaker on child abuse at the Paris Early Risers in Edgar County. Dan later pulled Ms. G. aside and indicated to her that our daughter might have been sexually abused and needed counseling. Ms. G. sent Dan some photocopied material: questions and answers to determine if one had been sexually abused, with the understanding that, if we needed further help, we were to feel free to give her a call.

We initially set up a family counseling session with Ms. G. and had approximately two per week for a short period of time. Then Ms. G. and Amy both agreed that Amy would benefit at this time to start individual sessions. Amy began these on about March 12, 1990. Amy saw Ms. G. as often as three times a week, the family would see Ms. G. one or two times a week and then son Roger (who was three years Amy's junior) began seeing Ms. G. one or two times a week. So the maximum of visits our family would make in any given week would be seven times.

Amy and the counselor decided that Amy was not emotionally strong enough to continue college at this time. So Amy temporarily dropped out and started living at home. At this point Amy was maintaining a 4.0 grade point average and was on the Dean's honor roll.

Satanic Cult

One thing led to another and it became apparent that Amy's abuse was not "normal." There were a lot of indications that Amy's abuse was "satanic." And not only the kindergarten principal was involved but several other people in the community whom we considered friends. (Please note that these conclusions originated from Amy's sessions with Ms. G.) And we were told from the very beginning that Amy's "memories" were being verified by a "leading authority on satanic cult abuse." One of the most unanswered questions that Ms. G. would throw in my direction was "WHERE WERE YOU WHEN THE ABUSE WAS TAKING PLACE?" as I was a non-working mother, staying at home and taking care of my family. This all allegedly took place fifteen years ago. And I have a difficult time remembering what happened last week, much less fifteen years ago. So how does a person honestly answer such a question? I just said that I had no idea. To the best of my recollection nothing abnormal had happened or caught my attention. My children were happy and well adjusted kids. Amy always did well in school and got along well with other children her age. (At this point, we truly believed the ritualism theory.)

Then, our son Roger began to have flashbacks of different events, yet connected to Amy's. One thing led to another and, OH, GOD!!! they were both abused. The main question was still "Where were you (their mother) when all of this occurred?" How did I never even suspect such a thing could be happening? My poor little babies. Also, "How could Roger (at that time two-and-a-half years old) remember the things that he was coming up with?" It just didn't seem possible that a child that young could remember the things that he was coming up with.

By this time our personal lives were a living hell. We didn't trust anyone, didn't dare tell anyone about all this for fear they would think we were crazy. We were also afraid to tell anyone for fear that they were involved in satanic abuse themselves. It occupied every second of every day. And all through this, Ms. G. was feeding us information and saying that this was all "being confirmed by a satanic specialist." After all, we were going to a highly respected mental health facility. This had to be the truth. It became a living hell just facing what must have been reality. The children began taking notes of their dreams and remembered very specific things: phrases, chants, descriptions of masks, ceremonies — All of which were "verified" by the "expert."

Ms. G. at first was working WITH us in trying to find out the who, where and why of Amy's alleged abuse. Ms. G. told us that cult abuse was a common occurrence fifteen years ago, just not publicized or talked about. Then Ms. G. told us that Amy was suffering from MPD (multiple personality disorder). One person was a young retarded girl, Sally (I think), another person had a masculine character and the third person was a "normal" girl.

Then, on May 31st (on Dan's birthday), Roger had a car wreck. He hit a very large tree almost head-on. Thank God, he was not hurt, but the truck was totalled. I called Ms. G. to tell her about the accident, and she told me not to be surprised if Roger didn't intentionally hit the tree. Sure enough, a few days later, Roger asked me if I had ever thought that he had hit the tree intentionally. I told him no. He said that he wasn't sure but he may have done it on purpose. (Roger said this after he had had a session with

Ms. G.) Looking back, we now wonder if Roger had been "programmed" to have a wreck.

A couple of weeks later, Roger told us that he no longer wanted to continue his sessions with Ms. G. We told him that it was okay with us. Roger and I would have some "mini" talks about his sister and how we both felt that she wasn't getting any better. Roger told me he felt that what was past, was past. And dwelling on it every minute of every hour was just allowing it more control over your life.

By this time, Amy got to where she wouldn't allow me to hug or kiss her. She would barricade her bedroom door at night, thinking that I would be coming in to harm her. She would even sometimes sleep on Bill's bedroom floor as protection. All of this behavior greatly disturbed us, but we kept reassuring ourselves that Amy was receiving good care and "this too shall pass."

Roger did continue to attend family sessions with us. At this point, Roger and Amy no longer were the close brother and sister they used to be. And Ms. G. seemed angry at Roger and purposely antagonized him. Roger and I seemed to become the "bad" influence at family sessions and Dan was the "golden boy". . . .

Ms. G. asked me, "Do you have any memories of when the kids were young? Did you ever take the kids to a circus? Do you have any memories of your father being involved in the abuse?" When I couldn't respond, she would say: "That's okay. Just give it time; it will come. It will come."

On Dan's birthday, Amy gave both Dan and Roger a cross necklace to ward off evil spirits. When I asked where my cross was, Amy just gave me a strange look and did not say anything. I guess that I was the evil.

At some point in our sessions, Ms. G. brought to light that Roger was the Anti-Christ and also had this "verified."

Roger's birthday is May 5, 1974 — or 5-5-74. The first two fives are okay, as is. However the 7 can break down to two components: 4 and 3. If you subtract 3 from 4, you have 1. Add the 1 to the remaining 4 (in 74) and you have 5. Thus, 5-5-5 equals the Anti-Christ.

Then in June, Dan started chemotherapy for leukemia. Amy was beginning to believe that I allowed the abuse to happen or perhaps even willingly participated in her abuse. This continued through the summer. She would flinch like a dog that had been severely beaten. Since it was obvious that Amy was uncomfortable in my presence, we discussed with Amy the possibility of getting an apartment. This would allow Amy her "own space" away from us. No, she didn't want to do that.

Amy Disappears

At this point we had grave doubts about Amy's mental health and wondered if Ms. G. was doing more harm than good for our daughter. So, even though we still believed that "ritualistic abuse" had occurred, we sought a second opinion from a professional in Small City. The psychologist agreed to do a one time evaluation of our children. Now, as Amy was a legal adult, we realized that we could not force her to go. We sat down and explained our fears and concerns to Amy, and she agreed to go and be evaluated, emphasizing that we could not keep her from seeing Ms. G. The appointment was set for Sept. 13th.

On Sept. 13th, Roger called me at work to say that Amy was "sick" and wouldn't go. I said, okay. Roger had no sooner left when Amy called to say she needed the van to get to an emergency appointment with Ms. G. We saw to it that she made her appointment.

On Sept. 14th, Amy picked me up at work for lunch

and we ran a few errands. She was looking forward to driving up to college for the weekend to see her girlfriend. She had bought a new nightgown to take with her. Half an hour after she dropped me off at work. While I was in a meeting, Amy called and left a message that she was leaving on her trip a day early and would call later. When I got home from work, Dan had just spoken with Amy. She said that she was at the college and some guy had almost run her off the road, but Dan said she sounded more angry than scared. Dan asked her if she had money, and she said yes, she had plenty, and that she would be home sometime Sunday.

On Sept. 15th, Amy's college girlfriend called to speak to Amy. Amy never made it to school. She lied to her father, the first time ever that she had deliberately lied to either of us.

I immediately called Ms. G. stating that Amy was not where she had told us and that we were extremely concerned for her safety. I asked Ms. G. what had happened yesterday at their appointment. How had Amy's state of mind seemed? Ms. G. evaded all my questions and answered them with other non-related questions, such as: Did I have any memories? Did I remember ever taking the kids to a circus? Did I have any memories of my father being involved in the abuse? Pissed, I hung up.

On Sept. 16th, I was at the police station filing Amy as a missing person when my son Roger pulled up and said some friends of his had seen Amy in Small City the day before having lunch with Ms. G. and three men! (We later learned that the three men were two Small City police officers and DM, an Edgar County deputy sheriff — the leading authority on cult abuse.) I went home and called Ms. G. to ask if she knew where our daughter was.

She said no. Then I said it was strange that she was seen having lunch with Amy on Saturday in Small City. Ms. G. said, "Yes, I did." Then I asked why she didn't at least call us and let us know that our daughter was okay. All Ms. G. would say is, "I do not know. I cannot say." She said that over and over. Dan screamed that she was a bitch, and after that she just hung up.

Since then, we have had two very confusing letters from Amy. One postmarked Dayton, Ohio, stating that she was fine and the car would be found at the airport in Dayton in long-term parking. The second letter stated that Dan and I had been abusing both her and Roger and that she had to get away from the abusive environment. She stated that she would have taken her brother, too, but "he is going through a denial stage, which is quite common when being abused by someone that you love." That letter was postmarked Denver, Colorado. . . .

The Search

It is now April of the following year, and Amy has been gone for seven months. The family has endured a local police request for Amy's fingerprints to compare them with an unidentified body found in St. Louis. It was five days before they learned that the body was not Amy's. After watching a "Geraldo" program on Satanism, they call a toll-free number and get referred to DG, a retired Ohio police officer who claims to be a "leading authority in satanic cult abuse." In return for expense money, DG agrees to investigate Amy's disappearance. Just before Christmas, DG calls to report that he has found Amy in a shelter under a doctor's care. She is pretty mixed up, he says, but prognosis is good for her recovery. But, DG can't tell them where Amy is or with whom because of her age.

The day after New Year's, they get a Christmas card from Amy — no note, just her signature.

April 13th — As time goes by, I think that both Dan and I are rapidly becoming emotional wrecks. I feel that my emotional stability is today as rocky as it was when Amy first left. It is so terribly wrong for anyone to keep loving and extremely concerned parents uninformed about their child's welfare. A part of me understands that legally these people are doing what is best for our child (or I hope to God that they are), but what about morally? When we last saw our daughter, she may have been an adult according to the law, but emotionally she was like a fragile and extremely dependent ten year old.

How can a person who has been hired to locate your daughter, keep specific information from you, such as: Where is she? What is her diagnosis and prognosis? Who is with her and how is her care being paid for?

Then, too, we wonder is Amy really in some sort of psychological shelter or is this information really accurate? Have we been coached and soothed into believing that, when actually she is in the clutches of a cult or some other group and being brainwashed, or God know what else?

I feel like my family has been raped and the rapist has convinced us to keep quiet, under the pretense that it is best for our daughter. When in fact what we truly need to do is cry "RAPE!!! RAPE!!!" at the top of our lungs. . . .

At this point, the family began seeing a counselor to help them cope with the situation. They met with lawyers and continued to gather evidence for possible legal action or at least public exposure of the nightmare they were enduring. They obtained copies of their mental health center files where Ms. G. was counseling them and discovered notes of comments they don't remember making and release forms they signed permitting Ms. G. to share their case with DM (the so-called cult expert who attended the lunch with Amy the day she disappeared) and an Illinois therapist, Ms. F. They had recently obtained a Chicago TV news report about a ritualistic abuse case in which therapist Ms. F. had been court-ordered not to counsel a five-year-old girl. The judge ruled that Ms. F. had led the girl into accusing her parents of satanic abuse. They found Ms. F.'s possible connection to their daughter extremely scary.

Illinois state police and Children and Family Services attorneys were now investigating the case. The family obtained evidence that local police knew a lot more than they were saying and often gave them the run-around.

In October, the family reluctantly filed a warrant for Amy's arrest. She had driven their car across state lines when she left — a felony. By February 1992, when the diary ends, the family has gathered even more information, distributing it to major TV networks and talk-show programs. Amy is still missing, and most of the law-enforcement cast members of this "Twilight Zone" episode are still stonewalling as to her whereabouts.

Marge, Sue, Brenda, Peg, Lori

Following is an account of the present status of our relationship with our five daughters who are making false allegations that they were sexually abused by their father and, according to one of the daughters, I was supposedly aware of what was going on and did nothing about it.

First of all I will give you fictitious names for the girls with their ages at the present time: Marge, forty-four; Sue, forty-three; Brenda, forty-one; Peg, thirty-eight; Lori, thirty-six. All five of the girls are well educated, three having Masters Degrees and all having responsible jobs at the present time.

Brenda

Brenda was engaged to be married and her fiance had told us that he was very frightened by her involvement in groups. He told us that whenever they went to a large city nearby, she would go to the Holistic center and copy the names of different groups from a bulletin board and write to all of them. The amount of mail she was receiving was astounding. Her fiance also told us that when she attended a meeting of a group new to her, she wanted to tell her story and be the subject of discussion for the meeting. Her fiance finally told her that if she did not give up her involvement in these groups, the engagement was off. She told him that this was her life and that she could not give it up.

After the breakup, she came to stay with us for a weekend with her two children. The children were from her second marriage and she did not want custody of the children at the time of the divorce. She did, however, have the children with her every other weekend. She told us at that time that she would be visiting us more often and we were looking forward to seeing more of her and the grand-children.

A couple of months passed and we had not heard from her so I called her on the phone. I told her that it had been a long time since we had seen her or heard from her. She then told me that she was having some unpleasant recol-lections of her youth and she did not want to see either of us. It is our understanding that she had been going to a therapist during this period of time.

Again, some time elapsed before we heard from her. We received a letter in the mail in which she made the false allegations of being abused as a child. We went to see her and she threatened to call the police if we did not leave. Her letter was very similar to a letter in the book, *The Courage to Heal.*

In a second letter, she told us that she had joined a feminist group and no longer needed men in her life. She wrote that she was very thankful for her 'new friends'.

Marge and Sue

We later heard that Marge was also claiming that she was sexually abused as a child. We were told that Marge, Sue and Brenda had met and Marge and Brenda asked Sue if she remembered being abused. We were told that Sue told them she did not know. I recently saw Sue and I asked her if she really believed that her father had abused her. Her reply was "my mind tells me no but my body tells me yes."

Marge's husband told us that Marge had been attending a weekly meeting in a city approximately eighty miles from her home. She came back to her home after attending one of the meetings and told her husband that at the next meeting the participants had to tell something traumatic that had happened in their youth. She told him that she had no idea what she could tell since she had nothing traumatic happen to her. The next week when she returned home from the meeting, she told her husband that the members of the group were all lying on the floor and she suddenly had flashbacks of the sexual abuse as a child. She wanted to come to our home and confront her father but her husband would not let her. He told her that her father would be devastated. Marge, after twenty-one years of marriage to her husband, came home from another meeting and told her husband that she could no longer live with him. We understand that the group told her that unless he joined this group, she would have to leave him. As a result, they are now divorced and she is living with one of the male members of the group. She now has her own group and she told me that she was very pleased with the number of people that had come to her first meeting.

Peg and Lori

Marge took our two youngest daughters, Peg and Lori, to a therapist for healing. We understand that they were hypnotized and both of them now believe that abuse happened to them also. I asked Marge why she had to get Peg and Lori involved since they had not been part of any of the meetings with the other girls. She told me that the entire family has to be involved before a healing process could be successful. The girls wanted me to go with them to their therapist and I refused. I talked to Lori on the phone one day and she could not believe that "I would choose their father over my five daughters."

Four of our daughters have been divorced once and the fifth daughter has been divorced twice, married for the third time and, the last we heard, is now separated from her third husband.

We are thankful that none of the ex-husbands believe that any of this abuse occurred. We are very good friends and we keep in contact with them.

It is our understanding that the three oldest girls are involved in the New Age movement. We have heard conversation regarding reincarnation, channeling, the healing powers of crystals. One of the girls believes she has god-like power. We have heard that repeated trips have been made to the state of Washington where New Age is flourishing. Many long-distance trips have been made and countless dollars have been spent on group meetings.

I could go on and on about our family situation but I have tried to condense it as much as possible. We do have one son who is in no way involved. His sisters have tried to contact him and we feel they would like to get him to agree with them about the abuse. We are very thankful that we still have him.

Yet Another Report of False Accusation of Sexual Abuse

Our own particular nightmare began, although we didn't know it at the time, when our daughter (I will call her Diane), announced that her physician had recommended "another kind of healing" to her. The recommended healing would be provided by a therapist who has offices in the doctor's building. (The therapist is a psychologist with an M.A. degree.) The suggestion was that the therapist would help our daughter deal with a chronic, and sometimes, life-threatening illness. We had no reason to question such a suggestion from Diane's doctor, a holistic physician (M.D.), who had probably saved her life when orthodox medical treatment had failed.

From the Start

Diane's recounting of her first meeting with the therapist should have, if not alarmed us, alerted us in some way. Diane described the therapist as having a "gift" in which she lays her hands on a patient and can "divine" things (both physical and psychological) about the patient. The therapist, *in the first session* with Diane, "knew" that Diane had been abused by her father. In retrospect, I can't believe that we didn't get upset. We interpreted that comment as meaning some kind of emotional or psychological abuse. Also, we had a great deal of confidence in Diane's M.D., his recommendations, and in the whole notion of psychotherapy as a beneficial agent. We had encouraged Diane in therapy before. Around the age of 19, she had asked if she could find a professional person to talk to. We were immediately supportive of that wish and set about to help her find such a person. Diane saw her psychiatrist (M.D.) intermittently for four years. In those many sessions, it seems likely that, if there had been any sexual abuse in Diane's background, it would have surfaced, but such was not the case.

Our conclusion about that first meeting with the recommended therapist was that she had recognized that Diane had never expressed any negative feelings toward her father and that it was time for that to happen – that it was "his turn." I, as mother, had experienced expressions of overt hostilities and blame as Diane was trying to deal with emotional and family problems. I felt this was normal for a young adult who had had to deal with a parental separation and a severe illness at the same time. But I also felt that we had been making real progress as a family.

At the start of her therapy (with the recommended therapist), Diane had just turned twenty-seven. She had come home again to live, after failing (for the fifth or sixth time) to stay healthy enough to work and live on her own. Both her dad and I felt a genuine relief that she was working with a trained professional – someone else to talk to about adjustment problems.

Diane's illness is ulcerative colitis, a disease she has been battling for eight years. Ulcerative colitis, or UC, is a devastating, life-threatening disease, the origins and causes of which are not only unknown but highly disputed. Unfortunately for anyone who is afflicted with it, it is one of those "causes unknown" diseases which got categorized a long time ago under the ubiquitous label of "psychosomatic." That translates into "not to be taken seriously – it's all in your head." For a long time, Diane felt guilty because she had not been able to cure herself. She felt that "if only she could get her head straight," she would be cured.

As she was growing up, Diane was always encouraged (as an antidote to my own repressive upbringing) to express any and everything that she wanted to, to us. That is the only reason we know as many details about her therapy sessions as we do.

The report of the initial meeting with the therapist faded as months went by, and Diane began to feel well enough to once again try living on her own. And once again, we moved her to a new apartment and she began yet another job. Some six months later, however, she was back again because of financial and health problems.

Finding the Source

About nine months after her therapy began, Diane reported the therapist as having told her that now they were ready to find out what had caused her illness. We said nothing. After all, Diane was almost twenty-eight years old. We felt we had no right to interfere; we were open to "alternative" approaches.

The therapist's investigation into the causes of Diane's illness began with general inquiries. Diane would come back from a session and ask me if I had ever disciplined her in an inappropriate way; if I had ever spanked her severely and/or continuously when she was small. When I told my husband about these inquiries, I saw a look of concern. A seed of doubt had been planted. I racked my memories and scrutinized my child-raising approach. The only thing I could come up with was the one time I had lost my temper and spanked her. Doubt and guilt. The focus then shifted to her father. Had he spanked or disciplined her inappropriately? We could think of only one incident of discipline where he had spanked her to impress her at age three or so, not to run out in the street. There then began to be reports of on-going "revelations" e.g., her father was jealous of her talent. Disapproval and disappointment were emphasized; he disapproved of all of her boyfriends because he wanted to control her; he used money in order to further manipulate and control her. At one point, Diane had tried living in Florida. When she moved home again, she found out that her father had been experiencing some symptoms of an ulcer. This fact was interpreted by the therapist as her father becoming ill in order to get her back home with him. We realized later that, systematically, a case was being built against him.

Then, almost a year to the day that the therapy sessions had begun, Diane came home and calmly announced that her therapist had come back to **the truth** – her father had sexually abused her as a child. We were in total shock. Surely the therapist would begin to see that this could not be true. But the allegation and its ramifications took on a life of their own. Things began to escalate rapidly. Diane began to report having "memories" of the alleged abuse. The first "memory" was reported to have been one of being molested at the age of six months. There were others. Diane came home after another session and said, "My therapist believes that the facts of the actual sexual abuse are much, much worse than first feared." Diane soon began to say that she had been repeatedly raped from the age of about four to seven.

We were devastated and horrified. Nothing her father or I said was listened to. We were immediately cast into the role of stereotypical, abusive parents: Of course, my husband would deny any such abuse. Of course, I would stand up for him against my own daughter and become angry at her for bringing up the matter. I protested that I was not angry. Diane said, "Yes, you are. The therapist said that you would react like that." Diane was soon prompted into "confronting her abuser," one of the absolute *musts* the abused person is urged to do, according to the book, *The Courage to Heal*, which the therapist urged Diane to read.

The "confrontation" was terrible — with Diane screaming at us and threatening that she could take her father to court. We were stunned. Her father tried to suggest to her that casually relaying the allegations to her friends could have serious negative consequences. He is a professional person and we all know of cases where a mere hint of an accusation such as this is destructive. He tried to explain to her that to impair him professionally could harm the family financially, and thus our capacity to provide for her. Her fury was uncontrollable. That her father would be concerned about his career at that critical time was outrageous to her.

Aftereffects

Things became so tense that it was impossible for us all to continue living under the same roof. The decision was made that Diane would find another apartment and move out of the house. That was in early May of 1991. Her father has not seen or talked with his daughter since. At first, she and I had a practical, albeit strained, relationship. I dropped by her apartment a few times; the last time I stopped by, which turned out to be the last time I saw her, was to discuss her request for additional money and why she needed it at that particular time. She became very angry and accused us of trying to manipulate her through withholding money we had promised and reiterated the concern, which her therapist had expressed: that her father would stop paying for her therapy out of retaliation, that we really didn't care about her pain. All this in spite of my efforts to express my sadness, my efforts to understand what she was going through – and yes, her pain. She demanded to know "once and for all" if I believed her not. I could not lie. I told her that after the most intense scrutiny of the past I could manage, I found nothing to support her allegations. She said that if that were the case, she never wanted to see or hear from me again.

The first reaction, after absorbing some of the shock and forcing oneself to recognize that, yes, this trauma is indeed really happening, is to want to *do* something. My husband consulted a psychiatrist in the area; one who we know is highly regarded in the medical community and who has been in practice for some forty years. The psychiatrist was appalled at the sequence reported, but could offer little but moral support. My husband then decided to contact Diane's doctor who had recommended the therapist. The doctor did not want to see him in person but did talk with him on the telephone. He voiced understanding for my husband's concern and suggested that in order to respond to these allegations, he needed to contact the therapist. The therapist refused a meeting but did consent to a telephone call. When my husband protested the allegations of rape, the therapist coolly replied "*that* word was never used"; when he asked about her gift of "divination, if she could explain it to him," she replied that "you wouldn't understand." He requested an appointment with her to at least be able to discuss the allegations which had been made against him. The therapist replied that all she had to go on were Diane's reports of the "memories" and "images" of what had happened and could only discuss the case if Diane would sign a waiver to that effect. Very shortly, her father received a letter from Diane. In it she emphatically refused to sign any waiver or give him permission to talk with her therapist. She expressed outrage at "his trying to invalidate her claim through her medical sources." She went on to relate, in graphic detail, what she believes happened to her as a child:

> — *Because the month of February has been a bad one for her during the worst periods of her illness, something terrible must have happened to her as a child during the month of February. (Diane also suffers from "Seasonal Affective Syndrome (SAD)." She, like many people, experiences headaches and depression during periods of prolonged, grey days.)*
> — *That as an infant (the age is now alleged to be between one and six months), she suffered inappropriate anal exploration by her father.*
> — *Nothing else happened to her until the age of four or five. (She adds, however, that ages six to nine are not to be ruled out). That during the ages of four and five, her father had sexually abused her.*
> — *That the reason her father cannot or "will not" remember any of this abuse is that it happened when he had been drinking.*
> — *With these revelations and remembrances, she finally understands the whole picture — everything makes sense.*

Since that letter, she and I had a few necessary telephone conversations about money, the time it was to be sent, etc. During one of those telephone conversations, I asked if it weren't customary for a therapist, in a matter which involves family members, to want to work with the family as a whole in some way; to try to begin a healing process. Diane replied that, "why would she? All we would want to do is to prove her wrong."

The Last Contact

In November of this past year (1991), I had my last contact with our daughter. During that final telephone conversation, she announced that she was finished with therapy and that she was totally and completely cured, and she had no symptoms of her disease. How triumphant the therapist must have felt to be able to cure UC when no one else ever has! What she doesn't know is that Diane can go for weeks, even months at a time, with no symptoms.

Diane also informed me that she was getting married and would be moving out of the state and that we would never hear from her again. She refused to tell me the name of the person she was to marry, or where they would be going. We have not had any communication from her since that time. We have no idea where she is, or how she is – if she is ill or well.

Of course we continue to hope that we will some day be emotionally reunited with our daughter, but incalculable damage has been done to all of us. We have been forced into an adversarial relationship, which we did not choose. We were given no opportunity to address the charges made against Diane's father. No one sought me out as the one person who was closest to both daughter and father, one who might have some insights about the matter.

How we grieve for her – that beautiful, intelligent, gifted young woman who is convinced that her father is some kind of monster and that her mother is an uncaring, ineffectual, cowardly person who refuses to stand up for her own child. She has been victimized in a most insidious way, led from "revelation" to "revelation" to the pre-ordained conclusion that her disease, and any other problems she may have had, were caused by sexual abuse committed by her father.

Only other parents who have also experienced this tragedy can understand what one goes through in a case like this: The initial shock, disbelief, feeling of unreality, and the deep, unrelenting sorrow. And there is another emotion — one of anger. Anger at misguided, arrogant (and I suspect, inadequately trained) therapists who are willing to risk destroying lives and families on the basis of some predetermined, unquestioned notion that they must first look for sexual abuse as an explanation for any and all emotional problems in their female patients.

How Long Can This Go On?

April 28, 1992
(Michigan)

Our older daughter, in her mid-thirties, lives in California. In a letter from her in September 1990, she accused her father of physical, emotional, and sexual abuse in her childhood. We live in the Midwest. She sent copies of the letter to her brothers and younger sister all living in the Midwest or east coast.

We were stunned, shocked, angry, and hurt. Our oldest son and youngest daughter living in the East have been supportive of us throughout the ordeal. The other brother and his wife live about three-and-a-half hours from us. They believe her story and have refused the father any contact with our four-year-old grandson. They said I could come to visit them but I have refused tearfully.

The daughter has cut off all communication with us. We continued to remember special holidays and other correspondence to her until several months ago when she refused to receive any more from us with threats to have her phone and address changed if we continued.

When I was on the West Coast visiting relatives in October '87, she had me come to see her and her husband. They were very hospitable. I agreed to go with her for a counseling session. However a substitute counselor met with us as her regular one was "unavailable," although it had been prearranged to meet with her.

She has been angry with her father for several years and we have not known why. She avoided him when she attended her brother's wedding in 1988. She informed her younger sister that she will not attend her wedding in May because we will be there.

She has belonged to a Marxist political group for over a decade. We have not been pleased with her choice but continued to accept her. This group claims her complete devotion and dedication like a cult group. When I visited her in 1988, she would not have me meet any of her friends.

As she lives so far away, we only have constant reminders of her beautiful growing years with us. We try, sometimes with difficulty, to live productive lives in the best way we can, including seeing our other adult children and our other two grandsons.

There has been some consolation in learning that others are suffering from this false-memory misery. We look forward to some combined effort to help us all. How long can this go on?

A Brother's Recollections

In August 1989, dad had his second bypass operation. The operation was difficult. During the procedure the liaison nurse came out and explained that they were having trouble cutting through dad's sternum. Due to accumulated scar tissue it had taken almost two hours just to open his chest cavity. Once inside they found it impossible to complete the operation as planned.

Dad's recovery was touch-and-go during the next two days, and his heart needed assistance just to keep beating. Paula, my sister, and her husband Tommy had come to Fresno to be there for the operation, but due to job obligations had to return to Reno before dad was fully alert. My sister, who was an emotional person, expressed a great deal of anguish about this. I comforted her and told her not to worry too much. Dad was beginning to come out of it, and looked like he was going to be fine.

About one month after dad's operation Paula called me and said she was having problems with her life. She said she was having anxiety attacks and had also had a problem at work. Paula was employed as a phlebotomist at a local hospital, and during a particularly messy emergency she passed out. She was embarrassed by this and felt she had let her co-workers down. I assured her it was a normal reaction under the circumstances. Paula then told me she was planning to see the hospital's psychologist. She felt she needed help dealing with her stress. I agreed it might be a good idea for her to see this person.

A Pattern

I had heard all this before. This behavior had become a

pattern in Paula's life. Over the years I had noticed that my sister seemed to live on an emotional roller coaster. One month she would tell us she had finally figured out her life and was feeling wonderful; she would get a new job, buy new furniture, meet the man of her dreams, etc. Then we would all wait for the inevitable crash. A depression would soon follow and she would then proceed to quit her job, change her residence, give away her furniture, etc. The reasons would vary from people whispering behind her back, to sexual discrimination, to her co-workers plotting her downfall, to any one of numerous other excuses. She would then get a new job and it would start off over again.

Contentment was something that seemed to elude my sister. She had always been a headstrong person. From the time she could talk you knew where Paula was and what she wanted. Though, as with all kids, she wasn't always happy with what she got. As she grew up she became more and more stubborn about getting her way. She was a classic example of the child who says black *just* because you say white. This attitude got her in some little trouble in high school where she was arrested for under-age drinking. She ran with a fast crowd and at times drove our parents to despair. My sister was never one to take advice, in fact, she would go out of her way to do the opposite of what anyone might suggest. Her impulsive nature would invariably get her into trouble, but as she was an adult, there was not much we could do.

I had never related my observations about her mood swings to Paula before, but now felt compelled to do so. I told her about the pattern I had seen unfolding over the years and suggested she may be suffering from manic depression. I also suggested she mention this to her doctor or psychologist. She seemed indifferent to this idea, but agreed to tell her therapist about the possibility. As we said good-bye I hoped she wasn't too angry with me for suggesting the things I had.

Her Discovery

About three weeks later Paula called me and said she had seen the hospital therapist. I asked her what had happened. There was a moment of silence and then she asked me if mom and dad had ever done anything to her when she was a little girl. I asked her where she had gotten an idea like that. She told me that the psychologist had listened to her symptoms and concluded she was suffering from some past childhood abuse. It was recommended she see a specialist in that field.

That was it! I lost my temper and we had a knock-down argument. I asked how she could possibly think mom and dad abused her when all of her life they had stuck by her through thick and thin: through her childhood tantrums, her difficult adolescence, her stubborn refusal to go to college, her three failed marriages, and endless financial difficulties. I told her mom and dad were elderly and needed our love and support, not ridiculous accusations. I reminded her that I was there too and nothing had happened to her while I was there. Our tempers finally cooled and I apologized for flying off the handle and she said maybe she had been mistaken about all of it. I asked her to keep in touch and reminded her we would get together at Christmas.

I didn't speak to Paula again until Christmas which was celebrated at her house that year. The holidays seemed all right to me, but my wife later commented that Paula had seemed subdued and not her usual hyper self. Looking back on it I had to agree.

About three weeks after the holidays I called my sister to see how she was doing. Her mother-in-law answered the phone and told me Paula had a nervous breakdown and was in the hospital. I asked her what had happened and why we had not been notified. She told me that Paula had been severely traumatized by something that had happened to her while she was a child in the care of some baby sitters. She also told me that Paula had asked her not to contact the family or to relate the facts of the incident to our family. Carol went on to tell me that this trauma explained a lot of Paula's behavior over the years. Paula's trauma had been so bad, she said, that the doctor thought her story would make a great book. Obviously Carol did not think she was breaking her code of silence by telling. Perturbed, I asked which hospital Paula was in and was reluctantly given the information.

I tried calling the hospital immediately and was put through to Paula's room. Paula was extremely surprised and very upset that I had gotten through, but after a few minutes agreed to talk to me. She eventually told me about an elderly couple that had baby sat her and that they had sexually molested her and forced her to participate in the ritual murders of several people. She said the sitters had been "Satan worshippers." As I listened I was numbed by shock. Paula was extremely paranoid and said she was afraid the Satan worshippers would now come back to get her since she had revealed their secret. This was, she said, the reason she had been so afraid when I called; she thought it was one of "them" tracking her down. Paula ended our call by making me promise not to tell our parents.

Later that day I spoke with my brother-in-law Tommy, and after a good deal of badgering, he told me some more details of Paula's experience. He said Paula had been forced by these people to cut the hearts out of several live victims in satanic ceremonies. She was also forced to place the severed heads of these victims on a shelf in some room and to participate in cannibalism. Tommy said this explained why Paula had a knife phobia and an irrational fear of dying. This was all news to me! However, at that time I accepted what I had been told and did not ask the many questions that were plaguing me.

The next day I again phoned Paula at the hospital and she told me she knew Tommy had given me the details and that it was all right for me to know these things. Paula then told me the memory had been revealed under hypnosis and also in group therapy sessions. Her breakdown had occurred, she said, when she could no longer cope with the memories. The next thing she told me I found extremely curious; she said she had the best story at the hospital and at her group therapy sessions she was looked up to because she was "being so brave" throughout her ordeal. She went on to tell me she had always felt different and that someday she knew she would be famous. I didn't know how to respond to these revelations. These phone conversations went on daily for about the next week or so. Every day new stories would be revealed to me, sometimes contradicting the ones previously related. I was very confused.

I told my wife about this and we both agreed that something in Paula's account was extremely strange. My wife then told me several stories Paula had related to her. These were told to my wife in strict confidence over a period of about eight years. In one story Paula said she had been raped at age sixteen by two of her male friends at knife point. This, Paula said, was the reason she had always been afraid of knives. She also told my wife that she had had a bad LSD trip as a teenager and that her friends (perhaps the same group?) had left her in a field for dead when they thought she had overdosed. Paula gave this as her reason for being morbidly afraid of death and why she was still suffering from panic attacks.

Another of Paula's stories concerned her son Joe. She said she had suspected her son had been abused at a day care center. Joe had been the same age as our daughter at the time, about four years old. When my wife asked about the nature of the abuse Paula was vague, and when my wife asked her if she had notified the authorities she had said she did not want to and would simply move her son to a different day care facility. This was at the time the television and newspapers were full of the McMartin Preschool scare. Even though some of the stories Paula had related were distressing on the surface, my wife had not fully believed them at the time because there had been too many inconsistencies to make the stories truly real.

Research

My wife, at this point, suggested we go to the library and do some research into various mental and physical disorders. I had to agree. Could Paula's new revelations or "memories" be a continuation of another pattern of her personality? I just had to try to find out.

The next day my wife brought home several books ranging from Dr. Torrey's book on schizophrenia to books on manic depression and victims of child abuse. She also brought a new book about mitral valve syndrome or MVS. I remembered that Paula had been diagnosed a couple of years before with a mitral valve condition. When I read this book it was as though it had been written about my sister.

Right down to the development of phobias about objects or places caused by associating them with panic attacks. I also remembered Paula had been prescribed medication to help her cope with the panic attacks which are extremely common in people with this syndrome.

By coincidence at that time there was a PBS series on the brain and its disorders. One of these episodes related the story of a woman who suffered from a low level of the hormone progesterone. While shopping the woman became confused and paranoid and attempted to stab a young girl she perceived was a threat to her. With proper diagnosis and medication the woman was successfully treated. Another story was about a woman who was hypoglycemic and had attacks of irrational behavior (sometimes violent) when her blood-sugar level was radically low. These stories reminded me of my sister. Her eating habits, which were atrocious, consisted of snack foods and diet sodas. I knew this was all supposition on my part, but after seeing the program and reading the books I was impressed with the delicate chemical balance in which the brain functioned.

It was at this point I decided to speak to the doctor. After several attempts he finally returned my call. He told me that Paula was suffering from the effects of a childhood trauma and that she was doing as well as could be expected. I asked him if he had done any tests on Paula to check for physical problems such as manic depression, schizophrenia, low blood sugar, hormone imbalances, etc. I also asked if they had performed any brain scans. His reply was to ask me if I was a doctor. I told him no, but that I was a very concerned brother. I also asked him to keep an open mind about what Paula was telling him since her initial symptoms could be attributed to definite physical problems. He assured me that all possible tests had been done and that he was positive Paula was not schizophrenic or suffering from manic depression. I then asked him if he was aware of Paula's mitral valve problem and he replied that he was. Something in his tone made me suspect that he was not aware of it, but I could not be sure. At this point I asked him if he had told Paula and her husband that he planned to write a book about her experiences. He replied that he hadn't exactly said that, but maybe it would be worth writing a paper about. I reminded him that he should maintain his objectivity about this case since, after all, this was my sister we were talking about. He assured me Paula would feel much better in a few months and expected her to be recovered within a year or so. I tried to feel reassured as I hung up.

Recollections

From the beginning I had been probing my memory for anything that might give me a clue to ANYTHING that could have happened to my sister. I'm five years older than Paula is so when the abuse was supposed to have happened I was already fifteen years old. I can remember nothing about Paula's behavior that would substantiate a trauma of this magnitude. Paula had been a bubbly, happy, active (albeit a handful) little kid. I can't help thinking that any human being, let alone a young child, could go through what Paula said she experienced and not exhibit some, if not all manner of dramatic behavioral changes. I realize teenagers are not the most observant of persons, but Paula was always Paula. She had a definite personality from the time she was born and I didn't notice a change until it became more exaggerated as she got older. I just couldn't figure it out.

By this time I had also probed my parents and other relatives for information. After much soul searching I finally decided to tell mom and dad the details of Paula's breakdown. I told them about the baby sitters, the Satanic ritual murders, the cannibalism, etc. They were absolutely shocked beyond belief. My mother told me Paula had stayed at the baby sitter's home for about one hour after school, but only on certain days of the week. She only went on the days I was not home which were the days I had golf practice for the school golf team. Paula went straight to the sitter's house from the bus stop. They lived about a block away from our house. They were an elderly couple who had grown children of their own. In fact, some of the children were friends of my aunt and uncle. The couple occasionally sat for children in the neighborhood. My aunt, who knew the family better than we did, said they were a nice family and well respected in the community. My mother remembers picking Paula up from their house and she always seemed fine, in fact, quite happy. As many times as my mother was in the sitter's home she noticed nothing unusual. It was just a smaller, older version of our house.

A day after I talked with the doctor I called Paula again at the hospital. She proceeded to give me much more detail about the Satanic rituals. She told me the victims were hobos (homeless men) who lived in the woods around the neighborhood, and that at least one was a young blond girl, probably in her teens. I thought I would ask her some questions about the details of her experience. I asked her if it was difficult for her, as a child of ten, to cut the hearts out of those poor people. She said she had been helped by a "hooded" figure who held her hand through the procedure. I could not help recalling our father's operation.

Paula then told me that she had a memory block when it came to seeing this individual's face. The doctor had told her that her "big breakthrough" in her therapy would come when she "saw" who this person was. But even under hypnosis she was unable to identify this person. She continued her account of what happened by telling me the victims were laid out on a large concrete or marble slab in the basement of the house (the sitter's) where the rituals were to have taken place. She then told me that the doctor wanted her to get out of the hospital and to get back to work. She was not comfortable with this idea and felt she needed to stay in the hospital until she felt a bit better.

A day later when I called her again she sounded really upset. Apparently, one of the nurses had told her to stop faking her symptoms and to just snap out of it. He felt she was just afraid of dying and who wasn't afraid of death. Paula was livid and the doctor had ordered the nurse to her room where Paula proceeded to chew the nurse out for what he had said to her. She said she had felt powerful and in charge when she had done this.

A few days later Paula went home. She also began working again part time. Paula called me at home a couple of days later and told me she wanted to get the family together in Reno so she could tell us face to face what had happened to her. At first she insisted the family session was her doctor's idea and not her idea. But when I talked to her husband a short time later, he told me that the doctor was against the meeting and had only agreed because Paula had insisted on it. Tommy also told me the doctor would tightly control the session and to be prepared for this.

The Confrontation
In early March of 1990 the entire family drove to Reno to

attend the family session in the doctor's office. He began the meeting by stating that Paula was suffering from the aftereffects of a severe childhood trauma. And that the trauma had occurred while under the care of her mother and father. Her memory of these events had apparently been suppressed for the past twenty-nine years of Paula's life. The doctor then added that he was sure that this had happened to my sister and that when something like this occurs the family often goes into "denial."

Paula then began to relate some of her story to our mother and father. Part way through her recital mom interrupted her and told Paula she had never ever showed any signs of distress or upset when she had been that age. I noticed Paula was rigid with anger and through clenched teeth she began to argue with mom. The doctor stopped the exchange and reminded Paula of the self-control exercises they had worked on. She regained her composure and continued to relate her story to us. Before she got to the really gruesome details, the doctor stopped her again and told us the "details" of her experience were not important. Paula then told him that there had never been any communication in our family and that no one ever took anything she had to say seriously. At this point I decided to bring up the rape story that my wife had related to me earlier to see what Paula would say. It had been a date-rape situation, she said, and she had been threatened into having sex with them by knife point. Mom at this point brought up the fact that Paula had been a physical virgin at the time of her first medical examination at the age of nineteen. This exam preceded Paula's first marriage and mom had gone with her. Since mom was a registered nurse she knew what had been revealed by the exam. Paula was utterly enraged by our mother saying this, and began to change her account of what had happened. She began to contradict herself and became confused and more upset. She said she had not actually been raped, but had fought her would-be rapists off. I felt Paula was trying desperately to cover up a falsehood she had told. The doctor, however, stopped Paula again and reminded her that the "details" of this were not important. He suggested we get behind Paula and support her through her trying time. Of course we were willing to do this so the session proceeded and the tension ebbed. Paula seemed to dwell mostly on the relationship she had with our mother and her wish that their relationship were a better, closer one. We ended the session by giving Paula a big hug and telling her we would always love her. She then invited us back to her house for an informal visit.

The next morning we again met at Paula's house and everyone settled into the kitchen for coffee and sweet rolls. I noticed that Paula was not around. When she finally did appear she was like a caged animal pacing up and down the room. I was confused by this since we had left her the evening before in a cocoon of family love, understanding, and support. Finally she couldn't stand our nervous small talk any longer and screamed, "Look what they made me do with my hands!" We were all stunned into complete silence until dad quietly asked her to tell us what happened to her and to leave out none of the details. Mom and dad still had not heard the complete story from Paula herself. Shaking with emotion she began a description of the rituals and finished by screaming at mom (not dad) her frustration with them for coming to her home and trying to "sweep everything under the rug" as usual.

We sat there with our mouths open, stunned. I didn't know what she had meant by the comment she made since none of us had said anything. But I got up and hugged her, telling her to remember I would always love her. The entire family joined in the hugging and support of my sister. After a while Paula went to lie down. We talked quietly with her husband about Paula's "memories." A short time later my sister left the house in the company of her husband. This gave us some time alone to sort through all that had happened within the last twenty-four hours. We were drained emotionally and physically by the morning's proceedings so we just sat around trying to absorb what we had witnessed.

When Paula and her husband returned she told us she had an audio tape she wanted us all to listen to. She said the doctor had given it to her. It was a recorded lecture given by a woman who claimed to have been horribly abused sexually, physically, and emotionally by her father and other live-in male household members. She provided a very detailed description of her ordeal and went on to explain that later on in her life she began to exhibit all manner of physical maladies that directly related to specific acts of abuse that were performed on her body. She then related her theory that all physical problems people have that have no other explanation such as back pains, numbness in the extremities, strange muscle cramps, illness and depression, to name just a few, were the direct result of childhood abuse. She said that this was so even if the person in question had no knowledge or memory of the abuse. The lecturer said she was getting her life together and was planning to become a psychologist. She could then help others like herself "remember" the abuse so as to begin the "healing process."

The tape was about half over when Paula turned it off. I asked her if we could hear the remainder of the tape, but she said it was of no importance. I realized at this point that Paula wanted us to hear only the part about the physical manifestations of childhood abuse. Paula went on to tell us that all the illnesses she had suffered through the years were because of the abuse she had endured. She even went so far as to deny having had a virus (Valley Fever) that was medically documented a few years earlier.

I couldn't believe a professional would give a disturbed patient a tape whose premise was so obviously flawed. I did not think I could argue the fine points with my sister at this time. The day progressed without further incident and by the end of the day Paula was feeling assured of our love and support. We left Reno early the next morning for San Diego.

More Memories

After that time I spoke to Paula maybe five more times on the phone. At this point I had decided to try and just listen to what Paula had to say about her experience. I would try not to question her too much even though I had my reservations about many parts of what she told me. I continued to gather information from the rest of our family still living in the town where the abuse was to have taken place. Unfortunately it became increasingly difficult for me to "just listen" since Paula was beginning to insinuate that our mother might be the "hooded figure" in her flashbacks. She talked about this fact a lot until she finally admitted it was probably her anger towards mom and dad, especially mom, for allowing this abuse to have happened to her that was making her feel like this.

I was curious about her flashbacks so I asked her to describe one of them to me. She explained that she mentally returned to the age of ten and would re-experience the trauma. She also made a point of telling me that it could happen at any time of the day or night. They always started with her heart beginning to pound rapidly and then a wave of extreme fear and nausea would sweep over her. The impulse to run would come next. It would be a couple of hours before she would experience the memory of the trauma. I asked her if these attacks reminded her of a mitral valve attack. She then wanted to know why I would ask such a question. She became very defensive.

I had brought this up because the attack Paula had described was a textbook description of a mitral valve panic attack (caused by abnormal brain chemical activity) with a trauma memory tacked on. To me it seemed logical that, if the panic attack had been trauma-induced, the sequence of events would have been reversed. Needless to say, I did not point this out to Paula at this time.

Sometime later Paula called me and complained she was having trouble dealing with her job. She was also having trouble sleeping and often would wake up at 2 a.m. with a panic attack. She began to relate a theory she had about the significance of this. Paula told me she was now having flashbacks that revealed she had been removed from our house in the middle of the night (at age ten) and forced to participate in the rituals. Shocked, I told her that I had no memory of anything like this happening and that living in the same small house surely I would have been aware of something like that. She said she felt mom and dad knew something about all this but were "in denial." I didn't argue further since it seemed pointless at that time.

A couple of days after this I telephoned Paula. Tommy, her husband, answered and said Paula was at work. I asked him how he was holding up and he said it was tough, but that he was fine. He said Paula was spending money like there was no tomorrow and couldn't wait for her to get back to work full time so the mountain of bills, medical and others, would begin to get paid. He told me they were already over $10,000 in debt. I asked him why Paula was spending money they didn't have and he replied that the doctor was encouraging her to relive her lost childhood, and Paula complied by going out and purchasing toys, dolls, handbags, eye glasses, whatever she fancied. He also told me something I found very strange. Paula now wanted to be called Paulie as she had as a child. I found this queer because Paula had told me not two days earlier that she was finally a woman now, an adult for the first time in her life, and no one was going to treat *her* like a child again.

I then asked Tommy about the latest addition to Paula's story (her theory about being removed from the house at 2 a.m.) He said he had purchased a book on Satanic Cults (one of many books the doctor recommended) and in the book it explained that the rituals were only conducted on the nights of the full moon. He also confided in me that he felt the purchase of the book was a big mistake because Paula was incorporating more and more elements from the book into her own story. It was then he told me he was beginning to have feelings of doubt about Paula's story and asked me how I felt about it. I told him I, too, had my doubts, especially since I had been there too. This was the first, and unfortunately the last, time Tommy expressed any doubt about all this being true.

I told him about the books I had read and in particular the information I had found out about Mitral Valve Syndrome. I told him about the panic attacks described in the book and about the subsequent developments of phobias associated with the attacks. There had also been a comment in the book about the frequent occurrence of panic attacks striking at 2 a.m.! I also related some of the information I had found dealing with manic depression. Tommy seemed interested. He expressed great concern that, if the story were not true, the alternative was almost scarier; the alternative being mental illness. Tommy also mentioned Paula was extremely paranoid about him talking to anyone on the phone and sometimes she would listen to his private conversations on the extension in the bedroom. I sympathized.

The next day when I came home my wife was on the phone talking to Paula. From the look on my wife's face I could tell it was not an amiable conversation. My wife handed me the phone and, as I said hello, Paula said, "I understand you had a conversation with Tommy yesterday." I told her yes, I did, and from the tone of her voice I could tell this was going to be a difficult conversation. She said Tommy had told her that I didn't believe her story. She was absolutely livid with anger. I tried to explain that I just wanted to get to the bottom of what really happened, if anything, and to find out what was really going on.

She was not interested in what I thought or what I had found out about the people she was accusing of abusing her. She just didn't want to hear it. At this point I felt I had nothing left to lose so I decided to challenge her story. I brought up all the points I found to contradict her story. This, of course, led to an argument where we, the family, were placed in a no-win situation of being "IN DENIAL." I also tried to point out that her physical symptoms could be caused by a physical condition; that people with MVS often had panic attacks. She countered that she was only having flashbacks! Besides, she said, she no longer had a heart valve problem and that it had cleared up along with all the other physical problems that used to plague her. I reasoned that it was a congenital defect and that it just couldn't "clear up." We went back and forth like this for a while until Paula finally told me to mind my own business and to "look after my own little family" and leave her alone. She then hung up and that was the last contact I had with her. It was May 1990.

Suit, Countersuit

In July 1988, one of our daughters, who had just completed a year of medical internship, acknowledged that her drinking had become a serious problem. She notified her medical board and us that she was checking into a treatment center for substance abuse. She had been under tremendous pressure during internship working extremely long hours and having to deal with the emotional stress of divorcing her second husband. We wrote to her commending her decision, wished her well, reminded her that we loved and supported her. We called her in early August to see how she was doing, only to find out that the program hadn't been totally successful. She said she was going to get further treatment/counseling. We spoke to her again a week or so later and found out she had been in a serious automobile accident. Medication she was taking made her so drowsy that on the way to work she rear-ended a truck. The car was demolished and the people who pulled her out said she was lucky she wasn't killed. In the meantime, she started attending a counseling group and attempted to work at a local clinic. Although we have never learned the details regarding the problems that developed while working at the clinic, she apparently only worked there a short time.

The Charge

We didn't hear from her for several weeks, so the evening before Thanksgiving, we called to wish her a happy holiday — Thanksgiving had always been a very special family holiday and she had usually been home with the rest of the family to celebrate it. When she answered, her voice was like ice and she said, "We have to talk." I responded, "So talk." She didn't want to talk on the phone, she said, but indicated she would write us a letter. Then she exploded, "You made me sick and abused me for twenty-five years and I'm angry." I wasn't sure how to react to that lightning bolt! I asked her what the heck she was talking about, and she replied "You know. Incest." I was shocked and could really not believe what I had heard. All I could say was, "That's not true." Her answer was: "They told me you would deny it." I suggested that maybe she should write that letter – soon – and we ended the conversation. Obviously, whatever had happened to change her attitude happened in October 1988. She called her older sister and brother and repeated the accusations of child abuse. Her brother was particularly angry with her, asking why she was trying to hurt us. An interesting point she made to him was that when she told her therapist that she had had some awful thoughts about her parents but was sure they couldn't be true, her therapist countered, "Of course they can! You'll feel better if you talk about it." Her brother indicated that until she apologized, he didn't think they had anything more to talk about. Her older sister also told her that whatever she thought had happened, didn't.

At Christmas, 1988, she sent gifts to her siblings and to us, but no cards and still no letter. She sent her siblings books: *Adult Children of Alcoholics* and *Healing the Child Within*. We only talked to her once more – in January 1989 – to inform her that one of her godparents' sons had been killed in a bicycle accident, and we thought she might like to send them a note. After that, we didn't hear anything from her. She called her younger sister in February 1989 and repeated the accusations. Her younger sister wouldn't confirm her ideas either. We sent her a birthday card and when her grandmother passed away in June

1989, we sent her a telegram but received no acknowl-
edgement. In September 1989, she wrote her two sisters
about going to a treatment center for incest survivors in a
nearby state, which was paid for, at least in part, by people
with whom she worked. At Christmas, we sent her a card
but it was returned marked "No Forwarding Address." She
had moved and would not tell anyone in the family her
new address. The operator told us she had an unlisted
telephone number.

The Suit

On May 7, 1990, we were served with the complaint
and summons of a Civil Lawsuit that she had filed on
October 16, 1989. We didn't find out for several days why
it hadn't been served until seven months after it was filed
and why we had gotten almost daily phone calls and when
I would answer, no one on the other end would respond.
In this lawsuit, she charged us with physical and verbal
abuse, substandard parenting and negligence, inserting
foreign objects into her body, molesting her, electrical
torture, satanic ritual, and false imprisonment. Knowing
our daughter's childhood, it was unbelievable to us to the
point that we wondered if someone was playing a practical
joke on us. Since there wasn't any truth to her allegations,
we knew there couldn't be any evidence to prove it, so
what attorney would accept a case so totally void of cred-
ibility unless there were ulterior motives?

We took the complaint to our attorney and he said he
would handle it if it was a civil case but that he did not
handle criminal cases. He said he would have someone go
down to Superior Court and find out why there had been
such a long delay in serving the summons. His explanation
made the serving of the Civil Lawsuit summons pale com-

pared to the story he told us about our daughter going to the police accusing us of murder. The first experience seemed unbelievable. This event was ludicrous. Our daughter had gone to the police the month her grandmother died, June 1989, and claimed to have had three children before she was twelve years old (biologically impossible) and that we killed them or caused their disposal. The police conducted an investigation of her allegations during the period prior to our being served, and had requested her attorney not to serve the Civil Lawsuit lest we destroy possible evidence. They had sent detectives out-of-state to interview our daughter and her ex-husband. They informed our attorney that, at that point, they had found no basis to file any charges, but that they were not closing the case.

The attorneys proceeded with the daughter's civil suit. Demurrers that were filed with the court to dismiss the suit on the basis of various legal technicalities were denied. Discovery commenced with the subpoena of all kinds of records and the scheduling of depositions from everyone in the family. In August 1990, our plaintiff daughter came to town and gave her deposition, which our attorney video-taped. She refused to state her home address or place of work and her attorney said all communications were to go through her office. Her deposition took three days during which she claimed to have 112 personalities to deal with the "terror" of her experience. The alleged events involved all members of the family, relatives, godparents, neighbors, members of our church, and most importantly, parties that we could never identify. During the deposition, she disclosed that the counseling group she attended for over a year had been disbanded because of problems the therapists were unable to control. We were able to watch the first of the nine tapes before we gave our depositions.

That one tape told us that either our daughter was very, very sick or had been duped by some very methodical brainwashing, or she was playing a role to the hilt. Everything was too pat, too organized and well-planned.

Through September, October, and November of 1990, all of the rest of the family gave depositions. Everyone refuted the allegations. Our attorney even told us that he felt her attorney no longer believed much of whatever her client had told her.

The Countersuit

After all of the depositions were completed, our attorneys filed motions with the court regarding our daughter's failure to produce records which they had subpoenaed. We had discussed with our attorneys the merits of filing a counter suit for malicious prosecution, attempted extortion, slander, and defamation of character. They said it would be possible to file a cross-complaint in the same court, so we told them to go ahead. After a couple of months of legal maneuvering, the attorneys broached the subject of a possible settlement. The first suggestion by the daughter's attorney included our payment of money and we told our attorneys absolutely not. We felt payment of any money was tantamount to admission that her charges had truth to them. We told our attorneys to pursue our cross-complaint, and because our daughter had indicated in journals that she maintained during counseling, and which we obtained by discovery, that she wanted to hurt and humiliate us, see us in jail, kill us, and indicated she wanted to write a book, so we asked for an injunction against her publicizing her false story and identifying either directly or indirectly members of our family or friends whom she had falsely accused.

On March 15, 1991, just before our attorneys were able to go take depositions from our daughter's two principal therapists and ex-husband, our daughter dropped her lawsuit! Her attorney suggested we drop our cross-complaint. We said no. Then she suggested that we drop our suit and each pay our attorneys' fees. The court had awarded us a judgment in the amount of $8,400 for court costs but nothing for attorneys' fees. We continued to pursue our cross-complaint with our attorneys, filing motions for more monetary compensation, and her attorney filing motions to invalidate the cross-complaint. Her attorney even said that if we succeeded in obtaining a larger judgment, her client would file for bankruptcy and we wouldn't collect a dime, which to us just appeared to be another part of what was meant to be a carefully orchestrated scam.

Finally in July 1991, our attorneys rescheduled depositions for her therapists and ex-husband in late August, and obtained a tentative trial date in the latter part of September. Due to the unavailability of one of the therapists, the date for depositions had to slip into September. Our attorney then advised us that a settlement conference was scheduled for the day before the depositions were to take place. This caused mixed emotions because a trial would have been a very trying experience with no assurance of the outcome, but we wanted some answers out of those depositions.

The Settlement

On September 4, 1991, the settlement conference was held. Our daughter was present and this was the first time we had seen her since 1987. She was accompanied by the same woman who came with her for her deposition. Not once did our daughter look at us or speak to us. We remembered how as a little girl she couldn't look us in the face when she lied. Even more remarkable, she never smiled, and the judge also commented on that. This was a daughter who always had a sense of humor and smiled often. This was the first time we had seen her since May 1987 at her graduation from medical school and we were very upset with her condition. We wanted very badly to have an explanation of what had happened to our daughter that would cause such a catastrophic change in her behavior and personality.

The settlement agreement hammered out that day included the injunction, payment of the judgment within three years, agreement by the daughter to continue psychotherapy, and to have a psychiatric evaluation by a doctor of our choice. We requested our attorneys to draw up the settlement and file it with the court so that if there were problems at some later date, it would minimize the work and time necessary to resolve them. After several months of ironing out the details of performing the psychiatric evaluation, the agreement was signed on December 4, 1991 and filed with the court on January 5, 1992. Because of the settlement, the depositions of our daughter's therapists and ex-husband were canceled. We were unhappy about this and felt that possibly there had been some manipulation of events in order to prevent us from obtaining information concerning our daughter's therapy and related activities.

The psychiatrist we selected performed the evaluation on January 24, 1992, and we had a conference with him the following week. He concluded she was not "crazy" but, like an increasing number of cases across the country, had been subjected to some unscrupulous and inappropriate counseling. Therapists who, thinking that they are "rescuing" adults who were allegedly abused as children, are, by suggestion and projection, making their clients believe that they have indeed been abused sexually, verbally, and emotionally. He says the process causes the patient to become alienated from the family and dependent upon therapy for an extended period of time. He feels that some counselors are even advocating that their clients sue their "perpetrators," usually parents, for alleged damages, a practice which was confirmed by VOCAL (Victims of Child Abuse Legislation) leaders. As a result of our discussion with the psychiatrist, we are now doing research on "repressed memory" counseling and obtaining all the information available on this subject from the "FMS" (False Memory Syndrome) Foundation. This information conclusively proves that there are many other cases just like ours across the nation.

Although our troubled daughter is a self-supporting adult and has been on her own for fifteen years, we feel that in view of the events of the past three years, we can no longer assume a passive role in this matter, and must take whatever prudent steps are warranted to protect the interests of the family as a whole and assure our daughter's recovery.

An Open Letter to Our Daughter's Therapist

Our daughter's therapist is a medical doctor who has practiced family medicine for almost forty years. He also taught at a leading North American university. Now semiretired, he maintains a practice as a family therapist and conducts seminars and workshops based on his self-help book. He claims that our self image is formed in infancy, that the parents convey to their children feelings of being unworthy of achieving happiness, and that this buried information can be contacted, updated and revised (presumably with the help of the right therapist). Only then, when a person is released from the constraints forced on him in his infancy by his parents, can he find true happiness.

We had the opportunity to talk to him two times. The first time we met him about two weeks after we discovered, indirectly, our daughter's delusion of being sexually abused by her father. The second time, about six months later, the visit took place after we were notified by her, in writing, about the horrible "abuse" she was exposed to between the ages of two and fifteen. We have no doubts that it was the "therapy" that led to recollection of events that never happened. At the same time we are aware of the sad reality that at this time, the therapist is probably the only person who could lead our daughter out of the maze of the fabricated "memories," if he only wanted to. After our second visit, mother wrote him a letter, in a desperate attempt to elicit his sympathy and to enlist his help. We are going to share with you this letter, which was slightly changed to protect our identity.

March 28, 1992
Dear Dr. R.

I am writing to you because I am convinced that, at this time, you are probably the only person who can help Jennifer to get rid of her delusion of being sexually abused by her father, and who can assist in the restoration of a normal relationship between her and her family.

For the past year we have been trying in vain to understand what has happened to her, what is the root of the fierce, totally undeserved hostility towards us. Approximately a year ago, her behavior changed abruptly and inexplicably. One day last March, she phoned and told me that she is seeing a family therapist. I was surprised, since I was not aware that she needed one. True, she had some problems at work, and a chronic illness, for long time in remission, flared up unexpectedly, but Jennifer seemed to be coping well. What surprised me even more was the fact that she was seeing a family therapist, as if her family was in some way responsible for her predicament. I asked her whether, since she sees a family therapist, the rest of the family should also be involved. She said that it was not necessary. Then she asked for her father. When he picked up the phone, she accused him of severely beating her when she was a child. He was astonished, speechless, horrified. When he told her that he did not know what she was talking about, she ridiculed him for having amnesia. Several weeks later, she and her fiance came to Our Town to pick up her belong-

ings, but she refused to explain what has been happening. We tried to keep the line of communication open, so we phoned every two weeks or so, but her responses grew colder and ruder. We tried to rationalize her behavior. Perhaps we were too protective and she wanted to "cut the apron strings," and she was doing it in an extreme way so that we would get the message. Or she thought that we disapproved of her choice of mate and she wanted to put a distance between us to avoid possible criticism. Still, even such rationalization somehow could not explain the depth and abruptness of her alienation.

Then, sometime in August, Jennifer phoned her sister and told her that for some time she has been able to remember incidents of physical abuse and negligence in her early childhood, and that recently she recovered "memories" of being sexually abused by her father between the ages of eleven and fifteen. Later, she moved the onset of the abuse to the age of two. We were shocked, confused, worried, hurting. This was so absurd! We did not know what her intentions were— was her sister supposed to tell us or not? What were we supposed to do? We needed time, so we decided to pretend that we did not know. In the meantime, we tried to cope with our despair, to understand what had happened, and to find means of approaching Jennifer in the most gentle, conciliatory way. We contacted professor Elizabeth Loftus, a specialist in the field of false memories. She put us in touch with

"Jane Doe", who wrote an account of false accusation of her husband by their grown-up, educated, intelligent daughter. We read and re-read the "Jane Doe" story and we were astonished by the similarities. All of a sudden, we did not feel alone. This article finally convinced us that we should let Jennifer know that we are aware of her accusation. We sent her the article hoping that after she and her fiance read this story, they may start having doubts about the validity of her "suppressed memory" recollections. In a letter that accompanied the article we suggested (as several times before) that we meet and try to get to the core of this tragic situation. Jennifer refused our proposal. Instead, she delivered her final blow. She sent to us a six-page handwritten letter, a separate copy to each of us. The contents of this letter are incredibly cruel, but even more frightening is the fact that it is completely delusional. Sexual abuse at the age of two, vaginal penetration at the age of three, oral sex, sodomy, savage beating that ended in rape, almost a complete list of the most repulsive crimes that can be committed against a human being. And all this from the pen of our beloved, pampered and admired daughter! I don't know whether you can imagine our mental suffering, horror, feeling of utmost absurdity; and on top of it, a deep worry about Jennifer's mental health, since a person of sound mind would not be able to fabricate something so sickening.

You may say that it is not a fabrication of an impressionable mind, but a reality. I must as-

sure you that if only a small fraction of the violations described in the letter, indeed if only one single incident happened, I would be the first one to take an action, I would take the children and leave immediately. You met Henry twice. Does he look like a pedophile, rapist, sexual pervert? Do I look like a subservient doormat who would tolerate this to happen? Moreover, if we were such perverts, it would surely show somewhere else as well. But the fact is that we are absolutely normal people, as anyone who knows us can confirm. We have a sense of purpose in life, we like ourselves, we are appreciated at work and in the community. We have a stable marriage based on love and mutual respect. There was not a single case of infidelity in the thirty-three years we have been together. These are certainly not the attributes of a pedophile, a rapist, and his accomplice.

Let me go back in time and briefly describe my perception of our family life in general and of our relationship with Jennifer in specific.

As you know, Jennifer was born in Central Europe. She was born after five years of marriage, and since the day she was born she was surrounded by love. Our love, her grandparents', uncles' and aunts' love. She was a delightful child: witty, inquisitive, intelligent, fun to be with.

When she was eight months old, she had a seizure. You seem to be attaching an extreme importance to this event. Surely we were concerned, but we were told by the pediatrician that this is quite common in babies, especially during a fever (which was the case). You came to a conclusion that since we showed Jennifer concerned faces in the days after her seizure, we destroyed her self-esteem. She "stored" somewhere in her subconscious the belief that she failed us, her parents, her "gods." You dwelt on this notion during both our visits, so you must be really convinced about its validity. But the fact is that we were as much concerned as parents whose child has a flu or an ear infection. In other words, our behavior was not any different from a behavior of millions of other parents. Moreover, it is quite human to worry once in a while, to show concerned faces to people we love, without destroying their feeling of self-worth, just the opposite. Besides, by worrying we destroyed, in your opinion, our daughter's self-esteem, and if we did not worry, we would have been branded as callous, not caring parents. So it seems to be a no-win situation.

In the late '60s Henry's parents, our daughters, us, and eight other relatives came to North America. Thus, in spite of leaving the country of our birth, we have a large extended family here, a fact greatly appreciated by both our children. Shortly after our arrival, Henry and I were hired by a large manufacturing firm in Our Town and we have been with the same employer ever since. Both girls learned English effortlessly and settled into life in a small, friendly community.

Throughout her elementary and high school years, Jennifer was an avid reader and an original thinker, but her marks did not show it. She was attractive, but she did not date. She did not have too many friends—she seemed to prefer books and nature to people. When she was fifteen, we moved to a larger house and she changed school. Shortly after, she started to exhibit signs of an emotional distress. She cried a lot, did poorly in school, and she manifested hostility towards both of us. Our family doctor and the psychiatrist who examined her explained her behavior as typical for the transition from childhood to adolescence. Later we found that in the new school, there was a gang of bullies who picked on her, ridiculed her for her accent and made her life miserable. However, by her second year in the new school she found a good friend, she settled down, and everything returned to normal.

We spent vacations and weekends with our children, we went for ski holidays every year, we camped and hiked together. We were always available when they needed us. We provided them with emotional stability, intellectual stimulation, and material security. Both girls told us on many occasions that they appreciated the good life that we had together. Of course, there were frictions, since nothing is perfect. There were frictions between me and my mother-in-law for several years and there were fights about Jennifer's sloppiness. Henry used to be what Jennifer called "sarcastic," perhaps a certain type of humor that rubbed her the wrong way, but we lived in peace and harmony most of the time. This is what makes her accusations so much more bizarre and incomprehensible.

Jennifer left home many years ago to attend universities and later to work. But she always liked to come home to Our Town for summer jobs. Later, she looked for a permanent job in Our Town, and only lack of opportunities forced her to move to a large city in the South. This is hardly a behavior of a severely abused child.

I assume that you have read her hateful letter. Please let me quote from another letter, which she sent to me for my 50th birthday seven years ago: " . . . You have accomplished a lot and therefore acquired wisdom. Specifically, you've been academically successful, brought up two happy and mature children, and have a husband who adores you more through the years. . . . Having lived fully, you know yourself and the world better and therefore have more to give to others. . . . Basically the same stuff applies to Dad. Show him this letter in June so I don't have to write again. . . ."

There is not much more to say. I am not going to try to analyze Jennifer's mental state and the circumstances leading to the profound change in her perception of her past. I am convinced that this absurd situation will not last forever. One day she will realize what has happened to her and how it has affected her parents, her sister, and indeed, the whole extended family. The problem is that we do not have decades to wait. We are at the age when time is more precious with each passing day. We have been robbed of Jennifer's love, respect, the pleasure of her company, and she has been robbed of the nice memories of the years gone by. Moreover, she has a problem, no doubt about it. Otherwise she wouldn't be so susceptible to "remembering" sexual or any other form of abuse that never happened. However, until she uncovers the real roots of her unhappiness and low self-esteem, she will never be able to move ahead. She will be forever locked in an emotional time warp.

When we asked you during both visits how we can help Jennifer to get rid of her false memories, you suggested that we examine our own childhood, that we get in touch and explore our inner "I." You also implied that Jennifer will learn about our efforts through "emanation," or some sort of telepathy. We have a great difficulty with applying your advice. First of all, we do not have an urge for regressing into our childhood years, nor do we feel compelled to probe our subconscious. We are happy the way we are. When we face a problem, we analyze the facts, do our best and move on with life. Also, we do not believe in telepathy. Instead, we would greatly appreciate your help in facilitating our meeting with Jennifer. Right now, she refuses to see us, to talk to us. We would like to be given the opportunity to meet her face to face, to initiate a discussion, and to try to correct this horrible injustice with compassion, patience and dignity. Thank you for reading my letter.

56 Personalities

"I'm a sugarplum," Heidi explained with pride to a friendly inquirer. She was a shining three-year old and it was obvious that she was secure in her knowledge that sugarplums are very special people. From sugarplumhood to womanhood, Heidi never lost that shining quality. Identified as a gifted child, she moved at an accelerated pace through her early school years and, with a fellowship award in hand, entered graduate school on a doctoral track.

Heidi's first marriage to a person for the sake of whose career she abandoned her own professional goals ended in bitter divorce. Shortly thereafter, without notice to family or friends, Heidi married a young man we did not know very well.

About four years ago Heidi announced that the tingling and numbness in her limbs had been diagnosed as multiple sclerosis. To assuage my grief, I read everything I could find about this degenerative condition, taking heart from the slow-moving progression of my daughter's sclerosis and praying for a medical breakthrough that might halt the ravages of the disease. Heidi appeared to be gaining strength from the support group which she had joined, a group of persons in various stages of disability from multiple sclerosis. It was about this time that she began speaking of the "dysfunctionality" of our family.

Dr. Faust Enters

About two years ago Heidi asked me to accompany her to the hospital where she underwent a hysterectomy, supposedly necessitated by problems related to multiple sclerosis. This was the first time I heard Heidi speak of Dr. Faust. Dr. Faust, she beamed at me, had told her that she was a "tough cookie." I assumed that Dr. Faust was the medical doctor who had ordered her hysterectomy; I have since learned that he is a psychologist.

Soon thereafter, Heidi reported that she may have been misdiagnosed, that instead of having multiple sclerosis she was suffering a multiple personality disorder. Heidi gave me the impression that it was Dr. Faust who determined that her problem was psychogenetic rather than physical. She related to me how Dr. Faust had apologized over and over saying, "The symptoms are so clear; I don't know how I could have missed it."

In relatively rapid succession thereafter, Heidi announced that Dr. Faust felt she had been sexually abused as a child. In the absence of any memory of abuse, Dr. Faust had suggested hypnosis as a way to get in touch with what had happened to her.

Under hypnosis, Heidi developed a feeling that she had been sexually abused by her father; in a short time, still without any specific memory of abuse, this feeling developed into conviction. The horrible things that Heidi described under hypnosis, her husband explained to me, could not have been made up; Dr. Faust had assured them that such words coming out of her mouth clearly indicated childhood sexual abuse. Further, Dr. Faust had identified fifty-six distinct personalities in Heidi's psychological makeup.

For months I was immobilized by doubts and soul-searching. It cannot be denied that there were problems in our home. My husband and I were not well suited to each other. When my husband told me that the problems were my fault, I accepted the responsibility for making our marriage work and set about with fierce determination to be a better person and to make a good home for my husband and children. As my mother had taught me, I complained to no one lest my problems should be magnified out of proportion and I would take action that I would come to regret.

I felt that I was, for the most part, successful in hiding my problems. I never ceased to marvel at the four beautiful children that had been committed to my care. To the extent that I was capable, every moment of my life was directed toward the nourishment and growth of these four incredible human beings.

Oddly enough, it was Heidi who came home from college one day and, after a stressful scene in which my husband stormed out of the room, turned to me and said, "How much longer are you going to take this?" Until that moment I had not realized that anyone looked upon the relationship from my perspective and the freedom I experienced in that moment allowed me, in due time, to seek a divorce and make a new life in a new community.

Supporting the Therapy

Against this background I have searched the depths of my memory for any indication that Heidi's father sexually abused her. Could I have been so blind and ignorant that I had overlooked signals of distress? While I wrestled with my doubts, Heidi announced that, in order to get well, she needed to distance herself from me; it would be better if I did not try to see her, talk to her by telephone, or contact her in any way until she could work out her problems.

I contacted Dr. Faust seeking advice as to how I might help Heidi, offering to attend therapy sessions with her in order to work things out together. He refused to talk to me at that time or at any future time on the ground that his loyalty was to Heidi.

In rapid succession Heidi lost her long-time job (a responsible position with a national trade association), obtained and lost a second job, and failed in at least two efforts to establish free-lance operations from her home. I learned from other family members that Heidi had expressed her intention to sue her father and me for lifetime maintenance on the ground of her disablement. The letter I received from Heidi, however, made no threat of suit:

> "... I would have given anything to change what has happened over the last three years. I frequently search medical literature for some other explanation for my emotional and mental stress, but there is none. I've been tested and interviewed by several professionals who specialize in treating people who've been abused and who suffer from dissociative disorders as a result of severe childhood trauma. All of them have agreed that I have MPD and all of them believe my memories of traumatic sexual and physical abuse. The memories I've retrieved so far seem to span from just under a year old to around the age of fifteen, plus later abuses suffered outside the family that had also been repressed. I don't want to have MPD and I mourn the loss of my image of my family life. ... I'm not really interested at this point in laying blame or pointing fingers at any one person. There seem to have been a number of people involved. At the same time, it seems unjust for me now to be alone in bearing the

> *burden of the cost of healing from things done*
> *to me over which I had no control. . . ."*

The closing of her letter is stained by the tears that fell when I read:

> *"In spite of our lack of communication these*
> *past months, not a day goes by that I don't think*
> *of you and miss you. I do love you and want*
> *someday to feel strong enough to talk with you*
> *and to work out a way to reestablish our rela-*
> *tionship."*

I responded initially by sending Heidi a rather large sum of money to be used for her own well-being; later, I sent another rather large sum to help her set up a business from home. Believing, from what I had read, that only through therapy would Heidi's fifty-six personalities be integrated, I began sending Dr. Faust monthly sums to assure the continuance of her treatment.

Satanic Conspiracy

Instead of improving, Heidi's condition deteriorated rapidly. She was several times hospitalized as suicidal. On one occasion she underwent surgery to correct a shoulder injury supposed to have been caused by the physical abuse I had inflicted upon her in childhood. Her list of sexual abusers grew to include an only brother in her immediate family as well as all the male members of her grandparental families, representing an extended family covering several states, hundreds of miles and a diversity of interests. Despite the fact that Heidi's contact with these extended family members was limited to occasional holiday visits or family emergencies, Heidi's charges now imply an ongoing conspiracy among these extended family members to sacrifice her to satanic worship and various forms of abuse. In an effort to confirm at least one such memory, Heidi and her husband recently paid a visit to a grandfather's farm for the purpose of locating the grave where she buried a baby that she remembers having been forced to kill. She believes there were numerous attempts to leave her in cold, dark places to die. On one occasion she was locked in an automobile trunk, weighed down by a dead pig that had been sacrificed in a cult ritual.

With her first accusation of sexual abuse, Heidi expressed concern that she had not done more to "save" her sisters. Since then she has been persistent in her attempts to get them to recall their trauma also. Her Christmas gift to Hannah, *Courage to Heal*, was returned with a scathing note. Hilda, on the other hand, while trying to maintain her objectivity, agreed to accompany Heidi to a therapy session with Dr. Faust. When Hilda questioned whether Heidi might be remembering events that she had only imagined to be true, but which had in fact not occurred, the doctor objected: absolutely not, the memories were real and there was not doubt that the abuse had occurred.

Despite her accusation of my physical abuse of her, I have sensed that Heidi has been reluctant to accuse me of any sexual or satanic abuse. Her explanation, I have learned, is that I, too, was abused and that the reason I do not remember it is that I am in denial.

Hilda Too

Under pressures from Heidi, Hilda made the decision to undergo hypnosis herself, if for no other reason than to set her mind at ease as to whether the charges had any foundation. A few days earlier Hilda had said to me, "I don't know what I would do if I didn't have my mother to talk to." A few days later she called to inform me that I had turned my back on her for the last time and that she wanted never to talk to me again. But first, in preparation for the suit which she and Heidi were going to institute against their father and me, she demanded that I prepare for her investigator (name withheld) an affidavit detailing all that I remembered of the family problems. Her brother, she informed me, would be offered a chance to plea bargain in order to avoid conviction for his part in the abuse.

All avenues of communication with my daughters have been cut off. I know they are suffering. I know that in the core of their being lies the knowledge that these tales of horror are false. I know that they suffer not only from this unscrupulous manipulation of their minds, but also from their failure to find relief for the present real conflict which led them to seek therapy in the first place. I know also that they, as well as I, suffer from the distance they have put between themselves and the love and support of their family.

I have a clear memory of my daughters' growing-up years. To say that there were no problems would be patently untrue, problems are a fact of life. But amid the problems I remember an abundance of laughter and love and understanding. What gives Dr. Faust the authority or the expertise to pronounce that imaginings "retrieved" in an hypnotic state are unassailably true against my clear memories otherwise. I was there; he was not.

Nor has Dr. Faust taken any steps to establish a confirming link between these fantasies and any verifiable event beyond the confines of his office. If I understand what *Courage to Heal* requires, it is confrontation with the abuser. Confrontation is not a new concept. It is a fundamental principle of our legal system and underlies any systematic approach to problem-solving. It implies a face-to-face meeting for the purpose of looking at and resolving differences in order to achieve solutions. The cutoff of all communication between an accuser and the accused is no confrontation at all. To the extent that I have been responsible for the problems my daughters are having I want to confront the problems and achieve understanding. To the extent that outside influences have a bearing on their problems, I want to support their coping.

My daughters are dearer than life to me. If I saw them in imminent physical danger, I would give up my own life to save them. It is no different now. Be warned, Dr. Faust. I intend to do everything in my power to save my daughters from your devastating mind control techniques and to expose your insidious evil to the world. I am a strong person and I have only begun to fight.

We Miss You Katie

The following is the story of my daughter's accusation of sexual abuse against my husband and me.

I will use the names of Irene (myself), Robert (my husband) and Katie (our daughter).

My husband and I are seventy-three years old, retired, middle income parents of Katie, age forty-nine, who has been in therapy since February 1990 for being sexually abused. She has accused others of sexually abusing her — one is now dead and she claims that she could not remember the face of the other.

I firmly believe that she has been abused. I went to one of her therapy sessions and watched her relive one of her abuses emotionally and then physically. It was very difficult for her and stressful for me to watch.

In mid-February of this year, Katie called from the Midwest with a request for a conference call with us, herself and a case worker. We later found that she was calling from a psychiatric hospital.

Record of conference call from Minnesota on 17 February 1992 between Katie, Robert, Irene, and case worker Anita:

Katie: *I remember you both abusing me. I am going to limit your phone calls or coming to see me. I will read your letters.*

Robert: *I categorically deny this.*

Irene: *How did this happen?*

Katie: *I can't tell you now.*

Robert: *What kind of abuse?*

Katie: *Sexual.*

Robert: *Who abused you sexually?*

Katie: *Both of you.*

Irene: *Katie, this didn't happen.*

Case worker: *Sometimes it is too painful to remember.*

Robert: *I have no guilt — I am shocked. I want to know where, when and how this happened.*

Katie: *I can't tell you now.*

Robert: *Can we tell the family?*

Katie: *Yes, if you want to.*

Robert: *How long will you be there?*

Katie: *I don't know. If you want to write me, Carl has my address.*

Robert: *What about us?*

Katie: *You can write me. End of conversation.*

Both of us felt sick and drained after this conversation.

Our feelings after the phone call:
Irene:

Angry

Incredulous

Sad — I feel that I will never again have a good relationship with Katie. I feel that she is losing her mind. How can she accuse us of being pedophiles?

Robert:

Angry — Katie is looking for an out and I'm it.

Disappointed with Katie

Shocked

Helpless to defend myself

Frustrated

Reactions of Katie's siblings:
Ruth — Bizarre.

Susan — Weird.

Ellen – Katie acts as if she is an outsider looking in. She is distant.

Erik – I'm knocked out. I can't think of anything that would shock me more. Do you think she is losing her mind?

Katie told me in November 1991 that she needed space. I have not called since then with the exception of calls necessary during the time before her daughter's wedding in January 1992. I made the dress one of my other grand-daughters was to wear in the wedding as a junior brides-maid.

I feel completely cut off from Katie and her family. The married granddaughter's husband graduated from college a few weeks ago. Ordinarily, my husband and I would have gone to the graduation ceremonies. We were not invited. All I could do was send a congratulations card.

Desperate Mom and Dad

THE MOTHER

Lori was in her first year in college, in Philadelphia, when all of this really started. She was very unhappy and just sounded real disturbed. She insisted on returning from school. This was six years ago. She'll be twenty-four in July.

She came home and said, "I have something to tell you. I'm bulimic." I really didn't know what that meant and so I said, "I don't know what that is. Please tell me." So she told me that she had had a weight problem for several years prior and she had reduced her weight. I guess it was constantly on her mind to keep her weight down. It became an obsession. As soon as we left her at school with her first roommate in her first apartment, she started to vomit after she ate. She got to the point where she was vomiting 12 or 15 times a day.

When she came home, she said to me, "I feel suicidal." I should have been astute enough to know that you are in deep depression the step before you're suicidal. She begged me to send her to an eating disorder hospital. I didn't know where to send her so I called the University of Pennsylvania and spoke to a doctor who was an expert in eating disorders and runs the obesity clinic at the University of Pennsylvania. He recommended a place in Chestnut Hill near Philadelphia. Lori didn't want to go back to Philadelphia. I said to her, "I just want to find the best place for your treatment." She kept getting hysterical — she couldn't go on another day, and we had to do something.

Treatment for Bulimia

Glenview Hospital was just about finished. We knew one family, whose daughter had a long-standing problem with bulimia, who had sent their daughter there. Since it was close, we figured we would take a shot and send her. She wanted to go and we drove her there and she signed herself in. We weren't allowed to see her for two or three weeks. Then, they had family meetings and stuff like that, and she was going through hell.

Their orientation was different – it was 12-Step. They had a psychiatrist on staff but somebody who spent only 15 minutes a day with the patient. Most of it was group therapy. Most it was Bradshaw-like. They had family meetings and they had family confrontations such as "It's your fault, you're dysfunctional, you're an enabler." A whole new vocabulary got passed on to me and the rest of the family.

The treatment was, "Blame the parents." It was five and a half weeks until she got out and they, I assume, had her do something radical to stop her vomiting.

Coming Out

She came out after about two months and we were told that she was not allowed to live with us. She has to live on her own. I said to myself, "Suppose we couldn't afford to send this child to go and live on her own?" What do you do in a case like that? I felt they were unrealistic.

They had her go for ninety days to recovery groups and her main recovery group in the beginning was Overeaters Anonymous. She attended these meetings every night, seven nights a week. At this point, she still had contact with the family. She had her own apartment. She had changed. Her eating procedure had changed. Her eating order had changed. It worked for her to keep her thin – she was very thin. One group met at Glenview and the rest of the time she had to go to outside groups and she became very involved in one particular OA group at South Miami Hospital that met on Sunday nights where all of the other patients that had been discharged migrated to.

She started to experiment. She went to ALANON and she went to AA and some other ones. She even went to Sex Addicts Anonymous. And I remember her saying that she couldn't believe the stories that were going on there. She never went back there, but she continued with OA and ALANON. When she went to AA, she would tell me that this was the "true recovery program." From this program everything else developed and she said it was very good for her — even though she was not an alcoholic — to hear men and women get up there and say that they were recovered alcoholics and that they had been clean something like 12 or 15 years. It gave her a feeling that she could maintain herself if these people could, because this was the "crystal palace."

We still saw her at this point. I don't remember if she went back to school or if she was working. I don't remember. And then about a year and half ago she started saying to me, "Do you know that when I was a little girl, (not mentioning the age) I used to put my Ken and Barbie in positions that you usually don't put dolls in?" I don't know at what age you become sexually aware. Maybe I did too when I was little. I just don't know. In my era we played Doctor. I listened and then she said to me, "I've also put things into my vagina." And I said, "What are you talking about?" She said, "I know that's not normal."

A New Therapist

A few weeks went by — maybe it was a month — she said to me, "I met a very rich girl in my OA meeting and she is going to a therapist and she said this therapist is saving her life. She's brilliant and she's wonderful, and I'm going." She didn't mention any sexual overtures that had to do with the family, she just said she was going.

I don't know the time period during which she separated herself from the family. The first thing I remember was a Sunday morning when she called me and she said, "I want you to know that my father has abused me." She went into detail. She was fifteen or sixteen and he was on the boat and he had stuck his finger up her vagina. I was stunned. I said, "Where were you? Where did this happen?" And she said, "Well, on the boat." I said, "Were you dressed? What happened?" And she said she was dressed and that she had shorts on. She said, "He was lying on the floor fixing something and that's when he did that to me. He ruined my life and I hate him and I'll never see him again." I confronted my husband right away. I said to him, "She has accused you of sexual abuse." He said, "It's a lie." And then I said to myself, "We're so close. Why would she lie?" I started to get suspicious. This happened after a couple of months of going to the therapist. She started to tell me that she also remembered when she was three years old or two-and-a-half that my son, who was five, had had sexual intercourse with her. She said it's hazy. "I'm not really sure — it's hazy."

I went bananas. When Lori was young, I was home all the time. My husband traveled constantly. I was with her mostly because the other three children were in school. When did this happen? When did this take place? What can a five-year-old boy do? I don't know. I really didn't know. Lori started to scream and cry, "Do you believe me?" I said, "I hear you but I just can't transfer it."

Separation

Then she stopped calling and stopped having anything to do with any member of the family. She still was living in town and she moved out of her apartment into another place and we didn't know where she was. She had gotten a job. We started to look for her and we found out where she lived and I walked in on her on Mother's Day (two years ago). I was so stunned and I said to myself, "I don't give a damn, I'm just going to walk in on her." And I did. She said, "I can't have anything to do with you if you don't believe what I'm telling you — that I have been sexually molested by my father and by my brother. My father ruined my life and I hate him." She said again that it was hazy when she was talking about her brother.

So I said, "Can we have a relationship? Can we communicate?" She said, "Only you, and when we're together, you are not allowed to talk about any other member of the family. It's only you and me." So I said okay.

We had dinner a couple of times and I happened to bring up a couple of members of my family, that my son was getting married. She just sat there and looked at me. The last time I saw her she asked for money which I gave her.

And I never saw her again. I tried to reach her and she wouldn't call. I tried to reach her therapist several times to maybe have a family conference. She never returned my calls and you could only leave a message on a tape machine. You never spoke to her. I left messages continually. I was very upset. My husband left messages that he wanted to see her, but his were more of a threatening kind because he was so stunned about what had happened.

It was my birthday and I knew where Lori worked. I got on the phone and I said, "You know it's my birthday." She said, "Oh, that's right — today *is* your birthday." And she hung up. I went off the wall. She was driving around in a new car and I called my husband who she has very negative feelings about. He told her to return the car as long as she has no contact with the family. "Return the car. Return the credit cards. Return everything." He wanted her to return it by midnight, which she did.

I went over there one night to see if she was all right and I didn't see her and it was late. I called the police. They came by and they banged on the door and they said she was in there and that she was sleeping. She came out and she said, "Don't you ever come here." Pointing a finger at me, "I don't ever want to see you again. I don't want to have anything to do with you again. As far as I'm concerned you're dead." I left and one of the policemen came up to me and I just got in the car and drove away.

About a month or two months after that, she moved to California with her boyfriend and we got a private investigator and we thought we had found out where she lived. My son just moved to California and he and his wife went over to the address. Either the people there covered for her or she wasn't there.

Court Action

Before she left, my husband was pursuing her to get together to just talk. She filed for a restraining order against him and he went to court. They brought him in the courtroom in chains so that he wouldn't attack anyone. She had the hearing in front of a judge that we all knew from our neighborhood and on either side of my husband was an armed marshal. Lori sat there with her therapist on one side and a female attorney on the other. It was decided that my husband had to stay away from Lori and her therapist for a year.

They had her come back for another hearing and so I

went down with my son and our attorney came out and he said, "Lori has just told the judge that your other daughters molested her – that the whole family molested her and that you knew about it but didn't stop it." And he said, "How that judge believed her – I just can't believe it." There is no recourse and there is no proof. Her therapist was there vouching for her. At the hearing, she won the restraining order and the therapist and her lawyer were applauding and they were hugging her, and I said to myself, "What the hell is going on here?" I walked out of there and that was the last time I saw her. Outside of the courtroom in a little park, I broke down. I really got hysterical. It wasn't a dream that I had come through. It was something that I cannot explain. I cannot believe it to this day – that this actually happened. It's like a hallucination – that's what it's like. Something so bizarre and distorted, not rational, not reasonable, not real.

Seeking Resolution

I went to a psychiatrist for help and he is a very good psychiatrist and I said you have to help me understand what is going on here. He said, "If you would have told me that she accused one member of the family, I would get a little suspicious – but the whole family – no way." He said, "I don't know if she'll ever come back and I believe she's been programmed."

We spoke to Doctor Harold Lief from the University of Pennsylvania many months ago. He said they're programmed but he doesn't know how they get deprogrammed and he doesn't know how she'll ever come back.

We were broken-hearted. My husband and I come from decent families with decent ethics and honor. There is no history of any kind of sexual behavior of this nature on either side of the family. It's such a shame that she has placed on the family. I try to think of her as sick. She went out to California — she met this guy in Philadelphia and his family took her under their wing. I caused waves there and I have spoken to the mother and really laid it on. I said, "Do you think I would leave myself open for liability with my name, address, and phone number if I were guilty?" I said, "You have children. How could you not tell me where she is — she's sick."

I don't know how to get peace for myself. I think she is a disgrace. I feel like I'm suffering from post-traumatic syndrome with no remedy. I feel the False Memory Syndrome Foundation that they have set up in Philadelphia is a good thing, but too many people want to believe incest and that's the media's fault. They would rather believe that this occurred than it didn't occur. Not being able to retaliate is my frustration. I've been suicidal. I don't believe in God. I don't believe in anything. I feel that if something so sinister can happen and destroy a family — I just don't believe in anything anymore.

We have been able to find out through private investigators where she works and my husband has asked me to call because he's not allowed to have contact with her. But I won't. I don't want to talk to her. I really wish she would evaporate. I know that's a terrible thing to say. I wish she never would have been. For the slander she has placed on this family; for the frustration that we feel because we have no recourse; and for knowing that I'll never see her again.

When I spoke to the mother she was very kind and decent and I said, "You know I've always been taught that you help one another." I said, "My daughter is sick." Fifteen minutes later my daughter's boyfriend calls me and he said, "My mother ran up to her room and locked the door and she is hysterical crying." I said to myself, "Good — I hope that she feels what I feel." She said she was the middle man and she couldn't give me my daughter's address or telephone number because that would be disrespectful to her son.

Her son said to me, "I thought we had an agreement that if anything happened to her, I would call you." In other words if she was dead or something. I said to him, "Let me tell you something — the only agreement that you and I will ever have is in a courtroom or in a lawyer's office." After that, I hung up.

A week later I got a phone call, two weeks after that I got another phone call. She sounded like a robot or as if she was drugged. Two weeks after that I got a Mother's Day card and two weeks later I got another card.

Some days it hurts real bad. It incapacitates me as far as doing anything. It's out of frustration of not being able to resolve matters.

THE FATHER

She accused me of climbing into her crib and forcing her to have oral sex when she was between the ages of two and six. She accused my son in front of the judge of having intercourse with her during the same ages. She accused my two daughters of fondling her and accused my wife of standing by and watching it all and doing nothing.

The judge could not conceive that it was true. They struck everything from the record and only granted the restraining order on the basis that I wouldn't leave her alone. Basically I was trying to force her into having a meeting. All of the sexual accusations were stricken from the record.

Then I start a lawsuit against Lori's therapist for $20

million, $10 million on behalf of myself and $10 million on behalf of my family. The therapist reported what Lori was saying to another therapist. So we charged her with slander and other things.

Then Lori left town. On October 1, she was no longer at her residence. We tried to go over there. My wife was there with the police saying, "We don't know where our child is. She's missing." Six weeks later, on November 15, my wife called the boyfriend's family. It was only then that the father got on the phone with me and said, "Yes, she's been in California now for six weeks." That meant they helped her get out there. I'm sure they gave her a place to live until she got a job. I said to him, "Are you aware what she has done?" And he said, "Well, I really don't want to know." I said, "You've got to know." Then I told him everything she accused us of doing. He was flabbergasted. I told him she was sick. She is psychotic and she needs to take medication. She is convinced that this family did all these things to her when in fact it didn't happen.

We didn't know where she was. Prior to the November 15 phone call, we didn't know where she was. We made an overture to the therapist's attorney – we would drop the lawsuit if she would sign a sworn affidavit that she has seen Lori in the last ten days and she is alive and well. Within 24 hours, Lori called and said she was doing well, but didn't say where she was. So based upon that phone call, we dropped the lawsuit.

We received two cards. One for Mother's Day and now we just got another card. The first card said things like, "We will never resolve our differences because you don't want to believe what happened to me." In the most recent one she doesn't refer to that at all. The card that we just got says, "I'm fine and doing well. It's beautiful out here and I'll call you soon." I'm hoping that my wife will make initial contact with her, because the restraining order against me doesn't expire until September. I suggested that we write a note to the boy's father and enclose a letter addressed to Lori. I don't know if we should do that and expose the fact that we have their address. Do we wait for Lori to call? My lawyer suggested that we write her a note saying that her mother would be happy to come out there and meet with her. We don't know if Lori is really sending these cards on her own, or if it is because of my wife calling the boy's mother and the mother might be putting pressure on the boy and Lori.

What we are concerned about is how to make her aware of what has happened to her. The brainwashing and all the accusations that really are not true. How do you get her back? We do not understand how she is angry at the whole family. She doesn't want to have contact with anybody. My mother-in-law, who is Lori's grandmother, called the boyfriend's mother two weeks ago and said, "Please have Lori call me." But she hasn't called. What we are concerned about is, can we make the knowledge that nothing happened to her available to her or do we use my wife initially as the envoy to go out there and just sit with her and talk with her, not mentioning the family.

At this point I really don't know what to do. It got to the point where I had actually contemplated physical violence against this therapist. And realizing that if any harm came to her, I would have to take my own life because I was not about to go to jail for doing it. I mean all kinds of crazy thoughts were running through my mind. I'm sure this has happened to other fathers in the same situation. I just don't know what to do. We are concerned with only one thing: Getting our daughter back.

Another Lost Daughter

"The pictures in my mind are so real that if they
weren't true then I must be crazy, and I know
I'm not crazy."

— a daughter

Once having these visions firmly established in her mind
— so real that the colors, smells, sensations are real — how
could she ever forgive the perpetrators? How could she
ever talk to them again? How could she allow them near
her children?

The itching was getting to be unbearable. It woke her at
night, she didn't get more than 3 or 4 hours of sleep at a
time. Between nursing her two-year-old and being miserable with the vaginal discomfort, she was becoming a total
wreck.

Her chiropractor massaged her spine with the promise
of relief — it didn't help. Her midwife who had delivered
both of her babies suggested an acupuncturist. The acupuncture brought relief — only temporarily. The dietary
changes suggested by her nutritionist at the health food
store had no effect — the increase in vitamins didn't improve the situation.

With all of the other New Age resources depleted, her
chiropractor suggested therapy.

She told her mother about the vaginal itch who then
consulted with a gynecologist. He said the itching would
go away when the prolonged nursing ended. (She nursed
each of her two children for more than two years.) She was
angered by this. "My mother thinks I'm stupid and don't

know anything!" she exclaimed.

The therapist diagnosed her malady within two visits. The vaginal itch and pain could only be attributed to sexual abuse as a child. Soon she was on a regime of four times a week therapy with a Reichian therapist who could help recall bad memories related to body pain. Each time she felt a new pain she went to see him. A therapist employed by the state mental health department was on the schedule, her group based on the Twelve-step program met once a week and used *The Courage to Heal Workbook,* and a feminist cult therapist was also scheduled once a week.

The cult therapist showed her a ritual knife. It looked familiar. That was the beginning of the recollections of Satanic abuse. With the aid of the cult therapist the memories quickly came back from her repressed memory.

She had been horrifically abused. A Satanic cult thrived in her community. She was forced to observe sacrifices of animals and babies. The blood of the babies was put into her baby bottle. She was not yet two years old when all this happened. They only do it to babies under two – so they won't remember – but the repressed memory never forgets. Her pain was the indication of all the torture that she had endured.

When she told her mother about these discoveries, her mother was naturally "in denial." Perhaps her mother was repressing these memories – if she wasn't a perpetrator she was a victim. Her mother had to know what was happening. She never wanted to see her mother or father again.

Healing would take a long time – perhaps a lifetime. With her family of origin banished from her life, she now created a family of choice. (Mostly other "incest survi-

vors"). Her children would grow up without their grandparents. The grandparents had lost their grandchildren as
well as their daughter.

Once they decided that a parent has abused them or not
protected them from abuse, they believe it. They think that
the parent knows what they know. What they have learned
in therapy is "truth." It is so vivid to them, how could the
parents not know? If the parent doesn't recognize this, he
or she is in denial.

Therapists Speak

The Therapists

The heartfelt and pathetic stories that parents have written about their experiences with alienated daughters have strong similarities. More than 500 such stories were documented between January and June, 1992. Some stories about alienated sons are documented as well.

In all of these cases:

- Adult children accused their parents of childhood sexual abuse
- In each case recollections of the abuse occurred in therapy
- The accusations were based on repressed memories uncovered in therapy
- The memories were all Decade-Delayed-Discoveries
- Many of the adult children participated in 12-Step Programs
- Many of the adult children read the book *The Courage to Heal*
- All of these adult children severed relationships with their parents and any family member who did not believe their stories
- The therapists refused all communication with the parents

We wondered about the attitude and ideas of therapists who treat adult children. We interviewed several of them. Following are slightly edited versions of our interviews. Their treatment methods are significantly influenced by the Recovery Movement. **Hundreds of thousands of therapists across the nation, many without formal credentials, are practicing therapy for adult children helping them to recall repressed memories.**

Interview with Therapist A

The Recovery Movement

Q. We have been hearing a lot more about the Recovery Movement in terms of psychotherapy. Are a lot of your clients involved in a 12-Step Program?

*A. All of them. I can maybe only think of one or two in my whole practice who are not involved in a **12-Step Program**. Either AA, NA, or OA. I have a lot of young bulimic women recovering and OA is so helpful for them.*

Q. So you recommend a 12-Step Program?

A. It's great. It's wonderful. In fact, they can be there for people in a way that I can't. They can be there for people 24 hours a day. You can go to a meeting every day. I can't be there for people that way. I can't take them by the hand and take care of them. So I get a lot of help as a therapist from the 12-Step Programs. People get tremendous support.

Q. So do people come from the 12-Step Programs to you or to you and then to the 12-Step Programs?

A. Well, what happens is that 12-Step people tend to talk a lot about their lives, so they'll talk openly about their therapy and then other people will say, "Who are you seeing? I see a change in you." So my whole practice has come from word of mouth.

Q. John Bradshaw implies that almost every family is dysfunctional and there is a need for everybody to recover.

A. I agree with that.

Q. So is there a mental health crisis in America?

*A. What we consider normal is somewhat **dysfunctional**. Normal may not be so dysfunctional that it's* *going to cause major problems. I think everybody can benefit even though they may not be experiencing major problems in their lives. They will get something out of listening to John Bradshaw. It's going to touch you inside and you'll leave there saying, "I never thought about that," or "I felt something that I didn't know was there." So everyone can benefit from* **Recovery.**

I openly say that I'm in therapy myself and people say, "You're a therapist — you're supposed to know everything." And I say, "Wait, wait a second. I live in this stressful world too and I didn't come from a perfect family because nobody comes from a perfect family and, in order for me to be a good therapist, I have to work on myself." Or else I'm just repeating from books that I've read. I have to know what it's like to be on that other side. That is what helps me do well as a therapist.

Q.   That's very common now with most therapists that are involved in the Recovery Movement. Is that right?

A.   I wouldn't trust a therapist that isn't working on herself or himself.

The Stages

Q.   There seems to be a lot of stories of women having been sexually abused as children. They have repressed the memories and now it's coming out.

A.   I work so much with that.

Q.   How does it start?

A.   The progression is that often there is some kind of an addictive behavior. They have forgotten all the sexual abuse and all they know is that they can't stop eating and throwing up or they are addicted to alcohol. Let's take the bulimics. That, somehow, is clearly linked to sexual abuse.

*A young girl finds that she's eating and throwing up, so the first step is to go to OA. So she goes to OA and she gets **abstinent** which is the word they use for eating what you are supposed to eat.*

*And then she starts hearing about therapy and how some of the people are in therapy and they are doing **inner child** work.*

Then she comes to the therapist and at this point it's all blocked out but little by little we get to the abuse. But they don't come in knowing about the abuse.

Q. *Is the abuse ongoing throughout their childhood?*

A. *It varies. It depends on who the **perpetrator** is. If it's an uncle that they saw once a year, then it's very different from a stepfather or a father.*

Satanic Cults

Q. *What about Satanic cult abuse —*

A. *You've come to the right person!*

Q. *Is that right?*

A. *Yes! I have three people that have **multiple personalities** from Satanic cult abuse.*

Q. *Multiple personalities?*

A. *Yes.*

Q. *So they go in and out of different personalities while they are in therapy?*

A. *Oh, yes. Switching constantly. It's fascinating to watch.*

Q. *So all three of your patients have been abused by Satanic cults and all three have multiple personalities?*

A. *Yes, to different degrees. There is a connection between multiple personality and cult abuse. You can't suffer that kind of horrible, horrible abuse without splitting into different personalities or you die.*

*I think special people have the ability to **dissociate** which means splitting off. So I think a lot of people grow up in that environment and just die or go crazy. Some very special, unique, miraculous individuals have this ability to split off so they can continue to function.*

One of my women has high level advanced degrees from universities and it's only because she has been able to split off that she can push it all away and function better than most people.

Q.   How prevalent are these Satanic cults?

A.   I am so sorry to acknowledge that I think they are everywhere. They are in every city. Jeffery Dahmer is in the news. No one has said that he is from a cult, but where does someone learn to eat a heart? This is classic cult stuff! He eats bodies — this is classic cult stuff! No one in the media has ever mentioned him associated with a cult.

Q.   But you definitely think that he is?

A.   Oh, I don't doubt it, and neither do my people doubt it. They know it. They recognize each other.

Q.   What are some of the stories of Satanic cult abuse?

*A.   It's **inter-generational,** so often the child is born into it and the abuse begins soon after birth. It's hard for people to realize how bad it is but I'll share some things with you: Blood given to them in a baby bottle early to get them used to the taste of blood. It has taken me a long time to be able to deal with this.*

That's one of the reasons that I go to my own therapy. I can scream my horrors in response to what I hear so I can come back to them and say, "Tell me more." If I don't get my stuff out, I will get shut down and I'll be a robot. I have to have an outlet.

I joined two societies of therapists that deal with this so we can share with each other and deal with it. These people are violated at an early age, any orifice in their body is violated. As they get older, there's usually an altar and they all stand around and perform killing and sexual acts. Somehow, their belief is that that would please Satan. This is gross, but they are doing everything opposite to what we think is the most Godly thing. In order to please Satan, they will kill newborn babies, and they have a variety of ways of getting them.

*My women were all **breeders**. As soon as they were able to be impregnated at a young age — thirteen or fourteen — they were, and the babies were aborted prior to them really showing out in the real world, and they were sacrificed and eaten.*

Q. Have there been police investigations?

A. No, and the reason why is that the programming is so sophisticated. When you are brought up in a cult, the programming starts very early. Some cults have brought Nazis over after World War II to help them learn programming techniques.

Forget the cult stuff and just take a child that's been sexually abused and the abuser says, "If you tell, I'm going to kill you and I'm going to kill your parents!" Often you see the child doesn't tell. Well, that's nothing compared to what the cult does to program you not to tell. My people have been programmed to go crazy if someone tries to get this information from them. They are told to just go crazy — do anything — but don't tell. And if they did tell as children, they were horribly abused.

Q. If this is so widespread, how come we don't hear about people being prosecuted?

A. They are too powerful. They know what they are doing. There is a brilliance to the craziness, and they are very well-protected.

Q. So, you think it's widespread and maybe tied in with government or police organizations?

A. A lot of women talk of people in the cult being high-level people in their town. These are small towns. The memories go back and they'll say that was the lawyer, that was the obstetrician and he was the one that helped pick the babies out, and even the mayor of the town.

I notice things in the paper. In the Keys a year ago, they found homeless people with their hearts cut out. Of course I know that was something to do with cults.

And then there was a baby-sitting incident here in a church and there was a whole big thing about how a young boy was baby-sitting and abused some of the kids in the church. That seemed like it was cult stuff to me. And that McMartin child care abuse in California where they all got off. I know that was cult.

The kids are frequently drugged during the sacrifices so they couldn't give clear information and said crazy things like, "He flew in his wheelchair." And so the court said, "Oh, what are the kids talking about?" They were drugged and they could be made to imagine a lot of things.

Q. Ken Lanning of the FBI claims that there is never any concrete evidence. All you hear is stories. You have to wonder if maybe it's hysteria.

A. No, no. It's real. It's just that they have such a good way to cover their tracks. After their sacrifices, they have ways of getting rid of the bodies and the bones and everything. I mean, they just don't leave any tracks.

Q. What happens when a client comes to you and talks about Satanic abuse? Normally, what is the rela-

tionship, at that point, with their families or with their parents?

A. The ones that I'm seeing that are able to really work it through have no relationship with their family. They have absolutely cut their families off. Some of them by choice and some of them because they died.

I would not see someone if the issue was Satanic abuse and they were still connected with their families because it's scary for a therapist to deal with this material. We are at risk of being killed — literally.

I don't know how these therapists go on Oprah Winfrey and these talk shows. Many refuse. Many in this community that I know who have been asked to talk about it have said, "No way." There was an article about it and the therapist did not have her name mentioned, and she still got threatening phone calls.

Q. I had no idea this was going on.

Multiple Personalities

A. We have a Multiple Personality Society and you would be surprised at how many new therapists are joining us all the time, saying that they need help, that they have this client — someone doesn't walk in and say, "I'm a multiple." It's after a year when they really trust you and there is such a strong bond that they feel it's safe for it to come out.

Not all multiples come from Satanic cult abuse. It is a fact that all multiples come from horrible abuse.

Q. Does anyone come into therapy knowing that they are multiple?

A. No, not really. Some do. The statistic is that most people have been misdiagnosed seven years in therapy prior to being properly diagnosed. They have been around many different therapists or psychiatrists.

Q. So what is the treatment for someone with multiple personalities?

A. All the personalities have to come out and tell their memories. The whole purpose of developing another personality is to hold the memories and protect the person from that memory of the abuse in the basement that day. Each personality has to come out and tell what their memory is and then integration just naturally takes place. The goal is integration. There are always children personalities in the adults.

Q. Has there been much success?

*A. I'm having success. It's a slow and painful process. Very slow compared to most therapies. It's hard for them. It's really painful. I think that the fact that I use **body work** makes it faster because I don't need to use formal hypnosis.*

They just lie down and it's like the body remembers every abuse that has ever happened. The head forgets but the body doesn't.

Somebody lies on the mat and then, all of a sudden, they go into an altered state breathing and then all of a sudden the body is kicking somebody away and the head doesn't know what's going on — the body remembers.

Q. Do they start speaking?

A. They start saying — and then one person was shocked because she said, "No, Pappy, no." And then she said, "Oh my God, it was my father and he did something to me." And it was just the whole body getting into that posture took her right back to that and she screamed, "No, Pappy, no!" And then her head, her intellect said, "Now I put it all together."

So by going through the body, it gets back a lot of the

traumas. Just sitting in a chair, it's harder to get it back, if the body has been violated.

Q. Do these people hold jobs during the day?

A. Yes.

Q. So they are not psychotic. If you meet them, you would think they are just normal people?

A. Yeah. In fact, psychotic is the opposite of multiple personality. It's like multiple personality is what they do to not become psychotic.

Parents

Q. I've heard stories about women coming into therapy and they have repressed memories of sexual abuse or Satanic abuse and then they get on the phone and they call their parents, "Daddy, how could you do this to me?" And the parents say, "What are you talking about?" The daughters break off all communication and there is a group of parents that are actually coming together and they are trying to get their daughters back.

Have you heard of any of this—what parents consider to be false accusations as a result of the incest movement?

A. When I'm working with someone and their body tells the story and their feelings are so connected with their body — I believe them very strongly.

I'm sorry, but I just don't side with the parents. My gut knows truth. I know when someone is bull-shitting — I can feel it. You can't fake feelings really well when they are deep down. It's really hard to fake it because people go back to being children.

So it's like I'm watching on my mat someone going back to being five and screaming, "Daddy, don't," or, "Uncle Roy, don't." I'm watching this with real feeling so

I just don't have empathy for these parents.

Maybe there are some therapists doing superficial work where someone just says, "I think I'm sexually abused," and that's the confirmation of it.

I know that with me, it's not real until it gets to a real strong depth.

Q. *There might be some therapists, like you said, who are doing superficial work. What often comes up is the book* The Courage to Heal.

A. *I don't know. My people read it but I've never read it.*

Q. *You don't recommend it then?*

A. *Yes, I do.*

Q. *Oh, you do?*

A. *Yes.*

Q. *But you've never read it.* ·

A. *No. It's not my personal issue of being sexually abused and I haven't read it, but I know it helps my people.*

Q. *So you haven't been sexually abused and you don't feel the need to read that.*

A. *Right, but yet I know that it helps because they come in and they say, "I read that section and it brought me back to another memory." So, I know that it's good.*

Repressed Memories

Q. *So it helps to bring up the **repressed memories**?*

A. *Yes, because it speaks to a feeling level. Sometimes it's people that are not so academic that can speak to a feeling level and that's why the fact that they are not academic doesn't mean anything to me.*

People are touched by what is written in this book.

Q. *Some people think that women are influenced by*

reading this book. Statements like, "If you think that maybe you were abused, then you probably were." Or, *women sit around in group therapy hearing story after story and maybe someone who wasn't sexually abused becomes convinced that they were.*

A. *Well, if I was a therapist in that group, I would say, "What's your evidence? You think you were, but how is your body confirming that? Tell me. Give me evidence." And if they just sit there and say, "I think I was," that's not enough.*

Most people who have been sexually abused want to deny it. They don't want it to be true.

I can't tell you how many times people come in here and say, "Oh my God, I think it was my father." And then say, "No, no, no. It can't be true. I won't accept it." I'm the one who has to say, "Okay it doesn't have to be true."

Just because they say it, that doesn't mean that it's etched in stone. I've said that a hundred times. I usually say, "You know what, let's see if future sessions bring it up again." "It might not ever come up again and then we'll forget about it." So, that's roughly the response — not what the parents say. The parents say, "Oh, you've gone to one therapy session and decided this." That's not the case, it's wanting to deny it because that is the worst thing you can ever get in touch with. And the body feels so disgusting and dirty.

*So I don't buy what the parents are saying. My sense is that they're **in denial** and they're protecting themselves. There might be exceptions here and there.*

I had a situation where a beautiful young girl came to me. She had been throwing her guts up in toilets for years. She was recovering and wasn't throwing up anymore. She came to me and she got in touch with the fact that she was abused by her father. He lived in town and he was a very powerful man and she was taking money from him.

It got to the point where she was saying, "His money is dirty, I can't take his money." It was so brave of her. At such a young age — at twenty-three — she was able to stand up and say, "I don't want his money." She said, "I don't want anything from you. I'd rather earn my minimum wage and live in a little apartment and not take anything from you because that feels cleaner to me, because I believe you abused me."

They know the truth is out. He had always controlled this daughter and now, all of a sudden, she was getting help here and he couldn't control her anymore. In his mind she is a malleable object to be controlled so the therapist must be controlling her. The idea that this woman is now developing her own mind and her own brain and her own power is too hard for them to believe, because they've always treated children as objects, so now it's the therapist that put all that in her head.

Q. What if someone were abused from when they were eight or nine years old until they were fifteen on a regular basis. Can these memories be repressed?

A. The older you are, the harder it is to repress memories. Unless you're a multiple — if you're a multiple, you can do something yesterday and repress it.

Q. It would seem to me that being sexually abused is such a traumatic event, people would remember it.

A. Opposite. It's so horrible that the body — and if you have no place to help you deal with it — I mean, my purse was ripped off my arm and I needed to deal with it. I needed to talk about it. I was really upset and I was really angry and that's something so small compared to sexual abuse.

These children don't have anybody to help them get through. If you don't have anybody to help you deal with it, you have to put it somewhere. Maybe you'd fall apart if you don't.

Q. *Do you do **inner child** work too?*

A. *All the time. It's like, "Let's take what you are having difficulties with now and see where it comes from. What are you re-creating here?"*

Women who feel comfortable with being verbally or physically abused today, obviously were treated that way as children, and that feels normal and comfortable.

Q. *But who says that it was the family? Maybe she was treated that way at school.*

A. *I don't think school would have enough power to really affect her present-day relationships. That doesn't come from school — that comes from the home. That's where we learn. Our parents are mirrors for us and how we see ourselves.*

Past-Life Regression

Q. *Some therapists believe that people can actually be regressed to past lives. Do you know any thing about this?*

A. *Brian Weiss is a psychiatrist with the most incredible credentials from Yale. He was working with a woman he calls Catherine and he wrote a book. She had symptoms and he got to her childhood stuff, but she didn't get better. He was so confused: "Why is she not getting better?"*

*He uses **hypnosis**. She went into a trance and she went to **past lives**. He couldn't believe it: "I can't believe I'm seeing this. She's talking about being Egyptian, and she's reexperiencing a death by drowning." She got better.*

He started doing this with more and more people and he wrote a book called, Many Lives, Many Masters.

I just went to hear him speak last Sunday and he has been getting a lot of publicity. People are taking notice because he is an M.D. and they are talking about it.

Q.   *So under hypnosis, they experience their past lives?*

A.   *It's happened to me too. Even though I don't use formal hypnosis, when people lie on the mat, and they breathe and they go deep — they go into an altered state.*

I had someone once all of a sudden go back to being in the Holocaust. She said she is standing on line going to a gas chamber and she is seven years old and she is so scared. She was exhibiting the fear and the shaking and the horror. "We are all so scared." I thought, "Wow, oh my God. What is this?"

Q.   *Have you ever experienced it yourself?*

A.   *Since then, it piqued my interest and I joined a parapsychology class and I was **regressed** to the life prior to this one and it was fascinating.*

Q.   *Just one time you did that?*

A.   *Since then, I did join Experta; she had a workshop and I did that at her house and I was regressed again.*

Q.   *Did you have the same experience?*

A.   *Totally different. How we come back with similar people. I find it fascinating and comforting because it's nice to know that we don't die, that we go on. So it's affected my spiritual beliefs separate from religion, you know.*

Interview With Therapist B
Session I

Q. Are you saying that people are turning away from drugs and alcohol and going into therapy?

*A. Well, I think they are hurting. I think particularly the **addiction movement** has made it real clear that addiction is pain plus learned relief, and we learn different ways of avoiding our emotional pain.*

In the past it was totally acceptable, and I think because of the addiction movement, certainly drugs and alcohol are not acceptable, but now eating as a way out is not acceptable; working is not acceptable; sex is not acceptable. All these things were acceptable before. I find people much more sensitized to anything, any compulsive behavior they have as a way of avoiding hurt.

Q. You say, "the addiction movement." Could you explain that a little bit more?

A. I think it's become "in" almost to have an addiction whereas, at one point, if you were an alcoholic, you certainly hid it. Everybody was totally ashamed. I think a wonderful thing has happened. I think that over the last ten years — I don't know why it's happened — I don't understand it. All of a sudden, it's just happened. You hear a lot of people coming out of the closet about their addictions. The fact that there is this addictive process, the fact that they do have a treatment for it that works, has started a lot of people looking at their own behavior, and finding it much more acceptable.

*I think in certain places, if you are not in a **12-Step Program** of some sort, you are really not "in."*

Q. So you are saying this is what works? This can be

adapted to any addiction, the 12-Step Program?

A. *Well, I can't generalize like that but I know it works very well for the people who have really engaged in working hard at their own recovery. And, whereas before, I think therapists talked a lot about* **obsessive compulsive behaviors***, we are saying the same thing when we say addiction.*

The addiction field now has developed a whole lingo connected with it. Recovery literature is a mega-million dollar industry.

The Recovery Movement

Q. John Bradshaw is very popular with his television show on PBS and his books have sold millions.

A. He is an incredible man. He has taken ideas from many different places and put them together. None of them, as I understand it, are original ideas. But what's so important about him is that he is able to take these ideas and synthesize them into something that's absolutely brilliant — clinically and otherwise. Have you ever gone to one of his workshops?

Q. No.

A. I really suggest it. Very intense. People learn a great deal. People don't have their own support structures around them when they do it. I have concerns about what could happen.

Q. Really. Why is that?

A. Well, you are almost **in a state of denial***. You grow up and terrible things happen to you. I grew up, I had terrible things happening to me, but they don't exist every day. And I sort of put them away and I deal with my life. And I can deal with my life if I'm relatively well balanced.*

To use recovery terminology: I'm not too hungry; I'm not too angry; I'm not too lonely; I'm not too tired; I have a decent job; I feel supported in my life; I'm doing pretty well. But if my daughter is sick or if I'm physically sick; if my spouse is an addict and coming home and beating me up every night — those are not normal stresses.

So I'm coming from a much more vulnerable place. For instance, it is kind of bad for me to then go and relive an experienced trauma I had, even when I was four years old.

There are people in the groups to hold me and help me mend and there are therapists there to help out at that moment. But what happens to the people who just shut down, who become flooded with emotion, numb out, walk out the door. What if they don't have a good support system? That's the down side.

The up side far outweighs the down side. You have gotten people to look at themselves. The whole inner-child movement — I was thinking about that stuff a long, long time ago. I didn't know how to put it across. People are putting it across and people are understanding it now. I think that's incredible. People are learning how to heal themselves. I think that's absolutely brilliant. I admire him a lot.

Q. And it works?

A. And it works. You know men are particularly attracted to it. That just blows me away.

Q. Tell me about the 12-Step Program.

A. Okay, 12-Step Programs are taking after the original AA program. AA is fifty years old. They don't cost anything. And you can make a contribution of a dollar when you go.

When you go to the meeting, they talk about the 12-

Steps. They read them out loud. They talk about the rules of the program.

Then people talk about their own experiences in their own lives. To the degree that they've worked the 12 Steps, their lives are working. They are much happier and much better. Then it goes around the circle, and everybody shares a little from their own experience and that's it. That's the meeting part.

The first three steps of that program deal with powerlessness and spirituality. A short form is, "I can't deal with this alone. I believe that there is someone that can and please do." So "I can't, you can, please do." Short form.

The next step is really so exciting for me because it's like a short-form analysis. The fourth step, people have to write their life story from their very first memory up through the present. So what they are doing is they are hitting the memories that shaped their lives which is what a therapist does.

Then in the fifth step, you take what you have learned, and you share it with another person, another human being. So secrets come out of the closet. Things that people have been hiding and ashamed of all their lives. A lot of acting out in addictions has to do with that shame.

Bradshaw talks a lot about that. When they can share it with another person, the other person doesn't go running and screaming from the room but embraces them and says, "Welcome brother, you know we're together in this." It's an incredible transformation. The next several steps have to do with eliminating character defects: greed; wanting to have it all; dishonesty. It's almost looking at some of the good coping mechanisms. What it does is it frames the character defect and this is my interpretation of it — it frames the character defects as a result of their history. But even though it's a result of the history, you have to let go of it if you want to live a healthy life.

And then there are parts about making amends to people that you've hurt in your life, and again, trying to deal with the self-hatred that caused a lot of acting out. I have a very varied background in therapy — in different kinds of therapy, in behavior therapy, in family therapy.

What these 12 Steps do — not in a very deep way — but certainly in the best way you could for a lot of people at the same time — is address some of the same issues that therapists direct.

Private Therapy

*Now there are some things that you don't talk about in those AA rooms. Because, although it's a program that's supposed to be anonymous, you have no guarantees of that. Take someone who has acted out sexually with his daughter, say a **perpetrator**. He is putting himself at intense risk to talk about that in those rooms. You don't know who is in that room. So this is a place where private therapy becomes very important. Having a private place to do that or a private room.*

*Also, the 12-Step Program gets at the stuff that's on the top, you know, like **snorkeling**. If you are snorkeling you can see a great deal but you are kind of removed from it. A therapist helps you **scuba-dive**. It really helps in the healing process.*

Q. There are groups where you can reveal your innermost?

A. That's right. It's a much more controlled visit. There is a therapist in charge to help you scuba-dive and it's much more controlled in the sense that people sign something about the anonymity.

It's exciting the way it's happening. I refer as many people as I can to the 12-Step Program. It helps my work enormously. It helped me enormously.

I went through a period where my daughter — it turned out she was a coke addict, using coke from the time she was about sixteen. She started with marijuana at fourteen and when I found out, I was absolutely devastated.

*I needed something because I couldn't help her. Here I was, a trained **lifeguard** and I couldn't help her get well. I needed a program to help me first take the focus off her and get back onto my own obsessive controlling behavior.*

Secondly, I needed to help her let go. And once I could help her let go, it helped me let go of her. She then had to face the consequences of her addictions and when she did face the consequences of her addictions, she could get into recovery.

She's been in recovery five years.

Q. You assisted her as far as facing her problem too.

A. I couldn't help her. She had to help herself.

Q. Well, I mean, you at least convinced her to help herself.

A. No.

Q. No?

A. I'll never forget at one point, someone who I had gone to for help, said to me, "You have to accept that strangers are going to help her." And it was the strangers at the 12-Step Programs that helped her. I couldn't help her. It was very hard.

Women

Q. I wanted to ask you about women in therapy. There seem to be so many women in therapy these days. I'm sure there's a good reason. Do you find it is mostly women?

A. Yes. I think women experience their pains. It's hard to generalize like that.

Most of the things women hurt about have to do with relationships. I think that's the way women are socialized. I think it's biological to some degree. We're going to have the babies. And we have to have relationships with our babies. We have to have a relationship with someone, a mate, to take care of the babies.

So relationships are very important whether it's a relationship with a mate, with children, and very importantly, with our family of origin. A family that we grew up in really shapes our lives a great deal and so how we relate to other people at our peer level is affected a great deal by our family of origin. So people are hurting because their relationships aren't working.

I deal with a lot of very successful women and you'd think that they come in because of issues having to do with their work. The men come in with issues having to do with their work, but women come in with issues having to do with relationships.

Q. Do you think it's more the relationship they have with their original family or the relationship they have with husbands and children?

A. I think it definitely has to do with their original family. They replay those original family issues in their relationships. Let me give you a more clear example — I have a client whose father died when she was seven. That's a very difficult age. Mother never remarried. Now, the kind of man that she is attracted to is usually a man who is not available. This is a very successful woman. And why does she keep going after men who are not available?

Well, there is a repetition compulsion that seeks to end

the pain or fill the hole, that loss that probably was never dealt with because she was so young. While other people were dealing with their loss, she put it inside for some reason and seeks to fill that hole. If a man is available, it doesn't fill the hole. She's got to go through the process of wanting, yearning, and then have the yearning fulfilled by winning over the man that's not available.

So all her energy goes to winning over the man that's not available. If he's available, there is no interest. He's here, so, you know, it doesn't matter.

Q. And that's not uncommon?

*A. Very, very common. And with the **adult children**, they replay the chaos. An alcoholic home most often is chaos. Someone, one of the parents, is using a mind-altering substance. So there can't be the order and the comfort and the safety that the child needs. There is a lot of chaos in the growing up. Well the adult child creates chaos in their adult environment. They become involved with people who are not reliable. They are not consistent in what they do. There is a lot of chaos. Sometimes I have to work with a client for a long time to reduce the chaos.*

Q. You see it from both sides?

A. Oh, absolutely. I have a belief that a therapist can't take a client where they haven't been themselves. If I can go through it, then we can kind of go through it together. But if I haven't been there, how do I know? I think most of us have had some trauma in our lives, and that trauma gets covered unless it gets really dealt with.

I know when I was raising my kids, I didn't know how to deal with my kids' trauma. I knew how to distract them. I knew how to make everything look nice. But I didn't know how to help them talk about it, really talk about it, really cry about it, be upset about it. And help them to process that.

Sexual Abuse

Q. There seems to be a lot of women confronting childhood sexual abuse.

A. Oh yes. A lot. Often a client will come in for something completely different. I had one client come in — I want to tell you about her, yet I don't want to identify her. Something had happened that really upset her. It's one of those rare situations where a woman comes in because of a job-related incident. We traced it back to find out that the reason she was so upset was because a man that she had worked with was shot and killed in a drug bust. She knew him very well. She knew his whole family and he had a little daughter who, of course, was left without a father, without any protections, by this death.

*So she was identifying with the daughter, and it later came out that she perceived a terrible abandonment from her own parents. She had been sexually abused by neighbor children for over a period of three years from the time she was three years old. Now where do you get something like that? Something she remembered — it wasn't something I had to do any **hypnosis** on to find out. But she had completely dismissed it.*

Q. It's something she was aware of her whole life?

A. That's right. Never told anybody. Completely dismissed it. She became a police officer, I mean, think about it. She became her own protector, and I find that a lot of people in their adult lives, and even in their professions, are doing something to help solve the child problem.

*One of the things that Bradshaw talks about a lot, about the **inner child** and healing the inner child, ways of taking care of the inner child. Sometimes our professions are ways of doing it, but we do it for other people* *instead of ourselves.*

Q. You mentioned hypnosis. I've heard a lot of stories about women in therapy. They don't realize that they were sexually abused. It comes out in therapy. Is that true?

A. There are two different kinds of memories that I see. Some are real clear memories — "I really knew that, I just haven't talked about it."

*And then there are what you call **body memories**. People have all these symptoms of having been sexually abused and their bodies respond in that way. Particularly in trying to have a normal sex life now.*

Sometimes by hypnosis, they begin to remember. But it takes a while because they have to really feel trust in order to be able to talk about that. Sometimes hypnosis cuts down the amount of time that it takes to get them to remember, and whether we know absolutely for sure that the person is remembering it accurately in every detail because, after all, a child does change perception. A child's perception is different than an adult's perception. But for that person, that experience is absolutely real. Sometimes they'll go back to look for verification, validation.

*I have a case I'm working with where a woman started to remember sexual abuse by her father. She doesn't have the memory yet, but she has everything around it. And it turns out her sister, working in a separate town with a separate therapist, found out the same thing. So there is absolute **validation**. Her sister is a little bit ahead of her in terms of recalling.*

You know children are very egocentric. They believe they are responsible for the whole world. They don't really know that they are not causing and creating everything. That's very intense when you're an infant, but it goes on, until you're eight, nine, or ten years old. And then they can realize that someone else is causing something. But since they believe that they cause everything in their environment, if they are treated well, they believe it's their fault. If they're not treated well, they believe it's their fault.

If a child is sexually abused, they feel guilty and ashamed that they *did it. On top of that, often you find that these kids have not had a lot of affection or attention from parents in other ways. So they really enjoy the attention and so do their bodies. You know, they have a biological response to pleasure. So they feel guilty about that also. They feel a deep shame about it and they want to hide it. I can't blame them for that.*

One of the things that these 12-Step Programs have is Alateen where they have children who are now adolescents, adolescent children of alcoholics, who unfortunately have experienced some of the damage of the disease in their families. They go to these meetings and they begin to share and talk with other children about it.

A client of mine, who sponsors an Alateen program, just told me recently that of twelve girls in her Alateen group, eight had been sexually abused.

Q. How do these girls find out about these meetings?

A. They are publicized in the schools.

Processes

Adult children take things on at a very young age because they have to. One parent is out of control. Another parent is so totally obsessed with that parent that they have no time for parenting their children.

The second parent — we call that one the **codependent** *— becomes so invested with control and making them all* look nice on the surface that the children have to function in service of that situation.

Sometimes it's the brilliant kids at school, the ones that look like they don't have anything wrong – they do everything right – super good kids.

Q. How does a successful patient of yours who has been sexually abused – this is the cause of her trauma – explain the healing process generally. Do they confront the parent?

A. No. The first thing is to talk about it. To have someone listen and validate.

You know some of these girls who have been abused by their fathers have gone to their mothers. The mothers either blame them or deny it or somehow try to push it away.

The first step is validation. The validation that someone believes them. Believes that they are hurt. You know I can't say exactly what it is but I can know that this child has been really really hurt. Validating their pain and validating their hurt is the first process.

Q. The therapist validates?

A. I validate. And then I often send them to join a group of people who have also gone through this so they are not alone.

I either send them to a group Project Resolve or to a group at my center or to a 12-Step group. But somewhere they'll have a community that will support and validate them. That's the next step.

Then comes the harder part. The going through the experience and mourning it. It is one thing to talk about some things and say, "My father abused me when I was eight years old." I might as well be telling you that you want a cup of coffee. But to go through the experience, kind of go back to it, in memory, and feel the feelings and *do the crying and do the mourning that people have to do to heal from this. To mourn the fact that they did not have a healthy childhood. To destroy the illusion of perfection of their youth. It's a heavy experience so the mourning is very important.*

Then we come to the question somewhere along this process of, "How am I going to deal with these people in my life?" There are many different solutions.

I think in the beginning when people were discovering their sexual abuse, they ran out and told right away and then were re-abused by families that continue to call them crazy and say that a therapist made this up.

Q. Would you say that's a typical reaction?

Role of Parents

A. Oh, yes. There is a wonderful book called The Courage to Heal. *In that book they have a whole list of expected reactions. They are very predictable. Very rarely do you get a parent that says, "I'm very, very sorry. How can I make it up to you?" Almost never.*

Even when the parent was not the **perpetrator***. Because they don't want to accept anything that's not perfect. So I really encourage my clients to be very careful about their decision to confront.*

Some people just pull back — pull away from their parents completely. I have a bias. I would like it if families could stay together and heal, and sometimes what I will do is, I will encourage a family member to come into therapy with healing in mind. And there has been some; I mean, we have been able to at least get people to talk about it — get it out of the closet. "You know what you did to me, dad, when I was seven years old was not okay!" "What did I do? What did I do?" "You know what you did dad! If you don't — if you want me to remind you, I'll tell you."

That often means that she is going to be re-abused, that he is going to call her crazy.

I have one woman that I was working with whose mother was abusing her and we confronted her mother, and her mother then got on a campaign to discredit her with everyone in the family. She called her old boyfriend. Her mother was saying, "Either you believe her or you believe me." So she factionalized the whole family. My client now has to deal with the loss of her whole family, so she may have been better off if she hadn't confronted — I don't know.

Q. Would it be possible to be healed without ever confronting the family? Is that a possibility?

A. I don't know. I really don't know. To some degree it is. There needs to be some kind of naming the truth. Otherwise you are living a lie.

And I don't know about you, but I wouldn't want my daughter with a father that had sexually abused me. I wouldn't leave them alone. And then he's going to wonder why — "Why don't you leave me alone with this person?"

If they are still using sex with someone that doesn't threaten them as a way of coping with their emotional pain, they could be abusive into their 80s. And there have been many cases that I have to deal with where grandparents are abusing children.

Q. I mean once the patient has reached a certain age — once she is in her twenties, it's not that common, I would imagine, to be sexually abused by a father who abused her when she was very young?

A. It's not so overt — it's more covert, it's like a grab on

*the ass, you know, or a touching of the breast. It's not just
women. There are men who have been sexually abused by
men and by women. So it's out there. It's really out there a lot.*

*People are **in denial** when they are doing it. They have
some kind of rationalization for it or they are under the
influence of something.*

*And don't forget, we went through the sixties where
young adults who had children were using a lot of drugs.
And they didn't know what they were doing. I'm beginning to see the outcome of that.*

*You know, Freud saw a lot of childhood sexual abuse
in his adult patients but he couldn't believe it was true.
After a while he named these women that he was counseling as hysterical. And he set the whole thing back years
and years and years by thinking it was figments of their
imagination He called it hysteria.*

*What's wonderful now is that people are talking about
it, coming out of the closet. People who have been hurt
are talking about it and they are trying to get healed.
And that's real important.*

*Almost every time you find a perpetrator, you find
someone in their lives who has hurt them. Abusers have
been abused. It's a continuous cycle. And they do it in a
repressed state — they don't know it. So a lot of times,
these people are coming from **dysfunctional families**
where they were abused as children and now it comes
out — the hidden secret comes out — and now they are
faced with their parents. And there is this conflict. They
don't talk to their parents anymore. And they have to
mourn their parents.*

Satanic Cults

Q. What are the stories of people describing Satanic

rituals? Have you ever heard of anything like that?

A. I have one client and it's horrible. It's unbelievable. It is unbelievable. I work with that. There is a book called Satan's Children — *case studies of children who were ritually abused.*

Q. Why do you think there are so many cases of these Satanic rituals? It seems so far fetched — you said, "unbelievable."

A. There are Satan worshippers and they believe that by inflicting pain and suffering, they increase their own power. It's the darkest part of the human mind as far as I'm concerned. Often I imagine that these people have been abused themselves and so they look for a way to be powerful.

*Now a 12-Step Program is a way of accepting your powerlessness over whatever addiction you have. But there is a paradox in that because in accepting your powerlessness, you become more powerful. You take responsibility for your life. You are not a **victim** anymore. You are in charge. You accept what you can't change, change what you can, and hope for the wisdom to know the difference; stop tilting at windmills. You suddenly feel much more powerful in your life.*

While a 12-Step Program is a wonderful way to empower someone, Satanism is the sickest way imaginable to empower someone. There are people who are doing it. I don't want to believe it. I don't want to believe it. There is enough evidence that it exists. I don't know if it exists in the numbers that are coming out though because the number of cases that are coming out are enormous.

Q. Do you think there is some type of hysteria here?

A. I don't know. It's hard to say if there is. I don't know. You know I wasn't there. Who am I to say?

What are you going to do — take two clients and say to one, "Yes, yours is real" and to the other "Yours is not?" If what's going on there is that their trauma was so horrible to them that they perceived it in this way. Their trauma is still as valid as it would be if this thing didn't occur.

At the end of our interview, Therapist B invited me to see her new clinic, just a short drive from her home where the interview had taken place. She was concerned with the decor, subtle colors, a Southwest look in the entry, rugs on the floors — seven small living rooms, each with couches, comfortable chairs and teddy bears of various sizes.

"This is where we create new families," she said. "Families of choice when the family of origin must be abandoned." She has seven therapists working for her. She looks forward to expansion. She is, after all, in a growth industry.

Interview with Therapist B
Session II

Recovery Movement

*Q. So, the **Recovery movement** has become very large.*

A. Yes. It's the beginning of a real important place in people's hearts. I think we needed it.

Q. Why is it so significant now?

A. Well, I'll tell you an interesting story. For a long time, I didn't know anything about addiction. I was in practice for about fifteen years before I learned anything about addiction.

I would have a client that would come to me and I would work my hardest with them, to help them. Someone that was maybe a spouse of an alcoholic or someone with a child that was using drugs. I would try to help them in a way that I knew how, and they would go to five meetings, ten meetings, and get more from those meetings than a year of my working with them.

Q. Why?

A. Because, I think, in those meetings, they weren't talking about anything theoretical. They weren't dealing with deep emotions and they were dealing with practical how-to's.

I think in those meetings, they told the truth and when you have been in pain for such long time, you know the truth when you hear it. And it's the truth about the diseases.

*Any kind of **obsessive compulsive** disease has the same kind of response in the whole family. When one person has the obsessive compulsive disease, it involves* *everybody who loves that person — everybody.*

When I say obsessive compulsive, I'm using that term very loosely to mean any kind of an addictive disorder. People can be obsessive compulsive about work too.

Q. *Now, I'm wondering, that seems to be something that's bad, and I'm wondering about that. I mean, you have to do something with your time, and what's wrong if you happen to like to work because your work gives you a great deal of pleasure and enjoyment? You might as well spend your time there as anywhere else. What's wrong with that?*

A. *It's not balanced. If the behavior is used as a way of avoiding dealing with emotional issues that you have to deal with in your life: relationship issues, historic issues. Let me take you back a little bit. What we are trying to do is help people recognize the pain, their early pain and where it comes from, but they have to take responsibility for **reparenting** that **inner child**. They can't blame other people.*

Some of the 12-Step meetings and some of the Bradshaw meetings do turn into blame games, but that's not the goal. The goal is recognition of how those incidents are hurting us right now.

I think a lot of it is an oversimplification.

Q. *People come with a point of view that, "This pain came to me because my father or my mother did something to me, and I'm going to give back the blame so I can heal."*

A. *Give back the shame — it's different than giving back the blame. The words are different.*

Q. *Well, I think there is just a little too much generalization.*

A. *I agree.*

Truth and Memories

Q. I am a parent of three children and I see their childhood much differently than they see their childhood. Their view would be the only view really validated or respected by the therapist because I'm not there to express my view.

*A. As a therapist, I validate their perception. That perception is not involved with **golden truth.** Truth is not what shapes their lives. It's their perception of what happened that shapes their lives.*

Q. John Bradshaw says 96 percent of families are dysfunctional. Bradshaw says that we live with shame and everybody has shame. Now, I didn't see that as I was raising children. What I did see as they left the home — they went to preschool, they went to other environments — they were hurt by other people and yet that is not addressed by Bradshaw. You could have had a wonderful childhood — many people did. Instead they are saying that most of us had terrible childhoods.

I think that my generation is really being blamed for what terrible parents we were because some of us used drugs and some of us used alcohol. And 96 percent of us might have done something to our children that we didn't know because we were drunk or drugged or something. And anything that is wrong in their lives today is because of what happened in their childhood.

A. I'm hearing the point that you are coming from and it's almost like, "God I tried so hard with my kids and I did such a good job. Why am I or my generation being blamed?"

You know people accept the nature of the ambiguity that you can be a wonderful parent and still hurt your children to some degree.

*One of the things I think about is what happened in the sixties. There was a lot of use of drugs in the sixties. It may be that that's part of it. I think that if people believe that they have been sexually abused, there is some chance that they were emotionally abused. And what that means is that they were emotionally incested. When, for example, a father has more interest in his daughter than he does in his wife. That's **emotional incest**.*

*Q. How valid do you think **repressed memories** are?*

A. I think they are. We can distort — the very nature of children is that they have a very huge rich fantasy life. So to some degree, their perceptions are not gold. It's not just a memory. It's the physical aspects of the other symptoms of sexual dysfunction.

*Some of the people I work with come to me and when we begin working, it comes out that they have known about this all their lives. It's a very clear memory. It is not something which is called a **body memory**. It is a very real memory. The next level is when they have all the symptoms and it seems as if something is going on and then they try and put them together.*

Now, very often, they don't believe — under hypnosis or if they get a flashback or something like that — they don't believe it. And then it takes a while.

A therapist that is responsible will say, "You will know after a while if it is true or not."

Parents and Memories

Q. How in this repressed memory can a child tell the difference between a fairy tale, a movie, or a television show that they saw and reality? Many people are treating these memories as if they are fact and confronting parents and suing parents.

A. I think it's a real dilemma. When it comes to confrontation, I have some real mixed feelings about it. If my daughter came to me and said that I sexually abused her, I would be shocked.

I think what I would do is I would say, "God, if I did that, I can't even know or think or imagine doing that!"

Q. *So you're in denial.*

A. Well, I may be. I would want to look at it. Let's work on this together.

As a therapist involved in some of these confrontations — my goal is healing.

Q. *What if one sees it one way and the other sees it the other way? What if the child says, "You did this to me, don't deny it, you're in denial."*

A. Then I would continue working with both until they can come to some kind of common view. Sometimes, it's going to be accepted. The important thing is not to re-abuse the child now. Sexual abuse comes in all forms. Sometimes, it's just looking at a child inappropriately. Another form is actual penetration.

Q. *Do children really have memories at the age of two and three? Can they actually remember that they were sexually abused at two and three years old?*

A. They don't remember it as sexual abuse. What they remember is fondling and feeling close and that they felt icky about it. Then later on, they will come to the assumption that they were sexually abused.

Q. *I think there are so many adult children who are going out there and saying, "My parents did something terrible to me. Something terrible happened to me somewhere!"*

Then I start thinking, what about the parents of adult children who feel the terror that they might have done something that their child is now so miserable about.

A. The research shows that when a child has a depressed mother, there is a lot of panic and fear that comes up in a child, "Does she want to be depressed? Is this her fault?" And trying to compensate for that with my own children I say, "I didn't like the way my mother raised me." As a result, when I had my daughter, I did exactly the opposite of what my mother did. As a result, my daughter is just like my mother. I tried to do the best I could. Every parent tries to do the best.

Therapy for Parents

Q. If a child believes that he was sexually abused, maybe by Satanic rituals, and if the parent knows that they did not perform Satanic rituals, would you then suggest to a parent to admit it and say, "Yes, I did this"?

A. Oh, no. I would suggest to the parent that they might have done it without knowing it. They might have exposed the child.

Q. But, what if the child will only accept an apology?

A. The only thing a parent can do is say, "I've looked. I've searched my soul. I've worked hard in therapy. I've gone to my therapist. And in my honesty, my truth cannot find it. What I must have done is, I must have hurt you somehow."

Q. But why did they hurt? Maybe the hurt came from someplace else.

A. It doesn't matter. Sometimes children tell their parents and the mother doesn't believe them.

Abuse happens an awful lot when the parents are on drugs.

There's a tremendous amount, especially in this society, of focus on sex and sexual performance and men are not getting what they need from their wives so they turn to their daughters. And the daughters, wanting to be loved, and not having affection in another way is one of the problems with this — they enjoy it. They feel very guilty that they enjoy it.

Q. One of the things that concerns me is, how accurate are memories? In some of the literature that I've been reading, there are a lot of people who have burned a lot of bridges and just abandoned their families, giving up their birthright, giving up their heritage because their parents will not confess to what the children say they did.

*A. I'm very concerned that you associate the Inner-Child movement with the aspect of **blaming** and **disconnection**. I feel very sad about it as a matter of fact. Most of the inner child movement has to do with healing and part of healing has to do with forgiving and part of forgiving has to do with acceptance.*

Families are getting healthier and healthier as a result of this. Wonderful things are happening as a result of recovery. See, when you are dealing with trauma, any kind of trauma, there is a lot of fear. So, to me, to believe in something greater than myself is, "I'm not in charge. I'm not doing it all. I can let go of some of it. I don't have to control everything." And therefore, I can deal a lot with my anxiety in a way that is much healthier.

People can "Turn over and Let go and Let God," as they say in the 12-Step Program. They just go from this — you see physical differences in people in their ability to let go. You know that it takes five generations to heal the pain.

I believe I was hurt. I believe my mother was hurt. I believe my daughter was hurt. My daughter says, "I'm doing the best I can with my son, but I believe he is hurt too."

We can change that by doing our own healing. If I live

in balance and if I live a healthy life, that will affect my children. And if my children live in balance and live a healthy life, that will affect their children.

There is a saying in recovery, "If you are not working the program you're slipping back." You can go to a John Bradshaw workshop and feel wonderful. Unless you continue your work, the early learning takes over again.

Unless people work on their recovery, they can very easily slip back into the dysfunctional ways of thinking.

Q. Well, you know there is just something about suggestibility. People get together and they hear each other's stories and it just sort of becomes their story too.

A. I think there are some people who are very suggestible. That means that they are affected about what happened differently.

Let's get away from golden truth here and then look at the effect. The golden truth comes in when confrontation comes in. If people keep an open mind in terms of confrontation, I think there can be healing.

Different Perceptions

Q. People see things differently, and each is absolutely certain he is right.

There are people who didn't have any idea of abuse until they went for some other reason to therapy and then it came out. And some of the symptoms, if you think you've been abused or if you are depressed, if you have pain — some generalizations are taking place.

I don't think there is anything worse than child abuse. Nothing in this world is worse. Because that is such a horrible crime, to be falsely accused of it is about the worst thing there is.

Nothing is worse than to be a child abuser; therefore, I

would be so cautious before making an accusation that somebody has abused a child because once you say that about a person, his or her life is ruined.

A. What these children need is a validation of their pain.

Q. But it must be validated properly. Sometimes it is improperly validated because they are accusing their parents and perhaps it's coming from someplace else. They are severing relationships. They are destroying parents. I've seen that side of it as well.

We should see that maybe the repressed memory is not one hundred percent accurate; therefore, pain is there for some reason. What you do is wonderful if you can help alleviate pain. The only thing is that sometimes it is misdirected or misplaced in the repressed memory.

A. So that's why I'm hearing this side from you.

Q. Because the other side has not been protected. It's not been spoken of recently. You don't hear that.

A. My advocate for the other side is an open mind and a joint search.

Q. A joint search is very important but there are therapists who will not speak with the perpetrator.

A. I know that you are concerned. Healing is where it's at.

It Can Happen to Anyone

If a person goes to a therapist who already assumes that most patients have been sexually abused in childhood . . .

And if that therapist believes that most memories of abuse are repressed . . .

And if the patient reads books that make the same assumptions . . .

And if the patient joins a group made up of women who all believe they have been sexually abused . . .

And if they all tell their horrible stories . . .

And if the patient has a suggestible personality . . .

And if the patient is led to believe by the therapist and the books that healing can take place only when the abuse is recognized and the perpetrator identified . . .

And if the patient spends months, sometimes years, in therapy and groups seeking the identity of the abusers – is it not likely that the identity of the abuser or abusers and recollections of the abuse will finally, after all that work, finally emerge?

How would you like to be accused of horrendous acts of child sexual abuse on the basis of such recalled memories?

And what if these reconstructed memories were ten, twenty, thirty, forty years old?

Beware!! It can happen to you. Accusations of child sexual abuse based on repressed memories that are decade delayed discoveries are running rampant – an epidemic is emerging . This is the mental health crisis of the decade – if not of the century!

The Power of the Book

Books Form Thoughts

Just how much influence can a book have over the lives of people? Hundreds of books, some with accompanying workbooks, have been written in the Self-Help Movement. Only now are we beginning to realize the powerful part they play in forming thoughts and ideas.

The Courage to Heal

Ellen Bass and Laura Davis have written one of the most widely used books in the movement for women who were sexually abused as children, *The Courage to Heal*. Bass' and Davis' assumption is that millions of women have been abused and many of them have forgotten or "repressed" that abuse. Until the abuse is recovered from the repressed mind and the perpetrator identified, healing cannot begin. The process is an arduous one and requires long-term therapy and continuing work in groups. In order to aid the process Laura Davis has written *The Courage to Heal Workbook*. Together, the book and workbook provide what is supposed to be a formula for healing. Instead it is a formula for confabulations.

The Courage to Heal begins with graphic descriptions of sexual abuse which are enough to make the average person nauseated. For a sensitive, troubled, empathetic woman these descriptions must be especially disturbing. Since Bass and Davis believe that sexual abuse is so widespread — it happened to one out of three women — it is likely many women have been treated in a similar fashion — and repressed it.

Bass and Davis utilize extremely masterful teaching techniques to elicit strong reactions. They use vivid descriptions, repetition, suggestion, and approval or validation.

All the quotes in this section are from the paperback edition of *The Courage to Heal* by Ellen Bass and Laura Davis, Harper & Row, 1988. We used restraint in including examples for each concept. Many more could have been quoted to illustrate each concept.

1. The authors are very persuasive in convincing women that the chances are very great that they were sexually abused and forgot it, and now need to create memories:

> *"If you are unable to remember any specific instances like the ones mentioned above but still have a feeling that something abusive happened to you, it probably did."*
>
> (p. 21)
>
> *"If you think you were abused and your life shows the symptoms, then you were."*
>
> (p. 22)
>
> *"You may think you don't have memories, but often as you begin to talk about what you do remember, there emerges a constellation of feelings, reactions and recollections that add up to substantial information. To say 'I was abused,' you don't need the kind of recall that would stand up in a court of law."*
>
> (p. 22)
>
> *"Forgetting is one of the most common and effective ways children deal with sexual abuse. The human mind has tremendous powers of repression. Many children are able to forget the abuse, even as it is happening to them."*
>
> (p. 42)

"Survivors often doubt their own perceptions. Coming to believe that the abuse really happened, and that it really hurt you, is a vital part of the healing process."

(p. 58)

"There are many women who show signs of having been abused without having any memories."

(p.71)

"Another way to regain memory is through regression. Under the guidance of a trustworthy therapist, it is possible to go back to earlier times."

(p. 73)

"Memories are stored in our bodies, and it is possible to physically reexperience the terror of the abuse."

(p. 75)

"If you don't remember your abuse, you are not alone. Many women don't have memories, and some never get memories. This doesn't mean they weren't abused."

(p. 81)

"If you don't have any memory of it, it can be hard to believe the abuse really happened. You may feel insecure about trusting your intuition and want 'proof' of your abuse. This is a very natural desire, but it is not always one that can be met."

(p. 82)

"Yet even if your memories are incomplete, even if your family insists nothing ever happened, you still must believe yourself."

(p. 87)

"Even once you know the facts are true, you may still, at a deep emotional level, have trouble believing it happened. Believing doesn't usually happen all at once — it's a gradual awakening."

(p. 91)

2. The authors reinforce the idea that you don't have to have actual memories of the abuse for it to have happened:

"So far, no one we've talked to thought she might have been abused, and then later discovered that she hadn't been. The progression always goes the other way, from suspicion to confirmation."

(p. 22)

"Women (who had been shown parts of the manuscript of this book before publication) *reported having nightmares, flashbacks, new memories. Several went back to therapy. All said their lives were changed."*

(p. 23)

"As the media focus on sexual abuse has increased, more and more women have had their memories triggered."

(p. 75)

"Often women become very uncomfortable when they hear another survivor's story and realize what's being described happened to them too."

(p. 77)

"So I'm going with the circumstantial evidence, and I'm working on healing myself. I go to these incest groups and I tell people, 'I don't have any pictures,' and then I go on and talk all about my father, and nobody ever says, 'You don't belong here.'"

(pp. 82-83)

"Emily, who was abused by her parents as a very young child, struggled for a long time against believing it happened.... When confronted with the abuse, her parents denied everything and her father offered

to see a counselor, take a lie detector test, anything,
to prove his innocence . . . . It was only when Emily
broke off all communication with her family and
established a consistent relationship with a skilled
therapist who believed her that she stopped doubting
herself and got on with her recovery.
Talking to people who believe you and validate
your experience is essential."

(p. 90)

3. **The authors encourage readers to get angry at**
alleged abusers and seek retribution whether there is
any proof of the abuse or not:

"If you're willing to get angry and the anger just
doesn't seem to come, there are many ways to get in
touch with it. A little like priming the pump, you can
do things to get your anger started. Then once you get
the hang of it, it'll begin to flow on its own."

(p. 124)

"There are nonviolent means of retribution you
can seek. Suing your abuser and turning him into the
authorities are just two of the avenues open."

(p. 128)

"Another woman, abused by her grandfather, went
to his deathbed and, in front of all the other relatives,
angrily confronted him right there in the hospital."

(pp. 128-129)

"There are many motives for wanting to confront
or disclose . . . . You may want to make the abuser,
nonprotecting parents, or others feel the impact of
what happened to you. You may want to see them

suffer. You may want revenge. You may want to break the silence. You may want financial reparations or payment for your therapy."

(pp. 133-134)

"*If your memories of the abuse are still fuzzy, it is important to realize that you may be grilled for details. Laura (Davis) received a letter from one of her relatives, full of demands for proof:*

> *'Rape and incest are among the most heinous of all crimes and he does not become guilty on the basis of 25-year-old flashbacks.... These are very serious charges and you had better present some factual evidence to back it up.'*

Of course such demands for proof are unreasonable. You are not responsible for proving that you were abused."

(p. 137)

"*One survivor told us the story of a woman who exposed her brother on his wedding day.*"

"*The initial confrontation is not the time to discuss the issues, to listen to the abuser's side of the story, or to wait around to deal with everyone's reactions. Go in, say what you need to say, and get out. Make it quick. If you want to have a dialogue, do it another time.*"

(p. 139)

"*This woman probably would not have actually killed her father, but it felt good to think about it.*"

(p. 143)

4. The authors encourage the readers to break off relations with their families:

"Many women try desperately to forgive.... But as Ellen (Bass) says in her workshops, 'Why should you? First they steal everything else from you and then they want forgiveness too? Let them get their own. You've given enough.' "

(p. 150)

"The abuser is not your primary concern. You say, 'I am my primary concern. Whether the abuser rots or not, I'm going on with my own life.' "

(p. 150)

"It is up to you to decide how you want to relate to your family. It is not a requirement of healing that you work toward reconciliation."

(p. 290)

"You do not gain by remaining part of a family system that undermines your well-being. In fact, many survivors have made great strides in healing by cutting the cord."

(p. 296)

"While it's not your job to educate your relatives, providing a little information may turn a skeptic into a supporter. You might want to give them this book to read. Then, if they're still antagonistic, you'll know it's not because of a lack of information."

(p. 302)

"It is painful to make a break with your family, but it is even more painful to keep waiting for a miracle."

(p. 305)

"When you experience a major loss, a ritual can

help you integrate the change and move on. Giving up your family, and the anguish that causes, deserves recognition."

(p. 305)

Quoted in book from Mary Williams: Attorney for Adult Survivors:

"Monetary compensation, even if it cannot undo the damage, is a form of justice, of being vindicated by society while the abuser is blamed and punished. Money is also helpful in a practical way, to pay for therapy . . . . Critics say it's bad for survivors to sue because it means cutting ties with their families, but I can't think of anyone who's come to me who has any healthy tie left to her abuser."

(pp. 309-310)

5. The authors give advice to those who have supposedly been abused about how to act with their own children:

"They do not need detailed descriptions. Instead, make a general statement that reassures them and speaks to their needs: 'I was hurt by my father when I was a little girl. That's why I've been going to so many meetings and crying a lot. I want you to know that if I seem sad, it doesn't have anything to do with you. I'm getting help now so I can feel better.'"

(p. 275)

"If a fourteen-year-old asks, 'What did Uncle Bobby do that was so awful?' you can say, 'He raped me and beat me.'"

(p. 275)

"But maintaining family ties for the sake of tradition does not help your children. You do not owe the molester an opportunity to have a relationship with your child, just as you do not owe your child the opportunity to bond with a child molester. Let the abuse have the repercussions it merits."

(p. 282)

"And if your relatives are unsuitable as a healthy extended family, consider surrogates — friends who can be loving companions and role models for your children."

(p. 282)

6. The authors encourage those who think they are incest survivors to create a new identity and lifestyle:

"One survivor, whose abusive parents were still very much alive, spent many months dressed in black, telling everyone her parents had died. Another woman wrote a eulogy for her abuser, imagining herself at his grave. . . . Rituals such as these can be powerful channels for grief."

(p. 120)

"Survivors often complain about how long it takes to heal, but there is an identity in being a committed survivor of sexual abuse. That identity has been closely linked to your survival, and it can be hard to give up."

(p. 163)

"You need to accept the fact that the healing process will continue throughout your life."

(p.167)

7. Even though they say that "none of what is presented here is based on psychological theories," the authors offer advice to psychotherapists:

"Be willing to believe the unbelievable . . . . It's imperative that you be willing to hear and believe the worst, no matter how disturbing."

(pp. 345-346)

"If you were not sexually abused as a child, explore those experiences in your history that come closest."

(p. 346)

"Refrain from discounting the survivor or judging her to be wrong about herself."

(p. 346)

"Believe the survivor. You must believe that your client was sexually abused, even if she sometimes doubts it herself. . . . If a client is unsure that she was abused but thinks she might have been, work as though she was."

(p. 347)

"Recognize the symptoms of early sexual abuse. If sexual abuse isn't the presenting problem but your client has eating disorders, an addiction to drugs or alcohol, suicidal feelings, or sexual problems, these may be symptoms of sexual abuse."

(p. 349)

"If your client says she wasn't abused but you suspect that she was, ask again later. Children often repress memories of sexual abuse, and your questions may be the trigger that reveals those memories, either now or later. 'No, I wasn't' may mean 'No, I don't remember yet.' "

(p. 350)

The Courage to Heal Workbook

The workbook is a teaching device. It has a major goal as do all teaching devices. Its goal: to confirm that you have been abused! The objectives are to identify who abused you, how, when, and where. You name the abuser or abusers, learn how to get angry, hate the abuser, and get even, then you can start to heal. Healing may take years, perhaps a lifetime, in therapy.

Fantasy and imagination play major roles in determining answers to suggestions made. You are asked to write as freely as possible, your thoughts and reactions to cues. This is a good book for developing literary talents, but for finding the truth it is purely a tool for confabulation – mixing fact and fiction to create new memories. It is dangerous because the techniques are so blatantly directed toward predetermined objectives that you could not possibly complete the workbook without locating an abuser or abusers – real or fictitious. When done alone, the workbook is dangerous, but with the assistance of a therapist or group it becomes pure dynamite. An inkling that someone might have abused you becomes a concrete reality as one exercise after the other leads to the undeniable conviction that there surely has been an abuser or abusers.

Think back to anyone who may have touched you in a bad way. If you don't remember, don't let that stop you – let your mind roam freely and write whatever comes to your head. After reading the book *The Courage to Heal* you already have examples of horrendous acts of child abuse in your head. If you have trouble remembering, suggestions are made. The power of suggestion is very strong. Your literary and imaginative powers are challenged. As you read your stories in a group, the tendency is to become more dramatic. Others tell similar stories. The group validates you and praises you and demonstrates its love and caring for you. You become increasingly eloquent.

Your grandfather, your grandmother, your cousin, or uncle or father or brother or baby-sitter are all suspects. Just imagine all the bad touches you might have had. Think back to when you were a child – ten, twenty, thirty, forty years ago. On the other hand, think of all the good touches that can easily be misinterpreted. Did you ever have a diaper rash? Did a caretaker ever apply ointment or baby powder to that rash to comfort you? Does any adult know the pain or discomfort of such a rash? Could a fragment of that memory now be recalled and misinterpreted as abuse? There is no room for doubt. That is not encouraged. Any touch to a sensitive part of the body is abuse.

Why do intelligent, well-educated women and men re-spond to this workbook? The answer is obvious. They are used to answering questions completely and sometimes eloquently, having been exposed to testing most of their lives. Many have been students for so many years they know how to answer any question the teacher may ask. They know how to respond to instructions. The workbook is brilliantly designed to take advantage of writing abilities, to overcome the fear of correction or to develop new writing skills. It directs and focuses thinking, at the same time it allows imagination free rein. Most important of all, when working through the workbook with a therapist or group, positive feedback and appreciation is provided. Unlike an ordinary classroom where criticism is consis-tently provided, the therapist is not a critic but instead is a validator. The group is not critical but is accepting and appreciative; the more grotesque the stories, the more supportive. The therapist interprets; the group supports.

As the person progresses through the lessons, confidence builds until the crescendo grows louder and louder in his or her mind. Finally the ultimate objective is achieved – the abuser is identified! He or she is then vilified and convicted – with the approval of the therapist and the group. It is time to celebrate with a ritual. The group is always there to replace the abusers and become the approvers, the new family.

Try it – writing like any other skill improves with practice. From the beginning lesson to the ending one, the skill for creative writing becomes well-developed. It is an excellent workbook for teaching a person how to become a great writer of fiction. The trouble is, the writing that results from this workbook is not treated as fiction, but becomes fact – cemented in the mind of the creator as if real and validated by a respected, and even loved, therapist and a like-minded group that displays more caring and sympathy than any family. That is precisely why they are there: to display approval – without challenge – for whatever you say as a victim. Families often challenge, tease, disagree – does that make them dysfunctional?

Is it any wonder that parents whose adult children are exposed to such activities become the central characters of the fiction and fantasy encouraged in this workbook?

As a teacher and a writer and publisher, let me tell you this workbook is the strongest teaching tool I have ever seen and coupled with the positive feedback of the therapist and group it becomes a powerful tool. Unfortunately, it has a nefarious objective – to describe abuse whether true or not true.

Sexual abuse is so serious an accusation that a person should be taught to be cautious before accusing anyone. Our jurisprudence system operates on the foundation that a person is considered innocent until proven guilty. The book assumes guilt not innocence. The book does not encourage independent thinking. It encourages one to focus on very specific goals, to create the story. It does not encourage one to seek verification – only validation.

This workbook is a masterful tool for indoctrination. It plays with the mind. With the suggestion that abuse has a broad definition and is prevalent, it includes anyone who "may" have hurt you, everyone can find someone who abused him or her. A brother who wrestled with you or teased you, a father who spanked you, a mother who applied ointment to a rash, a babysitter who accidently stuck you with a pin while diapering you, an uncle who hugged you too close, a grandfather who jostled you on his knee – let your imagination run freely – you can find more and more possibilities.

Following are some examples of the lessons in the workbook which help develop your imagination and writing skills. If you use the exercises in the workbook, it is sure that those skills will be greatly improved. Just remember you are writing fiction – not fact. Too bad the author doesn't recognize that. It is tragic that the people who use the workbook do not know that. Countless lives have been ruined because fantasy is being treated as fact!

We are not claiming that real sexual abuse is not ever uncovered by using the book. What we do claim is that imagined abuse may also be uncovered using this workbook – and that is horrendous.

This workbook is a perfect example of providing a suggestible person with a *formula for confabulation.* It encourages mixing fact with fantasy to create new memories. Some therapists recommend this book without reading it.

A Look at the Workbook

The major goal of the workbook is clearly stated, the objectives specified, built-in techniques for assimilation of information, and specific suggestions for feedback are provided. It is suggested that the book can be used by an individual survivor, or with a therapist or group.

Although written specifically for survivors, Davis says in her introduction, "If you're not sure you were sexually abused, or don't have clear memories, continue reading." The book will help you determine the abuse. Where the book *The Courage to Heal* was directed to women, the workbook has a broader audience – men as well as women. It is a masterful teaching tool, utilizing methods that get results. If subjects were taught in our schools with such proficient workbooks as this and with feedback as suggested in the workbook, all students would more readily excel.

The goal of the workbook is:

● To confirm and solidify that the person using the book is a survivor of child sexual abuse.

The major objectives are to:

● Build a support system of persons who believe you.

● Learn to deal with crisis situations that will occur as the abuse becomes more evident during the course of using the workbook.

● Believe that the abuse happened.

● Assess the damage caused by the abuse.

● Identify the abuser or abusers.

● Grieve and mourn.

● Confront the abuser or abusers.

● Get angry and direct that anger to the abuser and the people who failed to protect you.

● Deal with the family by letting go of the old family and creating a new one.

Those of us who have evaluated this workbook do not believe that a person could follow the book and complete all of the exercises without accomplishing the major goal of the workbook. In other words, if the workbook is completed – the person who uses it will reach the desired goal – he or she will have confirmed that sexual abuse did occur. Furthermore the person will likely sever all relationships with the family of origin and create a family of choice.

Davis is very much aware of the powerful impact this book will have on someone who uses it:

> *"Like* The Courage to Heal, *this workbook will evoke powerful feelings. Feelings are experienced in our bodies, so as you work through these exercises, you may experience unfamiliar feelings, body sensations, flashes of memory, or even sexual arousal. If you start to feel things you haven't felt before, or if you start to feel overwhelmed, know that you are not crazy. You are feeling. You are remembering. You are receiving images from the past.*
>
> *If you feel overwhelmed, stop. Go to the support list . . . Make some calls. Get support. Don't go through it alone. You already did that once. You don't have to do it again."*
>
> *The Courage to Heal Workbook*
> Harper & Row, 1990. (p. 7)

The workbook's "stream-of-consciousness writing" technique releases inhibitions. The idea is just to put pen to paper and go with it – without concern for grammar, sense, accuracy and any formal constraint. There are lists to check off, spaces to fill in and lots of space for the free writing exercises throughout the workbook.

When this book is used with a therapist who helps

interpret the ramblings of the writer, the activity itself becomes validating. In a group it becomes even more so. Once you write something, then share it with others, you own that information — fact or fantasy, it makes no difference. Pride of authorship becomes very significant. And the appreciation by the therapist or group for what you have written is very rewarding. The more horrific the story, the more the empathy. How hard it would be to recant a scenario that was presented with such great feeling and eloquence.

Preparing for a Safe Journey

The workbook is full of the "power of suggestion." It provides many cues for writing. It gets you started on an incredible, incredulous journey through your past.

The journey is so treacherous that Davis wants you to plan for the crisis you will inevitably encounter. Before embarking on this dangerous journey you are to develop a support system of friends, neighbors, people you've met in a recovery program who you might consider telling about your abuse and then the people you can call on for help. The book also gives you lots of exercises to help you find a therapist and counselor that will be supportive.

There's space in the book for a phone list for hard times and tells you what to do when you panic as revelations start to come out of your repressed memories.

Davis lets you know that "most survivors have suicidal feelings at some point in the healing process." Here's some advice, "If you are concerned that you can't control your suicidal feelings, take the time now to create a plan for keeping yourself alive." The plan includes space in the workbook for emergency numbers you might need to call as you proceed through the book. It sure builds up a tremendous tension. You are living through your own suspense novel — not knowing where it can take you — but be prepared for the worst.

We could find examples to illustrate what we consider mind-manipulation on almost every page of this workbook. We will limit ourselves to providing examples for three of the major objectives of the workbook.

Confront the Abuser or Abusers

Davis sets a determined tone for the exercises on "Confrontations."

> *"In a confrontation, you stand up as an adult and face the people who hurt you as a child. You name your experience as sexual abuse, express your feelings, and talk about the way the abuse has affected you. Confrontations can be incredibly empowering because you learn that you are strong and powerful."*
>
> (p. 340)

You are told to prepare for your reactions at a confrontation.

> *"What's more likely is that you will be discounted, called crazy or a liar, ignored, scapegoated, or attacked."*
>
> *"It is critical that you enter a confrontation because it will strengthen and empower you, not because you're hoping for a particular response."*
>
> (p. 349)

The core of this section is a seven-page activity on Making a Confrontation Plan. A thorough list of decisions needed is made clear by the suggestions:

1. How do I want to confront?
2. Where do I want to do it?
3. Do I want anyone else present?
4. When will I do the confrontation?
5. How long will the confrontation last?
6. This is what I want to say and do:
   (use additional pages as needed)
7. This is what I'm going to ask for:
8. When it's over, I'm going to:
9. If I start to lose myself, I will:
10. To take care of myself, I'm going to:
11. My backup support people are:

(pp. 353-358)

If the confrontation is not to your liking, here's what you can do:

"Reread the guidelines for freewriting on page 11. Then set a timer or alarm clock for twenty minutes, and write a eulogy for your offender. Imagine your offender dead (if he or she isn't already). Imagine standing up at the funeral. How do you want your abuser remembered? What's the legacy he or she left behind? What was his or her real impact in the world? On your life? Imagine the power of having an audience hanging on your every word. This is your chance to set the record straight. Spare nothing."

(p. 361)

You are finished. Your so-called abuser is out of your life. Perhaps you have given up your entire family. Now you can continue your new life as a proud survivor of incest.

Get Angry and Act

Davis furnishes thirty-eight pages on anger. She sets the tone by asserting: "You were the victim of an atrocity. You have the right to get angry and stay angry as long as you want."

After completing an anger inventory, you are helped to overcome your fear of anger. If that was not enough to rile you up, you are asked to look at "a child at the age you were when you were first abused." Write a letter to that child. Couldn't anybody (abused or not) imagine such a child and write a powerful, emotional, caring and outraged letter? How else can you respond to the suggestions?

> "Then think about the person who is abusing the child. Picture that person in your mind. Knowing what the abuser is doing and saying to that child, how do you feel? What would you like to say to the abuser? What do you want to do? What sort of revenge would you like to exact?
>
> Reread the guidelines for freewriting on page 11. Then set a timer or alarm clock for twenty minutes, and write a letter to the child's abuser. Start with the words 'You are miserable, rotten slime.' Continue from there. Allow your anger to flow."
>
> (p. 323)

Davis suggests you turn your anger into action. With so much emotion backed up, you are certainly ready to "talk to children about good and bad touching, speak out in the media, work for legislation to increase penalties for child molestation, or get involved in survivors groups and organizations." You can even build a banner to proudly display with your status as a survivor.

Deal With Your Family

Here is the real crux of the situation. Now you can learn how to get rid of that unhealthy family once and for all. Now is the time to sever those old relationships, never to be restored.

> *"Blood is not all that determines family ties. If your family hasn't been there for you, you have a much better chance of getting your needs met by an alternative family you create for yourself."*
>
> (p. 375)

You are helped to set new ground rules, to plan (control) family contacts, to develop realistic expectations of your family's response to your telling them about the abuse. Imagine the appropriate response to the following:

> *"In 'Confrontations' you looked at your fantasies in terms of one-time confrontations. If you haven't done that exercise yet (or even if you have), try it again in the space below, substituting the names of family members you pin your deepest hopes on:*
>
> *I wish   my mother   would:*
> * Believe the abuse happened.
> * Tell me she's sorry she didn't protect me. Ask me how she could help.
> * Stop protecting my father.
> * Stop drinking and stop telling me her problems."*
>
> (p. 401)

You are asked to give up the fantasy of a helpful, caring family again and again. Now you are asked to write a letter with a model provided and three full pages of writing space.

> *"Pick your abuser or someone in your family you are currently struggling with. Choose the person on which you pin your secret hopes for reconciliation. Compose the letter you wish they would write to you. Use their phrasing, their language, their writing style.*
>
> Dearest Sandy,
>
> This letter is long overdue. When you were a child, I did unspeakable and unforgivable things to you. I know now that I was wrong, that I never should have violated you to satisfy my own selfish desires. There is no excuse for what I did to you . . .
>
> . . . Love and continuing wishes for your recovery,
>
> Uncle Phillip
>
> *Reread the guidelines for freewriting on page 11. Then set a timer or alarm clock for twenty minutes, and write your own letter. Express all your secret hopes and dreams, no matter how unrealistic."*
>
> (p. 404)

You are now ready to let go and create your family of choice.

> *"Think about the alternative family you are creating (or would like to create). Who is part of that family now? Who would you like to be a part of it? How do you treat each other? How do you spend time together? What kinds of things do you like to do? How do you have fun?*
>
> *Imagine a family gathering with members of your new family. You're coming together to celebrate. You create the setting, the theme, the conversation, the activities, and the reason for your celebration. (Your*

team won the World Series. You had a story accepted for publication. Your abuser died. It's your birthday.) Let your imagination go. This is your fantasy."

(p.409)

The deed is done. You have a new life and a new family.

Powerful Tool

We believe that many families who have been cut out of their adult children's lives without any chance to defend themselves will recognize themselves as "victims" of the techniques described in this workbook and its predecessor book *The Courage to Heal*. It is not so easy for them to move from being "victims" to "survivors." That is just semantics.

The amount of suggestibility and the leeway for error in making false accusations in this book is very great. Untold numbers of victims – both the adult children and those parents who are falsely accused may suffer from the effects of this book and others of its type for a lifetime. Cutting off the sacred family bond is intergenerational: the present generation of parents, the grandparents, the children and those yet to come are all affected. Will the innocent family that might be so cut off ever heal from this brutal assault on its integrity? Shouldn't caution be advised before such drastic "cutting off" occurs? Shouldn't one be told to be absolutely certain, rather than going on "feelings," before giving up family, friends, inheritance? We think so. We believe that many of the more than 500 families who proclaim their innocence and are astounded by the behavior of their adult children will find recognizable patterns in this workbook. Many parents have been accused in a manner well-described in this workbook, confronted, denied an opportunity for defense and abandoned.

An Open Letter to Ellen and Laura

Dear Ellen and Laura,

Your book The Courage to Heal *and its accompanying workbook have reached a huge number of people. You are free with your advice. You suggest writing letters to "perpetrators." You think there are an immense number of perpetrators in America.*

According to you more than a third of the parents in America are criminals – they have horrendously abused their children. The crimes you describe could put these parents in jail. We always thought Americans were among the most caring, generous, loving people in the world – but you say that they rape and otherwise abuse their children in large numbers.

We are talking about terrible crimes here and we think you are confusing an awful lot of people. We think you're causing a lot of grief. You are encouraging adult children to accuse their parents of terrible crimes. You are saying that "if they think they have been abused then it is true." You are telling them to confront their parents on flimsy evidence but not to allow the parents to respond. You are saying that if parents don't confess to abuses that adult children recall from their repressed memories, they are "in denial" and should be forever banned from the lives of their children and grandchildren.

Ellen and Laura, a lot of innocent parents are suffering from the consequences of your books. If you advise someone to accuse a person of being a perpetrator and do not give that person a chance to defend himself or herself, that is not right. That is not justice. In American justice people are presumed innocent until proven guilty – or are you and the clients that you counsel above the laws we in America choose to live by?

The Recovery Movement

"Dysfunctional Families"

Millions of people across the U.S. are in recovery groups. It is the "in" thing today. And what are they recovering from? All sorts of "diseases" including alcoholism, drug addiction, sex addiction, shopping addiction, eating addiction. There are even recovery groups for messies and debtors. And then there are the codependent group meetings, for those who are close to anyone suffering from any of these addictions. In one three-day period in our community, the newspaper announced 42 recovery meetings — they take place morning, noon, and night.

And where do all these diseases come from? They are the effects of "dysfunctional" families. The addictions are diseases caused by living in families that pass down their neuroses. The "family of origin" is fundamentally unhealthy according to John Bradshaw and other leaders in the recovery movement.

Bradshaw used to claim that 96 percent of us grew up in dysfunctional families — now he says it is closer to 100 percent. Abuse is an intergenerational disease and Bradshaw and others say the cure is to break away from the evil effects of the family. He and other therapists claim that it is not only all right — it is even in many cases the right thing to do, to give up the "family of origin" and create a "family of choice." It is necessary for healing.

Bradshaw champions the "inner child" in all of us that has been destroyed by mom and dad. That child can only flourish when it breaks the ties that bind it. Many of the adult children who have abandoned their families in our stories have been and are participants in 12-Step Programs.

The 12-Step Programs of today are patterned on the AA

model developed more than 50 years ago. The main aspect of the program is to recognize that a person has a disease and is powerless over that disease. He or she needs a consistent plan of action to recover. The disease has such a tight grip that healing by oneself is impossible. Wellness requires constant group reinforcement. Perhaps for a lifetime. And the source of the disease is often "the family" according to some leaders in the Recovery Movement.

The 1980s witnessed a huge growth of the Recovery Movement. It expanded to include hundreds of seminars, books, and thousands of groups. It is estimated that more than 15 million people go to groups. The seminars, books, and groups produce a billion dollar industry.

John Bradshaw is probably the leader in the Recovery Movement. An alcoholic (once an alcoholic, always an alcoholic) former priest, Bradshaw is a true evangelist who is on the road constantly, traveling from city to city to spread the recovery gospel. He has written three books and has television programs that dominate the PBS airwaves in this field.

We've read a lot about Bradshaw and have spoken to people who know him. He started out modestly, growing up as he says "in a sick Southern family." He has reached the pinnacle, becoming the undisputed "King of the How-to-Heal-Your-Life" crowd, according to *Changes* magazine (Sept.-Oct. 1991).

Wanting to know more about this man of such tremendous influence and power, we read his books, listened to his tapes, watched him on PBS, attended his seminars, met with people who know him and read about him.

We find that Bradshaw is an angry man. He is mad at the family as it exists in modern life – and he lashes out ferociously. He speaks as if healing is the objective of all his activities – but to heal you have to settle first with mom and dad; dad was a drunk, mom if not a drunk herself was an enabler who had children just for her own advantage – to mold them into a pattern to suit her own needs. John is also sensitive. He does not like criticism of his own altruistic personality or message. Bradshaw's many friends and admirers include Oprah Winfrey, Barbra Streisand, Quincy Jones, and Nick Nolte. He claims that some people in the recovery movement have created vicious rumors about him – that he is drinking again. Bradshaw says, "There are people who are jealous of me, and I understand that." He thinks they are envious of the amount of money he makes; according to *Newsweek* he made a million dollars in 1990.

So this man who can lash out with tremendous vehemence against mom and dad, is defensive when personally attacked. Mom and dad can't defend themselves. They are sitting by helplessly and hopelessly when the adult children who go to Bradshaw's seminars and read his books come away from these experiences with hatred for their childhoods and with techniques for cutting themselves off from their "families of origin." Bradshaw has a victim practice rituals designed to break away from mom and dad. He uses a term which in our minds is vicious. That term – "emotional incest." Incest is the worst crime recognized in our society. And Bradshaw likens emotions that parents may have toward their children as incest, it is a rape of the spirit. Maybe in some cases he is right – but to condemn parents with such a broad generalization is just downright irresponsible.

Bradshaw won't like this, but we went to his seminars in order to find out what goes on. We had to see for ourselves how a "family of choice" can so readily replace a "family of origin." Thousands of families of origin are devastated and live in agony each day, abandoned by their adult children. How are these sacred bonds being broken? A Bradshaw seminar provides some answers. Together with his books, tapes, and TV shows this man has tremendous influence. We believe that the seminars most truly represent the man because it is here that you can truly see the interaction that occurs between him and his followers. You can see the power, mystique, and magic of the man. You can see the transformation in attitudes and emotions that occur in just a few days. You can see how the family can be destroyed in the name of healing.

In recognition of the power of the Recovery Movement, Hallmark has established a new line of greeting cards to celebrate the various stages of recovery.

John Bradshaw in Fort Lauderdale

John Bradshaw appeared in Ft. Lauderdale, Florida on April 9-12. Three of us attended, each going to a different program: An evening lecture, an all-day workshop, and a two-day intensive workshop. The four-day appearance was presented by Joan E. Childs & Associates, Inc., described in the brochure as "an out-patient counseling center for recovery.... The areas of specialization focus mainly on adult children issues with special emphasis on co-dependency.

"The Transformation Model, developed by John Bradshaw and Kip Flock, is used extensively in doing 'original pain work.' By employing an eclectic approach and embracing the '12 Steps,' our therapists help their clients to heal, reclaim, and champion the 'wounded inner child.' This approach effectively leads to recovery and self actualization."

April 9, 1992 – An Evening with John Bradshaw: "Sharing His Experience, Strength, and Hope"

Joan Childs introduced John Bradshaw as "the number one communicator of the 20th century" and the most effective person in the field of family development in "the history of the world."

Bradshaw discussed the damage done to society through the "PATRIARCHAL" system. He used the examples of China, Iran, Iraq and the incredible cruelty and abuse that occurs as a result. We, too, as individuals are the product of a family structure that creates incredible abuse. We have not all come from alcoholic/incestual family structures but most of us, if not all, have come from the patriarchal family model. "100% of us come from dysfunctional families."

Bradshaw described Patriarchy:

● Confuses love with abuse and thereby creates a "mystified" sense of love.

● Teaches blind obedience: "Obey me because I said so."

● Uses corporal punishment.

● Represses all emotion except fear. In doing so, suppresses anger which takes away our primal boundaries (we can't say no; every misfortune or mistake is our fault).

● Seeks to destroy the soul, but the soul doesn't quit. . . . "It (soul) may allow us to become addicted in order to survive but it is always healable."

● Teaches "toxic shame" as opposed to healthy shame. Healthy shame allows the moment's free flow of emotions; toxic shame is at the heart of "mystification" since it suppresses and freezes the emotions in time – making what is relative into an absolute. "It is a frozen state of being."

● Uses control which often leads to physical, emotional, and sexual abuse.

● Creates a "spiritual bankruptcy." "People who are raised on authority do not have a conscience." (This applies to religions as well.)

● Stresses happiness from the outside in. We call it spiritual bankruptcy when one can't generate happiness from within. "We used to call this co-dependency."

● Teaches us to polarize, absolutize, and set standards that all must follow. In a child's mind the parent is ALL good and ALWAYS right, leaving no room for the human dimension. This makes parents into gods which is true of any absolutized theory. "The second you

don't believe you have a Hitler as well as a Mother Teresa inside you, you're in trouble."
- "Brainwashes" children and causes them to become "stuck," "mystified," and "unimaginative." It forces them into a "hypnotic trance-like state."

This trance-like, hypnotic state is central to the inner-child theory. "Toxic shame" freezes us in the past creating mystified notions about understanding life. "Trances save our lives" by allowing us (the child) to go into hiding and avoid dealing with pain. The trance state causes a fixation of consciousness, creates delusions or illusions, auditory and visual hallucinations, and a kind of amnesia which enables us to forget, for example, sex abuse. Mystification allows us to remain in this trance. We go through life "fixed," dysfunctional and always on guard to avoid being exposed. We then choose partners in the same trance state who match our own level of dysfunction.

We continue to repeat dysfunctional behavior until we break our trance state. We must end our secrets and lies by facing what we have internalized about our parents. We must separate from that "mystification" — the core of which is toxic shame — and do recovery work. We shouldn't blame our family but "we must demythologize our family."

For Bradshaw, this process began back in the 1960s with his experience of the 12-Step Program. When he admitted his powerlessness and gave up his effort to "control," his healing process began. Eating disorders, sexual dysfunctions, phobias, and addictions are "almost all shame-based syndromes." The only way to heal shame is to embrace it and bring it out in the open. "That's why the 12-Step Program is so effective. . . . You come out of hiding and others still accept you." You begin to establish healthy boundaries for yourself by growing in "healthy shame." When addicts lose their enablers, they crash and "demystification" takes place. The healing begins when a "snapping" (word used in cult exit counseling) takes place and "soulful" living can begin.

Soulful living never polarizes, knows there are no magical answers, sets up realistic expectations for self and others, and allows the free use of the imagination – the faculty of the soul – to imagine great things and happiness for one's self. "Therapy is for people who have lost their imagination."

At the end of the lecture Bradshaw stated, "There is no John Bradshaw way. . . . We try to be unattached to any one theory." He stated his work is based on an "attitude" that believes each individual is of great worth and the objective is to get in touch with and be who you really are. "There is no one technique to break your trance. . . . There is no one-way salvation system out there."

Personal observations:
- *A lot of name dropping.*
- *Evangelistic style of speaking.*
- *Age group 30s-60s; more women than men.*
- *Standing ovation at the end.*
- *Surrounding environment very sales oriented (tables with books, tapes, t-shirts, teddy bears, etc.)*

April 10, 1992 – An All Day Workshop
"Creating and Maintaining Healthy Relationships"
I arrived early enough to take a walk through the empty ballroom of the convention center where the workshop took place. Seating was arranged in 12 groups of six from

front to back and 10 rows from side to side, so there were 120 groupings, seats for 720. In the first few rows near center, the seats were already claimed by people who brought teddy bears, pillows and coolers – they had obviously been to Bradshaw workshops before.

Out in the lobby refreshments were sold and tables were set up for a number of organizations hawking their products and services. The Joan Childs Institute – the official John Bradshaw counseling center which was sponsoring the affair – was prominent among the hawkers. Health Communications, also a sponsor (along with PBS Channel 2), displayed their publications and gave away copies of *Changes* and other magazines for adult children and others in recovery. There were various tables for mental health facilities, Bradshaw books, teddy bears, t-shirts, and tapes.

Several hundred people filled the ballroom as Joan Childs stepped up to the podium to introduce her "therapists" who would be available throughout the workshop for "your protection." Also introduced was the man who made the Joan Childs Institute possible, her wealthy husband. Gushing her adoration for the other man who has made her wealthy, Childs introduced John Bradshaw – "the greatest communicator of the 20th century."

Getting Started

Bradshaw took the stage attired in a gray double-breasted suit with a black undershirt. After stating how valuable the therapist community was, Bradshaw laid down a few ground rules for the day. Everyone must make a commitment to honor confidentiality. He asked those present to protect their boundaries and control sexual urges by not using the workshop as a place to come on to someone sexually.

To begin, Bradshaw turned on an overhead projector and outlined a process toward healthier living. The first step would be Behavior Modification – to take that first step toward working for better relationships. This first level could be joining a 12-Step group or attending a Bradshaw workshop. The second level was something that was not going to be covered at this workshop. What Bradshaw calls "original pain work," "feeling work" and "inner child work" must be done at a treatment center, in psychotherapy, Alcoholics Anonymous, or other 12-Step Programs. He claimed at this point that the Bradshaw method is not the new salvation and is only one of many methods. The third level is entitled Corrective Experiences, by reparenting ourselves we can establish the necessary skills for building a healthy relationship. Compulsive behaviors need to be changed. Behaviors which result from our dysfunctional upbringing need to be worked through with a therapist. The fourth and final level is spiritual work or what he calls "Soulfulness."

The audience numbered five or six hundred and hung on to every word. Bradshaw was at times humorous, serious, confusing, technical, simple, and always repetitious. He constantly referred to his alcoholic father and codependent mother and the nightmare that was his childhood. He assumes that everyone had abusive parents and deprived childhoods. A woman nearby had a teddy bear under her chair and was petting it as if it were a dog.

Toxic Relationships

The importance of relationships is emphasized and Bradshaw states that he is heterosexual, but his method also works for homosexuals. He claims that everyone has some shame that needs to be worked on. He speaks of the internalized mother in all of us that needs to be dealt with. He relates more of his personal experiences, how he stopped needing and began knowing his needs. Anyone who does not know his needs cannot be in a healthy relationship.

Bradshaw had spoken for about an hour at this point and gave the people an assignment. Everyone was to explore his or her past opposite-sex relationships by listing on a chart three or four names, the positive and negative traits of those named and why the relationship broke up. During this time, soft background music was played and many people got up for a break. After several minutes, Bradshaw requested that everyone form a circle within their group, introduce themselves and relate a feeling about past relationships. Including myself, there were five in my group. Of the other four (all women), two were in therapy, one had attended meetings of Adult Children of Alcoholics (ACOA) and the other was simply interested in healthy relationships. I said that I had read some of Bradshaw's books and that I came out of curiosity. The two in therapy loved talking about themselves and how much they have recovered. One women was in therapy at the Joan Childs Institute but not in a 12-Step Program.

After a 20-minute break, Bradshaw took us through a meditation or trance-like exercise for about 30 minutes. His hypnotic intonations separated by moments of silence with the lights very low and soothing background music provide the atmosphere for mentally returning to our childhood and the "source influence of our relationships." Our source relationships (parents) provide unhealthy unconscious factors in our present relationships and we must make peace with these source relationships — we must "leave home" to have a healthy relationship. Auditory and visual imprints from the past remain in our brains. We all hear an inner voice from the toxic past – a way in which we remain controlled and influenced by our parents. As a result everyone looks for someone like their parent in a relationship. For instance, the girl who grew up with an alcoholic father swears she will never marry someone like her father, but surely does. Bradshaw says, "You are most lovable when you are not yourself." In various stages we must work toward getting rid of "idealized and degraded images of our parents." He claims that parents plant a heavy dose of toxic guilt within us so that we can't have our own lives. "You are the source of your parents' admiration – they need you!" He states that the most damaging thing to any child is the unresolved lives of their parents.

Separation

Proclaiming again that the separation inside our brain needs to take place, Bradshaw took us back again via another meditative exercise. Relax, concentrate on your breathing, feel your clothes touching your body, the lights are dimmed, the gentle music begins, the hypnotic voice commands. Bradshaw led us back to our childhood again, this time asking us to imagine ourselves physically attached to the parent we feel most connected to. Then the adult in us appears, to rescue the child from the parental control. He told us to imagine our finger is connected to a laser beam and to literally detach our child from the parent. The child will then seek guidance from the adult and leave the influence of the parent. The adult must show the child that the parent is no longer needed because someone more reliable will now account for the needs and demands of the child.

During this emotional seance there is much loud weeping. The "therapists" quietly move toward the piteous sounds emanating from the wounded adult children purging themselves of the toxic guilt bestowed on them by their parents.

After lunch Bradshaw returned to the stage and repeated the necessity to separate from the influence of the parents. The child fights the separation, fearing something dreadful will happen if he thinks or says something bad about his parents. Recharged by the break, Bradshaw talked for an hour or so, sometimes rambling about the physiology of the brain, stating that being terrorized as a child leaves a permanent scar on the brain, affecting certain reflexes which cannot be cured, only controlled. He returned to the overhead projector and described his building blocks of relationships which also correspond to different stages of child development. This is his way of providing more detailed, technical information to make the audience feel as if these original ideas can be universally applied. He appears at times to be deliberately ambiguous. (Perhaps his books will provide the answers.) The audience laughs at his humor and is completely enthralled with his message.

A simple statement seemed to summarize the entire workshop: You will die psychologically if you don't separate your identity from the source figure of your relationships, your parents.

April 11 & 12, 1992 – A Weekend Intensive Workshop "Finishing Our Business With Mother"

In this workshop, with much self-disclosure, Bradshaw led about 700 people in small groups through a series of guided exercises and imageries to help them confront the parent (mother) in themselves in order to heal the wounded child within. Many of the people in the room have had problems coping with life: unable to form a relationship; addicted to drugs, alcohol, food, love, sex; unexplained feelings of fear, sadness, anger, panic. Many have been emotionally or physically abused as children. I overheard several people say that their therapist had suggested they attend this workshop.

The central idea of the workshop was that by going through a process of confronting the parent-child relationship in the psyche, a healing relationship would be formed and the person could move on to become a functioning adult.

Finding My Way In

I was put off by the greeters at the entrance who didn't hesitate to ask me if I needed directions to the ballroom — as though I were a wounded child, as if there wasn't a great big sign pointing up the escalator to the BRADSHAW EVENT. I said I was looking for a cup of coffee.

I was put off by the lavish display and the high prices of the coffee and food outside the ballroom. To say nothing of the exhibit tables where everything from books, t-shirts and teddy bears to tapes of lectures and music were on sale. To say nothing of the number of adults, often in childish clothing, who were holding, dangling, even hugging teddy bears. At least one well-known psychiatric hospital also had a booth offering services for most of the well-known problems of our age: bulimia, anorexia, addictions of every kind, adult children of alcoholics.

I joined a small group inside the ballroom and we introduced ourselves — strictly on a first-name basis. Naturally, we each had to explain why we were there, and I said I had seen John's TV program the previous month. I had come out of curiosity. I was a teacher and thought I could pick up something useful about teaching and learning. Plus, John Bradshaw appeared to be so popular, I was just curious to hear what he had to say.

About ten minutes late, things got underway. Joan Childs introduced about 20 therapists, including her daughter from California. They walked across the stage as she said their names. A great deal was made of the fact that these people were there to help keep us safe and that if we felt like we were losing it, we were to raise our hands and someone would help us. Then Childs introduced John Bradshaw who strode energetically onto the stage and took the microphone.

Parents Are the Problem

His voice seemed unreasonably loud at first. He was definitely in charge. He began with a lecture illustrated by drawings on the overhead projector. This is what he said.

There is a definite association between one's experiences as an infant and later addiction. If needs for nourishment and basic care are not immediately met, the totally helpless infant experiences rage. Object-splitting is the way infants cope with delayed gratification. The child perceives two polarized mothers (or caretakers). One is good; the other is bad. In the early months, the infant is totally tied up in a relationship with "mother" to meet its basic needs.

Gradually, the child experiences a need to separate from its mother in a process called object constancy. If, by the age of 25 months, the child has not successfully separated from its mother, it will never be able to have a normal relationship later in life. Bradshaw calls this experience of separation a "psychological birth."

At some point here, Bradshaw issued a warning to journalists. To protect his privacy, details about his life, which he lavishly uses to illustrate his lectures, were not to be carried from the room.

Adult children are those who have unresolved issues from their childhood. They are grown-ups with the needs of children. They have deficiencies, what Abraham Maslow calls dependency needs. When mother is an "adult child" with her own unresolved issues from childhood, she will never let you separate – let you experience your psychological birth.

For this reason, Bradshaw agrees with Jung that the most damaging influence on children are parents with unfulfilled lives – parents who use children by having inappropriate relationships with them. "Use is abuse." Example: At a workshop, Bradshaw received a note from a man in the audience. The man wrote that when he was two, his mother "went down on him" – she wanted to be his first "girl." The man was unmarried and now 42 years old, still living at home with his mother. The question was: had this man been abused as a child? The audience responded appreciatively to this rhetorical question.

The point is, according to Bradshaw, Mom should not use her child as her boyfriend or her best friend. It deprives him or her of a childhood. Mom should get friends her own age. She should get a life!

This also happens when mothers live vicariously through their daughters – convincing them to marry a doctor, for instance, because Mom failed to marry a doctor. No matter what you do to try to please such a mother, she is never satisfied and you are always disappointed.

Polarity characterizes people who never separate from mother. They see things as all good or all bad. They do things to excess – drink to oblivion, become addicted to control. If a child does not separate from its mother, co-dependency results.

For example, Jimmy Swaggart, the minister, preaches clean living but keeps getting caught drunk with prostitutes. Swaggart once said that all psychologists are secular humanists — an all-or-nothing sort of attitude. Bradshaw believes that all religions teach this kind of polarity.

In another aside to the press, Bradshaw says that often he comes to town, reporters interview him and then call a professor at the local university for comment. The professor has never been to a Bradshaw workshop, calls the whole thing too simplistic and junk food. Bradshaw says he knows this because he has said the same thing when being called for a comment on other therapists. His frequent, humble self-disclosure has a way of disarming us.

Bradshaw defines "emotional incest" as a mother flirting with her child. It is inappropriate parental behavior. It confuses the child, is a form of abuse and leads to "enmeshment" between mother and child from which the child derives a "false self." If a child does not separate from its mother, it retains an illusion of impotence. An infantile memory of mother stays inside its head.

Bradshaw makes the charge with some vehemence that normal parenting is inherently abusive because it is patriarchal. He says humanity has made great progress in achieving political democracy but we have not yet democratized the family. Parents still think they "own" children. They still use them and often abuse them. His views on this are more fully explored in the TV program, "Bradshaw: On the Family."

The Mother in Our Mind

Now Bradshaw makes a strong point that his workshops

are not about flesh-and-blood, real mothers. Rather, they deal with the mother-inside-our-head. He wants to get that very straight with us because the press often accuses him of encouraging people to blame their parents. The quarrel is not with our real parent, but with the parent part of our psyche. This is a point of some confusion in our group throughout the day. Do you have to confront your real parent in order to heal? Or can you do it privately in guided imagery? Opinion is divided. And, judging by the crying and angry words I hear during our first meditation, I believe the confusion is general.

We are now introduced to our first guided imagery. The lights are dimmed, the music plays – swishing sounds of a mother's heartbeat heard through the amniotic fluid of the womb. Bradshaw likens it to ocean sounds from whence we evolved and out of which we are born.

Although I bow my head and close my eyes, I do not allow myself to be lulled by John's powerful voice and the hypnotic music to remember my moment of birth and the first sight of my mother. I chiefly remember the pace of my own heartbeat in tune with the music. As the sobbing starts and, yes, the primal screams, I become unnerved. I am very tempted to get up and leave but I succeed in controlling my instinct for flight.

When the imagery is over, we are told to share our thoughts and feelings with the small group. We are instructed not to give each other advice and to refrain from touching, hugging, or patting each other no matter how sorry we might feel for someone. Those with sex or love addictions are cautioned against acting out. Everyone must take responsibility for their own behavior so that the workshop will be safe for all.

Everyone in the group but me has been brought to tears

by the imagery in their minds and feelingly share their thoughts. I do the best I can to say something sincere about my heartbeat and the music. These are awfully nice people who really had some bad things happen to them when they were young – ranging from being called ugly, to being hit, witnessing family fist fights, and being locked in closets or bathrooms for hours when they misbehaved. My feelings for the group have been activated and I decide to stick it out for today.

We take a coffee break and return for another brief lecture.

Images of Mother Hurting Me

The workshop will cover three healing stages. In the first stage we will try to visualize our "mother hunger" – presumably that special symbiotic relationship between infant and mother that we all experience. Then we will grieve our own grief, hurts, and disappointments.

Bradshaw says that if our own parents are also wounded children, they, too, must go through these stages before they will change. He implies that it's rather pointless to confront such parents or try to explain our own feelings. He describes the typical parent response: "There's nothing wrong with this family. You're the problem. You're the one who is crazy." The audience appreciates this comment very much, as though they have experienced it.

He describes the standard grief process: Shock, Denial, Anger, Remorse, Acceptance. He encourages us to seek therapy or the assistance of an appropriate 12-Step Program if we get stuck in any of the stages after the workshop ends. We move into the next guided imagery. Again the lights are dimmed. Lullabies are played, as well as a soft-rock song "The Child Will Remember" by Richard Wagner.

You can buy tapes of the song in the lobby. It is the high
point of the imagery judging by the sobs it evokes. It is a
maudlin song and I am beginning to feel exploited.

John begins by asking us to breathe deeply for several
minutes, feel the clothes on our bodies, the seat beneath
us, and the floor below. Since I know that "highs" are
induced by the infusion of extra oxygen to the brain, I
continue to breathe normally. John asks us to focus on the
number three, then hypnotically says numbers, first from
one to ten, and then increasingly at random: 11, 89, 47 —
for quite a long time. Then he goes back to three, then
two, then one, which we are to visualize as a door which
we open and enter into a room in a house where we once
lived. We see our mother as she was when we were a child.
This goes on and on until the lights go on and we are
instructed to write a letter to this mother telling her all the
times she hurt us. We are to do this with our non-dominant
hand presumably to enhance our childish feelings from a
time when we were just learning to write. I use my left
hand and it is a very interesting experience to be so incompetent. Unfortunately I can't think of much to write but I
do the best I can.

We are left to do this for a long time and I am stream-of-
consciousness writing anything that comes to mind just to
appear involved and because it is such an odd feeling to
write with the left hand. Then, oh no, we have to read our
letters to the others in the group. I volunteer to go first,
and luckily the others go easy on me, probably because
they want to move on and read their letters, which are
really touching and I feel for them.

Before we break for lunch, John makes a point about
young people experimenting with drugs. He says there's
nothing wrong with experimentation. There's no harm in

trying drugs. The problem is that kids from dysfunctional families are the ones who get addicted.

Lunch Break

Heading outside in search of a restaurant, I meet one of the men in my group and we end up having lunch together. He is an awfully nice fellow and I like him. To show my empathy for him I try to mention as many crazy things about my life that I can think of. I find myself really opening up and saying things I don't normally tell anyone. This echoes several comments from others in the group throughout the day. There's something very freeing about meeting with perfect strangers whom you will never see again and sharing your innermost thoughts and feelings. It is just not something you do normally. Or at least I don't.

During lunch, I begin to feel so comfortable that I confide to the man my feelings of skepticism about the program. I say I'm withholding involvement for fear of getting sucked in, that I feel a little exploited by the whole thing. He said, "You mean like a cult?" My very thought. He said it is possible to get sucked in to some of these things and you do have to be careful. It has happened to him. He appears to be keeping an open mind now.

We are a little late getting back from lunch and find John again issuing a caution. Some of the experiences he is conducting us through are very scary. If one is too scary, we shouldn't do it. Trust your own judgement, he says, and just pull back, or raise your hand for therapist assistance. In over five years he has led workshops for half a million people and nothing bad has ever happened. This is because he arranges safety precautions – a safe room, plentiful therapists. During one imagery, that involved the primal screams, I did open my eyes and look around. The therapists were quietly walking around among us, presumably looking to head off trouble.

A woman stands up at this point and says that John is wrong. Something bad could happen and he should be extremely careful. He tries to soothe her and even tells her that if she wants to leave, he will refund her money, even though this is not official policy. He mentions that sometimes people write him with similar concerns.

Learning About Anger and the Adult Child

That blown over, we move into the exercise which involves anger. John begins by describing some of the symptoms of adult childhood. You have to have four or five of them, such as addiction of one kind or another, depression, or age-inappropriate behavior, before concluding that you are an adult child. Some forms of depression, for instance, can be chemically treated. Others may have been induced by a traumatic experience (the death of a loved one, a divorce) which has nothing to do with childhood abuse. One symptom of adult childhood is the expression of anger as rage – belittling a person (especially a little person), shaming them, hitting them when you are angry. It is possible to express anger respectfully.

People can be helped to deal with past anger. In a clinic situation they are sometimes given batika bats – soft, padded sticks with which they beat furniture and other inanimate objects. Bradshaw said he wouldn't issue batika bats at this workshop for fear of someone getting hurt, for which I heave a sigh of relief.

Another way to deal with your anger is to embrace your inner child. You must get rid of your rage, or it will keep you in the same place. The whole point of therapy is to finish it and move on. Bradshaw disagrees with Susan

Forward that you have to confront your offending parent and sever connections. You have to move on. He describes some of the ways a person can get stalled in the healing process – getting addicted to the 12-Step Program, getting addicted to groups or to workshops. This is not the point. He does admit that he still occasionally meets with his support group for "reality checks."

Another symptom of adult childhood is post-traumatic stress disorder. If you were hurt as a child and had no control over it, when you're older, you want control. A desire to control other people's lives is a symptom of adult childhood.

Confrontation and Seeking Safety

The next exercise involves going back to the room in the house where we had pictured our mother that morning. We find our inner child elsewhere in the house, take it by the hand reassuringly and ask it to talk to mother. We are to tell it that we will protect it from harm no matter what it says. The idea is to have the inner child confront the inner mother, charge her with whatever she did to us and ask her why she did it. Again emotions are strong and some people are unable to convince the child to confront. Those who can't acknowledge that this is an area they will have to work on in the future.

After a break, we return for the final exercise of the day, in which we are taken back to a place where we feel comfortable – the beach, park, a woods – wherever. We meet with our inner child and try to talk to it. To help us feel stronger, as a kind of talisman, we are told to touch the thumb of our right hand to one of the other fingers of our right hand. Later, whenever we do this, we will remember our special comfortable place and feel a surge of strength or courage or maybe safety. I'm losing it and can't remember any more details. I believe that before it's over we do embrace our inner child. Some people take this a lot more literally than others, especially those with teddy bears. For some, I think, the teddy bear is a stand-in for the inner child. I think this would be an awful way to go through life, but then, I haven't walked in their moccasins.

Overnight

Before closing, John cautions us to take it easy tonight, that tomorrow will be even more emotional than today. We might want to share phone numbers with our group. We should avoid taking any mind-altering drugs.

Our group does not share phone numbers but we agree to meet in the same place tomorrow morning. I feel a surge of fellowship with them. At the very beginning one of the members had said that sometimes groups don't click, and one of the members has to be asked to leave. I knew that if that happened, I would be the one asked to leave. It made me feel good that this didn't happen.

I go home, have three beers and go out to dinner. By four a.m., I'm up and writing this report. By ten a.m. I'm back at the workshop for Day Two. My husband thinks I'm crazy for going back. I hadn't really planned to go. But I feel my group would be disappointed if I didn't show up, feeling perhaps that they had done something wrong. They don't need this now. My husband then says it may do me some good. Maybe it will.

Three members of my group are there when I arrive. Ten minutes into the session the last member arrives. And we are a group again. I can see how this can get addictive!

Handling the Mother in Our Mind

John begins with another cautionary note. We must

beware of getting polarized — thinking there is only one way to heal, one road to salvation. His model is only one of many. There are other ways to heal.

We must not get stuck, addicted to being angry or addicted to being a victim. Some people get off on that for years, for life. It's a role one learns in the family and it's hard to break. That is not the point. We must move on.

John goes to great lengths to validate our pain. We must have our pain validated before we can move on. We can't relax and move on until we stop viewing our mother as either a saint or a monster. This is infantile object-splitting. We have to get to the point where we accept our mother as a human being — a real person.

Again, Bradshaw stresses that we're not talking about flesh-and-blood mothers. We're talking about the mother in ourselves. Children have a vivid fantasy life. It doesn't matter if mother did what we think she did. Maybe we fantasized it. Young children interpret things very differently than adults sometimes. But if we think it happened, we have to deal with that.

John's model has three stages. In the first, we grieve our grief, as we did yesterday. In stage two, we grieve our mother's grief, demythologize her, and forgive her. This we will do today. In the final stage, we complete the separation which never occurred when we were 25 months old. We become our own mothers. We learn how to nurture ourselves. We become the heads of our own household. We champion our inner child. We parent ourselves.

How do you know when you're healed? There are signs. First your energy about this problem diminishes. Next, you stop obsessing on your mother. Finally, you get on with your life: out of a destructive relationship, into an adult relationship. Be careful, he says, if you're not moving on in your life and getting empowered. Stay away from people who try to keep you dependent on them.

John describes growing up. Until we are seven or eight, we view our parents as gods — we mythologize them. Then during puberty or by our twenties, we start seeing their faults. This is part of growing up. The Kachina ceremony among Southwest Indians depicts the process. Youths are taken to a dark lodge. Adults in the costumes of gods and goddesses spring into the room, dancing and singing. Then two of the gods take off their masks. They are mom and dad.

As adults we sometimes mythologize people — movie stars, presidents, and so on. John thinks this might have something to do with our human fear of death. But, he says, don't put anyone on a pedestal. Don't put HIM on a pedestal. He has been put on a pedestal and he doesn't like it. It's very uncomfortable. Sometimes in therapy we transfer our relationship with a parent to the therapist. One day we will see the therapist's feet of clay. And all the rage we feel toward our parent will be transferred to the therapist. This is why Bradshaw tells us so much about his life — so we will see his feet of clay and not put him on a pedestal. There's nothing wrong with the word "guru" — it means "teacher" — but it also has a mythological connotation. John says he does not want to be anyone's guru.

Beware of cults, even religions, with all-or-nothing philosophies, he says. He is working on a new TV program about cults right now. People who are adult children tend to get into cult situations because of their own childish polarity. Toxic shame creates this polarity.

Learning to Forgive Our Mother

The first exercise of day two involves drawing a chart listing our mother's ideal or goddess qualities (saintly, unselfish), her degraded or monster qualities (controlling, abusive), and in the middle column her real qualities (deprived, rejected, whatever). Drawing this chart about anyone you have a relationship with is often useful: father, siblings, friends, mates – it helps you sort out the real from the unreal.

The point of forgiving your mother, he says, is to enable you to move on to freedom from the bondage of hate and resentment toward your mother. Sometimes parents are so resistant to this moving on – they are still "acting out" – then you have to cut off the relationship at least until you're strong enough to relate to them in a different way.

In the next exercise, introduced by something called "paradoxical breathing," from which I refrain, we are taken back to the comforting place – the beach, the woods, etc. – we visualized yesterday. We sit comfortably with our inner child and see our mother coming toward us at her present age and gradually visualize her growing younger until she is the same age as our inner child. We encourage our inner child to go and speak with our mother as a child and ask them to talk. Some people cannot do this, as becomes apparent later in our group when we try to tell what the children said to each other. This is an area they will have to work on.

In the next very emotional exercise, we enter a cemetery and see our mother's gravestone. We go to her as she is dying, forgive her, and go through the grieving of her death. There is a lot of very heavy sobbing in this one. Again, in subsequent discussion, some people can't forgive and realize they have to work on that. Since I have actually experienced the death of my real mother, tears come to my eyes during this exercise, and I am very happy to report this to the group. It has already been noticed and I am given a pat of encouragement for making progress. John gives us permission now to give each other hugs if they are requested. We make the rounds, and I try to participate. I know that everyone is aware of my squeamish feelings about it. Several times, based on whatever revelations I have made, a member of the group tentatively diagnoses me as an overachiever. I don't know whether this is a symptom or a disease. He says I may have worked through most of my problems but I may still have work to do. It takes a lifetime, he says. And I agree by saying something along the lines of "nobody's perfect." And I do agree with John Bradshaw who periodically quotes the line about the unexamined life not being worth living.

Another Self, A New Family

In the final exercise, to lively music heavy on the drums, we meet the wild woman or wild man in us all. We all have a strange woman or man inside us. We are taken to a dark forest where we come to a clearing. From out of a swamp a very wild woman emerges. She begins to dance and we join her. It is wild. Then we move toward the light and climb a high mountain. To the sound of waves pounding on the beach we leap into the ocean and come ashore covered with seaweed – in much the way we were born – only now we are reborn, presumably as a real adult. No one cries during this exercise and we all feel sort of calmed, uplifted by the experience. Everyone LOVED the music. Someone said he wanted to get a tape of it. I said, with a bit of a smirk which he recognized, that it was probably on sale in the lobby. Sure enough, John named the music and told where we could get it in the lobby.

In closing John gave us a pep talk on parenting ourselves. We have to learn how to do this – to become our own parents, to nurture ourselves. In order to reenact their childhood, some people actually live the role of a child for several years in a house with people who role play as parents. But most of us don't have the time or money to indulge in that.

He advocates joining a support group but to be careful in picking one. Beware of those where people give advice. What you need is high-quality sensory interpretation, a group which can name your feelings and give you a reality check. Avoid enmeshment, entrapment. You can't be in a normal relationship, whether with a person or a group, unless you can leave it, or feel free to leave it. He even suggests we might want to form our own group, perhaps starting with the one we have been in this weekend. This does not sound like a good idea to me. By their silence, the others in my group appear to agree.

You need to find a new family affiliation (I don't know what this means exactly). You need to find a new source of potency. It's the hardest thing – to become your own person.

It's also hard to ask for help. Even though you are now the source of your own potency, you can ask for help. I presume this means going to a therapist.

You also need a "higher power" – whatever God is for you. John is writing another book about this. You should leave your mother's religion, at least for a while. You should give yourself permission to evaluate the rules and values you live by. You need to protect your inner child by having some sort of social group you can go to – maybe a therapy group, maybe something else. I'm getting vague on the details here.

Finally, admitting that he's part preacher (and he definitely is), John gives a beatific sermon on the rewards of this process we've been through. He says something like the following:

The gift of working through your separation is to give life to yourself. The differences that make us unique as human beings is our identity. We have a right to be our own person. He quotes Gerard Manley Hopkins: "I am me. That's why I came." We must quit trying to change our mother and start changing ourselves. Bradshaw has been through this and says "I love my mother now more than I ever have and I hope the same will be true for you."

We share a group hug. One woman passes out her phone number in case we ever need to get in touch. We wish each other luck and we say good-bye.

An Open Letter to John

John Bradshaw suggests that the best way to get something resolved is to write a letter to the person involved. In fact he often writes to himself — as a Little John, the inner child or Big John, the abused child as an adult. So I write him the following:

Dear Big John,

You counsel people to write letters to express their emotions. So, I'm writing to you, to let you know what I think about you.

You've certainly developed a formula for success — books, workshops, TV. You've earned the title as the "world's greatest communicator." What are you communicating?

We all grew up in dysfunctional families — 100% of us — and you are going to save the family? Are you saving the family by destroying it? John, I know hundreds of well-meaning, caring, thoughtful parents who have been abandoned by the adult children who cut them out of their lives after taking the advice you gave them, and the advice of the therapists who think of you as a "guru" whether or not you like that.

I wanted to learn why you are so popular; what is your message that appeals to so many people? Frankly (you do want me to be frank, don't you?) I'm appalled.

You say we weren't put on this earth to take care of old mom and dad. I recently spoke to an "old dad" on the phone. He's seventy-nine years old. His fifty-one year old daughter cut him off and took her children out of his life forever. Why? She learned from you that he "emotionally incested" her. He doesn't know what the heck she's talking about. All he knows is that the good times they had in the past, helping each other, spending holidays together, are gone. Is that "healing" the family? John, I could tell you more than 500 similar stories of frantic parents, who love their children and thought their children loved them. That is, until these children read recovery books, joined a 12-Step recovery group, went to therapy to recover their inner child, or went to one of your seminars.

I have read you are a sensitive person, you have many prominent friends who love, respect, and consider you as a mentor. I thought you should also know that there are many people who don't like you so much. They think you helped destroy their families by creating a mood in this country that it's all right to be angry at your parents and disown them. They don't like your idea of abandoning the "family of origin" to create a "family of choice." Parents don't like having their adult children blame them for raising them in bad shame. They don't like being labeled as perpetrators and being accused of doing things they didn't do. What many of them are accused of are visualizations that come out in a seminar, not reality. They don't like the fact that they are not allowed to defend themselves.

Sorry, John, that you had such a bad time in your childhood that you think everyone did. It's just not true!

The Language of Recovery

Giving an idea a name is a powerful thing to do. The name or "concept" conjures a whole set of emotions and feelings. Once the word is understood by a group of people, they have a special language or way to communicate.

Adult child – *Adults who have not confronted and healed their inner child are really children with adult bodies.*

Boundaries – *The need for "space" and privacy. Don't expect too much from a person – respect his or her "space."*

Codependent – *A person who provides too much help to someone with an addiction.*

Core issues – *The true source of a person's problems. With a trained therapist the patient regresses to childhood to find the trauma that is causing all the trouble.*

Dysfunctional family – *A family in denial. Communication is lacking and people hurt each other.*

Emotional incest – *When the parent ignores boundaries and expects too much of his or her children.*

Enabler – *A person who allows a perpetrator to be abusive.*

Family of choice – *When an adult child's family of origin didn't nourish the inner child, a new family is necessary. Bradshaw recommends you find "a new, nonshaming, supportive family."*

Family of origin – *The birth parents and siblings.*

Grief work – *After confronting the trauma of childhood, it is necessary to grieve for the neglect and the shame the child endured.*

Higher power – *Term used (for God) in 12-Step Programs and Recovery literature. According to the 12-Step Program, it is necessary to surrender your will to your higher power in order to become abstinent. If not God, your higher power could be the therapist or the group.*

Incest — *The imposition by a family member of sexually inappropriate acts or acts with sexual overtones that violate the trust between the victim and the dominant perpetrator who has an ongoing emotional authority or bond.*

Incest survivor – *A victim of childhood sexual abuse. (Also, adult survivor)*

In denial – *Not recognizing the fact that you have an addiction, even though it is obvious to others. Not recognizing the bad things that happened in your past. Denying the bad things you did to someone else.*

Inner child – *The true self or identity in a person. The only way to a healthy and happy life is to heal the wounded inner child within. Everyone has a wounded inner child.*

In recovery – *Having recognized an addiction and seeking to heal often through a 12-Step Program. (Sometimes a lifelong process)*

Original pain work – *The intensive therapy that is necessary to discover the basic trauma that your inner child experienced growing up in a dysfunctional family.*

Perpetrator – *The person responsible for the childhood abuse of the adult survivor.*

Reparenting – *The adult child must take responsibility for being the parent to the wounded inner child by recog-*

*nizing and confronting the shame experienced in child-
hood and by forever protecting the inner child from
unnecessary trauma.*

Toxic shame – *The reason why Bradshaw claims all
families are dysfunctional. The constant shame we all
experienced as children is the source of all our present
deficiencies.*

12-Step Program – *A recovery program which follows
the plan established by the founders and practitioners of
Alcoholics Anonymous. (Overeaters Anonymous, Gam-
blers Anonymous, Narcotics Anonymous, Incest Survivors Anonymous, and more)*

Validation – *What you say in group or to the therapist is
accepted as true – they believe you even if no one else
does.*

Victim – *Someone who has been abused and not yet
taken control of his or her life. When he or she takes
control, in recovery, he or she becomes a "survivor."*

Working on your stuff – *A common phrase used in the
Recovery Movement, it refers to the process of actively
being in recovery by attending group meetings or private
therapy, or better yet, both.*

The New Age Movement

New Age

New Age provides a huge umbrella for a potpourri of ideas. Visit your local bookstore. Under New Age you will find books on the following topics: astrology, psychics, acupuncture, crystals, moon signs, dream interpretation, Oriental mythology, magic, ghosts, gemstones, goddesses, sun signs, astrocycles, out-of-body experience, Tao of symbols, creative visualization, Tarot cards, astral projection, hypnotism, fortune telling, UFOs, paranormal experience, auras, ESP, healing, focusing, life-extension, age regression, reincarnation, channeling, homeopathy, mind-body connection, macrobiotics. The authors range from the uncredentialed to PhDs from our most prestigious universities. It does not seem to matter.

What ties New Age thinking together so that all of these diverse ideas can fit under one umbrella? Maybe the fact that the ideas do not fit anywhere else. The ideas in these books could not be categorized under science, health, psychology, philosophy – the more traditional, recognized disciplines. So if it doesn't fit anywhere else, it's New Age.

What all of the New Age topics have in common is that they don't need to rely on the scientific method to come up with answers to anything. They rely on intuition, imagination, hearsay, superstition – forget logic, data, analysis, the need for replication in an unbiased setting.

The New Age movement assumes that a rational, scientific investigation into the mysteries of the mind, body, and universe is inadequate and outdated. New Age adherents subscribe to a "new consciousness" which is characterized by mystical beliefs in such things as magic, astrology, numerology, the occult, sorcery, and shamans. Influenced partly by Eastern mysticism, New Age offers the promise of achieving "self-actualization" and reaching a higher "consciousness" through meditation, yoga, and holistic body healing. Magical charms, ancient myths, and the healing powers of crystals and pyramids are prevalent in this belief system. The belief in outer-body experiences, past-life regression, and contact with spirits from other dimensions are readily accepted. Many of the daughters who have developed a childhood history that their parents don't recognize, are adherents of New Age ideas. How do New Age ideas influence these women?

New Age provides answers to everything: nutrition, health, the great philosophical questions of who we are, where we were, and where we are going. Gurus of New Age thinking have "the" answers. Finding peace within oneself as a prelude to planetary harmony is one goal of New Age thinking. Neo-paganism, witchcraft, goddesses, and Druids offer religious alternatives to the traditional Western religious beliefs.

New Age techniques include visualization, imaging, chanting, meditation, fasting, sensory deprivation, hypnosis, body massage. These techniques all can have a very profound impact on the thought processes. In addition to the many New Age seminars, groups, and books, there are tapes as well. The tapes are hypnotic; many of them carry subliminal messages. How significant can subliminal messages be? We just don't know.

New Age has become very influential in the United States. A president has been known to be influenced by astrology, movie stars by channeling, and other well-admired celebrities use these and other New Age techniques.

Why is New Age dangerous? Because it doesn't face reality. It speaks about a holistic approach to life, the mind-body connection. Excluded from the holistic approach are scientific responses to health and other problems.

With all the answers to life available in New Age thinking, what happens if an adherent who follows all the prescribed guides to life has something go wrong? Who is to blame? Certainly not the person herself or himself or the guru or the New Age concept. The problem has to be outside of that person – something done to her or him. Then age regression becomes the prescribed therapy. Through visualization, imaging or hypnosis, answers can be found. Generally it is a parent or other caretaker, not an adherent of New Age, who is at fault for the problem. New Age healing rejects modern medicine; cancer, MS, diabetes are all caused by psychological trauma. No bacteria or organic causes for anything. Healing of such illnesses can only take place with therapy, or imaging away the illness.

With this mindset it is easy to see why parents are blamed for all the problems these women have. If therapy, hypnotism, or visualization do not discover the person (in this life) who is the culprit, regress or channel to a previous life – that's where the problem may lie.

With science and non-science mixed in unequal proportions, as it is in New Age, we think this movement provides a breeding ground in which confabulations can thrive.

The Language of New Age

New Age has its special vocabulary allowing New Agers to readily communicate with one another. Here is some of that language. We are providing definitions for you since you're not likely to find them used this way in the dictionary.

Anchoring – *Using specific body movements and key words in a repeated process (chant) enforced by hypnotic suggestion to implant positive experiences or messages into the subconscious.*

Biofeedback – *Using mental persuasion to lower blood pressure, body temperature and heart beat to relieve stress.*

Bodywork – *Using complex yoga-like physical exercises and postures to release the psychic tensions hidden by the conscious mind.*

Ceremonial healing – *Using a specific public communal ritual usually as a part of a religious experience to activate physical, mental, or spiritual renewal.*

Channeling – *Communicating to or from another dimension or level of reality through another physical being.*

Chi – *The life-giving energy force of the cosmos.*

Clairvoyance – *Receiving information from or about an object, person or event through nonsensory means.*

Consciousness – *Being aware of something and able to hold a present image of it in the mind.*

Cosmic counseling – *Helping an individual establish a proper relationship with the life force of the universe by* *which all beings have their subsistence.*

Dream theory – *Recollecting when awake visions during sleep to reveal goals, desires, and events that influence an individual's consciousness and actions.*

Faith healing – *Using a chant, a laying on of the hands, or other religious ritual to enhance consciousness and call upon the Supreme Being or saint to accelerate or activate physical, mental, or spiritual well-being.*

Guided imagery – *Creating or re-creating, under the direction of a therapist, visualizations of properly-aligned reality enforced by repeated affirmation. Usually involves mind-body synthesis, beginning with relaxation techniques, followed by breathing exercises.*

Holism – *Integrating into an interwoven whole all organic, environmental, psychological spiritual systems.*

Homeopathy – *Stimulating the body's healing ability by treating the patient with the same substance that sickened him/her.*

Human potential movement – *Using a wide range of self-help techniques ranging from group therapy, hypnosis, and subliminal or motivational techniques to release the boundless capabilities of the human psyche and the unlimited powers in the human spirit leading to self-realization.*

Illusions – *Perceiving reality, one's self, one's personal control, or the future with attributes beyond what is actually the case.*

Imaging – *Replacing negative mental images (or memories) with carefully constructed positive ones, out of which a new reality can be created.*

Mantra — *Hindu scripture words or phrases which possess spiritual powers when repeated in a chant.*

Meditation — *Systematically quieting the mind and senses to increase internal awareness of thoughts, meanings, sense of direction, decisions to improve the quality of one's life.*

Mystical manipulation — *Making intense physiological or psychological states appear spontaneous through planned and engineered activities.*

Neurolinguistics — *A form of therapy that requires the careful analysis and structuring of behavior and body language, to help a client overcome phobias, insecurities, and neuroses.*

Precognition — *Having knowledge of an event or circumstance prior to its occurrence.*

Psychometry — *Receiving information from an object, person, or event through nonsensory means.*

Rebirthing — *Using proper rhythms of inhaling and exhaling to expand one's conscious capabilities as in birth itself.*

Rolfing — *Realigning the body through deep massage so the body is in concert with gravity and the energies of the earth.*

Sensory awareness — *Bringing to consciousness and recollecting the sensations recorded by each of the senses, especially touch.*

Visualization — *Creating an altered frame of reference by imagining circumstances as one would prefer them to be.*

Feminism

The Feminist Influence

The feminist movement has a broad appeal for women. Many of the mothers who have been accused of being perpetrators or enablers by their daughters in this sex abuse phenomenon are feminists. So are their daughters. But their views of feminism are wide apart. The mothers see feminism as a way of thinking that liberated them to do many things in their lifetimes. Feminism provided the support for them to become doctors, teachers, writers, and mothers and wives at the same time. It broadened their possibilities. Many of these women are grateful to Betty Friedan and Gloria Steinem, leaders in the women's movement, who spread the notion that women could and should do all things. The consciousness raising groups were places for these women to go to lessen their isolation and strengthen their commitment to political altruism through mutual revelations of common experiences. These groups originated as a structured series of meetings by and for women, and to bring new recruits to feminist ideology. For many women the group experience opened their eyes to all sorts of possibilities.

The women's movement was always home for a wide range of ideas. While many women with husbands and children join feminist groups so do women who are lesbians and they too are welcomed.

Lesbianism is becoming more than a way of life – it's more than who one wants to choose as an intimate partner. Lesbianism is now a political movement. In its extreme, lesbianism isn't just seeking the right to be recognized for the decision to be gay. It is now a movement which decries the patriarchal society in which, according to this radical thinking, we are forced to live and which has ruined the world. There are many books which expound upon this point of view.

Sonia Johnson is a leader of what might be called radical feminism. Johnson joined the women's movement in the 1970s when the Mormon Church, to which she belonged, opposed the Equal Rights Amendment. She formed Mormons for the ERA and later ran for U.S. president. Her book *Going Out of Our Minds* addresses feminist spirituality. She recommends group meditation or "self-hypnosis" to gain understanding of the pervasive nature of male domination or patriarchy. She sees herself and all like-minded women as prophets and believes that only by "going out of our minds" can women boycott patriarchy "emotionally, spiritually, and intellectually" and thus transform society. Not only does patriarchy rule the world, it destroys the soul of women because it allows men full control over them. Here are some quotes from *Going Out of Our Minds*:

> *"We have not been warned that Daddy is our enemy, or Grandpa, or Uncle Steve, or brother Harvey.*

> *Like rape, despite rhetoric to the contrary, incest is not only encouraged, it is insisted upon; not just condoned, but blessed.*

> *Like rape, incest is not accidental. It is an* institution *of patriarchy — like the church, like the law: absolutely necessary to maintaining male privilege and power.*

> *Not with fear and dread, but with hope and love, we can leap out of our minds, free of patriarchy, into a celebration of life. I believe there is no other way.*

> *I decided that this time out I am going to begin to*

*learn to use — despite patriarchy's scorn — the immense
and various resources of my spirit and deep mind.*

*Hand in hand now let us leap off this stinking
rubbish heap men call "civilization," out of our
limited, lightless, dying patriarchal minds, and
reach for our lives — for all life — deep into the cosmos that is our own souls."*

Another book with influence in the radical feminist
movement is the *Great Cosmic Mother* by Monica Sjöö and
Barbara Mor. This book is credited with showing that the
religion of the Goddess is our ancient heritage. The religion
of the Goddess "is tied to the cycles of women's bodies,
the seasons, the phases of the moon, and the fertility of the
earth — was the original religion of all humanity." Sjöö is an
artist and theoretician of the Goddess religion. Mor is an
American poet. We will let them speak for themselves in
some of the following quotes:

*"Reich pointed out in the 1930s that the prevalent
male sexual fantasy in male-dominated society, is
one of rape.*

*And it confirms what too many people do not want
to know: that the first "God" was female.*

*Truly, our very sanity is at stake with continuing
patriarchy and the denial of the cosmic self — the
Goddess — within us all, and us within her.*

*Women who cannot or will not accept taboos are
still punished, as we've been punished for two thou-
sand years in the patriarchal world — as Lesbians,
unmarried mothers, thinkers, artists, witches. One
form of punishment is culturally mandated rape.*

Women, in the Judeo-Christian-Islamic-Buddhist-
Hindu-Confucian traditions, are seen as some kind
of functional mistake. Nature is a mistake. Life is a
mistake. And the male mind was born to correct it. "

This is just a small sampling of feminist literature that
provide the rationale for a new way of life to rid the earth
of the evils perpetrated by the patriarchal systems that
have governed our lives since the beginnings of the Judeo-
Christian period.

Berkeley, California, is a center of feminist thought and
it is here that one can see the movement in full flower.
Why Berkeley? Because it has always been a tolerant city,
home of the University of California it attracts people with
diverse opinions. Berkeley is across the bay from San Fran-
cisco, where gay men congregate in large numbers. So the
men and women are close enough to share the gay movement in ways that help both groups, yet separate enough
to enjoy their individual domains. They can build and
experiment with strong support networks.

The level of concern about rape and sexual abuse including incest is at a fever pitch in Berkeley. Workshops
and 12-Step Programs which address these issues are held
regularly. Rape and incest are on everyone's mind. It is a
good climate to push extremes. "Man is to be feared and is
the enemy" becomes a recurrent theme. Defense against
this enemy is an ongoing concern.

The same vitality that was used in the 50s for Civil Rights
and the 60s against the Vietnam War is now being applied
to feminism. The week of March 16-20 was set aside as
Sexual Assault Awareness Week. The town was plastered
with flyers. Here are some of the activities for incest survivors that took place.

One Week's Schedule

Monday

7:30 p.m. Poetry readings by contributors of *OUT!* – a magazine for and by survivors of physical and sexual abuse.

7:30 p.m. Women Survivors of Childhood Sexual Abuse Grof Bodywork Therapy Group

Tuesday

6:30 p.m. Survivors of Incest Anonymous

7:00 p.m. A talk "Recovery from Ritual Abuse" discussing creative ways to heal from sexual abuse that occurs in cult-like groups.

Wednesday

11:00 a.m. Speech "Recovering from Incest"

6:30 p.m. A talk "Ritual Abuse and its Impact on Women"

Thursday

7:00 p.m. Incest Survivor Therapy Group

7:15 p.m. Support/Discussion Group on Incest/ Childhood Sexual Abuse for Lesbian/Bisexual Women

Friday

7:00 p.m. Newcomer Incest Survivors Group

8:00 p.m. Women Survivors of Incest Anonymous

Saturday

1:00 p.m. Pagan Support/Recovery Group

7:00 p.m. "Why We Burn" a consciousness raising play with readings of quotations about women from eminent churchmen and male philosophers.

Sunday

12:00 noon March for Women's Lives

Flyers were posted on bulletin boards:

Childhood Sexual Abuse: Group and Individual Counseling for Adults

"Inappropriate sexual advances can be very confusing and traumatic to a child. As an adult, those past experiences can have a lingering effect on one's self-esteem, intimate relationships, and sense of personal effectiveness. Whether your experience was that of incest, sexual molestation, rape, or the subtle blurring of relationship boundaries through inappropriate sexual overtones, your rights and personal needs were not respected. The impact this has had on your life is real and important to address."

Healing Celebration

"I invite you to come to a warm and soothing place, to a sweet scented land, that is your own, where your heart will unfold itself to you, where you will taste the sacredness of your tears and hear the stars in your laughter. Come to a place where you will remember your own special walk, where your walk is healing. Come to the warm place of your heart. Come home to yourself."

"I offer a supportive therapy in a nurturing environment, designed to suit individual needs and goals. To do this I draw upon my unique training and experience with Growth process facilitation, Intuitive problem solving, Relaxation and Visualization, Self-Esteem, Gender Empowerment, Goddess and Earth Spiritualities, Healing and Ritual, Reiki, and the Expressive arts."

Many other groups met on their issues, 26 in one center alone. Handouts were abundant: (a) a reading list on women's issues available at Women's Resource Center, (b) a flyer from Survivors of Incest Anonymous, (c) "Bitter-sweet" for those in 12-Step recovery programs, (d) a listing of 47 chants, and (e) newsletters from each support group. *OUT!*, a newsletter published by and for survivors of sexual abuse, headlined three emotional articles about sexual abuse and incest. In an article entitled "The Rules," the editor discusses asserting independence from patriarchal dominance. The following recognizable theme appears:

> *"My father is not the only family member to have graduated me into sexual abuse. (This is where it gets really painful and icky.) My mother must also be looked to for the responsibility. Granted, she never physically abused me in any way, but she did one very damning deed: she didn't save me. (Ouch!) She supported the rules and my father's breed of 'discipline' by default."*

(OUT! p. 3)

The newsletter also includes sixteen graphic poems on sexual abuse. Among the items included in the "Where to Go for Help" section are *The Courage to Heal* — "This book is the best I've read" — and ten different 12-Step Programs.

Gloria Finds Self-Esteem

Many women who are mothers of these adult children feel gratitude to Gloria Steinem because she spoke out and championed their causes. She was a role-model: articulate, intelligent, energetic, ambitious, and attractive. Yes, attractive— many women still like to be thought of as attractive. She seemed to have reached the pinnacle of success — one of the best-known, revered women in the world. It turns out that Steinem was not a happy person. Most of those years when she carried the banner for women, she was riddled with self-doubt and anguish. She was lacking self-esteem. However, she now bares her soul in her new book *Revolution from Within*. She has discovered her "inner child" and is now thriving. This inner child had been destroyed by, what else, the patriarchal society in which we live. Steinem has embraced the tenets of Recovery, New Age, and radical feminism. They are all melded together into one big mess – one big confabulation. The women who gave her their honor and respect in the 70s and 80s will find a new Steinem in the 90s – one who is less pragmatic and more spiritual. She now has turned inward to find someone to blame for all that happens, to an unhappy childhood that we've all experienced living in a patriarchal society. She provides a complete rationale for radical feminism using the constructs of Recovery and New Age.

We will let her speak for herself, from her book *Revolution from Within*.

Steinem writes with great admiration of a woman named Marilyn Murphy. Murphy evolved from a timid young girl who married at age eighteen and lived a "life that was expected of her" for many years to a strong woman who in 1975, having separated from a second husband, began to understand "the soul-killing depth of male dominance." After leaving this man, "to her surprise, she fell irresistibly, head-over-heels in love with another woman."

"Suddenly, she began to feel an inexplicable sense of rightness and naturalness, as if she was finally living her own life. The world seemed open and 'free form' unlike her heterosexual past in which every-

thing had rules, guidelines, customs and traditions."

(p.47)

According to Steinem, Murphy has come to see incest and other childhood sexual abuse as, in her words, "a preverbal sexual terrorism that breaks the female spirit, and makes women continue to believe terrible things will happen to them if they tell men's secrets." What a powerful idea! It appears that men plot together in their patriarchal society to rape their daughters in order to control the society.

So, incest is not an act by a violent, crazy, individual psychopath. Instead it is an act of oppression of men against women to keep them under control. We see patriarchy for what it is, a system ingrained in society to keep women in their place. Men start with little girls to ingrain this attitude. Women who have been incested cooperate by repressing these atrocities and accepting male discipline.

Steinem talks about "voyaging to the past." She quotes John Bradshaw:

"I believe that this neglected, wounded inner child of the past is the major source of human misery."

In order to find her inner child and reparent herself, Steinem visits a psychotherapist whom she says is "an experienced travel guide for journeys into the unconscious – that timeless part of our minds where events and emotions of our personal past are stored along with the wisdom of our species."

Steinem enters a state of meditation, trance, or self-hypnosis under the guidance of her therapist. Even if you are skeptical, Steinem suggests that a person should proceed "as if you believed. Your unconscious may surprise you."

So Steinem accepts the whole concept of New Age regression therapy without ever questioning whether or not this unconscious mind, whose veracity she so respects, could be confused and without even suggesting that memories need confirmation from other sources. The unconscious can be confused by many things – every "scientist" who has studied the mind knows this. Memory at best is unreliable. It is made up of fragments that we fill in with details. It is subject to suggestibility. Memory is tricky – it confuses what we see, read, and experience. A child's memory is especially easily contaminated by visions from TV, movies, pictures, other people's experiences. Doesn't Steinem know that? Does she really believe that the little girl she visits in a trance-like state is the real little Gloria? Doesn't she know that little girl is a confabulation, a mixture of fact and fantasy? Doesn't her therapist know that?

These are just a few examples to indicate that Steinem has left the left side of her brain behind (the practical side) and now relies just on the right side (the intuitive). She has a great influence on millions of people. She is one of the most respected women in the world. We wish she would use her whole brain and return to some logic and critical analysis as she pursues the goal of encouraging women to search for self-esteem.

Satanism

Satanic Hysteria

The phone rings – the horror begins. The first phone call is about child abuse – maybe a baby sitter, neighborhood teenager, uncle, teacher – before long it escalates. You, Mom or Dad, are guilty of the most horrendous, unspeakable, incredible, atrocious crimes imaginable. You were part of a satanic cult. Knowingly or not, you participated in the sacrifice of animals or babies to Satan. And you forced your daughter to participate. You gave her blood in her baby bottle. How can she ever forgive or forget? All she can do is rid herself of her crazy family including grandma and grandpa because satanism is multigenerational. The only way to work toward a cure is to relinquish all family ties. Where in the world are these stories of satanic cults coming from in 20th century America?

Why are respectable, sincere, caring families being accused of such atrocities?

At about the same time that therapy-induced memories of childhood incest became common, grotesque stories of ritualistic abuse by satanic cults began emerging from therapy sessions. A growing number of licensed therapists are involved in these cases. Some therapists claim that they have patients who are victims of an international cult of satanists operating in virtually every town and city in America. Satanists, they claim, have infiltrated the highest ranks of government, law enforcement and other professions useful to guarding the secret conspiracy.

A national network of investigators, therapists, social workers, doctors, preachers, prosecutors and others has helped create a recent hysteria that devil worshippers are killing babies, impregnating little girls, and forcing bizarre and violent acts of sexual and physical abuse on children.

Newspapers report every exaggerated incident as if it were real. Geraldo Rivera, Larry King and other popular television personalities have millions of people believing these confabulated tales by giving proponents of this satanic conspiracy a national forum. Since the early 1980s hundreds of cases have been investigated. Many people have been charged with crimes and imprisoned. Yet, there is absolutely no concrete evidence of any organized satanic cult.

During the mid-1980s therapists made the association between patients with multiple personality disorder (MPD) and satanic ritual abuse. Hundreds of patients in therapy have related the same incredible stories of being born into multigenerational satanic cults, being abused and tortured at an early age, forced to partake in violent sexual rituals with black-hooded figures gathered around an altar, sacrificing animals and babies to Satan. The victims claim they were brainwashed and prevented from telling anyone because of terrible threats. The stories eventually are told in therapy sessions, with a therapist "trained" in dealing with MPD and satanic ritual abuse. Hypnosis and guided imagery are often used by the therapists to "help" the patient recall the details of the painful "memories."

Therapists believe these incredible stories of satanic cult abuse for a number of reasons. Ken Lanning is an investigator for the Federal Bureau of Investigation (FBI). He has been investigating claims of satanic cult abuse for several years. Like many people, Lanning initially believed the media reports of satanic cults. After years of investigating these claims, he has found no evidence at all of a national network of devil worshippers.

Lanning believes that not just therapists, but police and prosecutors are too emotionally involved to rationally ex-

plore the issue. Lanning warns police investigators that
seminars on satanic crimes, conducted by self-proclaimed
experts, often mix fact with fantasy and can be very convincing:

> *"Almost any discussion of satanism and the occult
> is interpreted in the light of the religious beliefs of
> those in the audience. Faith, not logic and reason,
> governs the religious beliefs of most people. As a
> result, some normally skeptical law enforcement
> officers accept the information disseminated at these
> conferences without critically evaluating it or ques-
> tioning the sources. Officers who do not normally
> depend on church groups for law enforcement crimi-
> nal intelligence, who know that media accounts of
> their own cases are notoriously inaccurate, and who
> scoff at and joke about tabloid television accounts of
> bizarre behavior suddenly embrace such material
> when presented in the context of satanic activity.
> Individuals not in law enforcement seem even more
> likely to do so."*
>
> (Lanning, p. 8)

After nearly a decade of research on the subject of
satanic ritual abuse, psychiatric anthropologist Sherrill
Mulhern believes that these far-fetched tales of bloodthirsty
satanists result from fundamental changes in psychotherapy
methods. Many therapists see early childhood trauma as
the reason for later psychological problems. Many therapists believe that traumatic childhood events are blocked
out through a process called dissociated memories, so that
a person can survive the trauma without having any conscious memories. Therapists treat their patients by having

them recall and reexperience the childhood trauma. Hypnosis is often used to uncover the memories.

Federally funded research about hypnosis during the 1950s indicates that some people are more susceptible to hypnosis than others. Between 5 and 10 percent of the population are so highly hypnotizable that they can instantly be put into a trance. During the 1970s, Herbert Spiegel studied this phenomenon of highly suggestible people – which he called the Grade Five Syndrome – and concluded that they would invariably confabulate detailed experiences on whatever topic the hypnotist suggested.

According to Mulhern:

"Research confirms that hypnosis is anything but a truth serum; recovering memories through hypnosis does not *ensure the material's historical accuracy. Controlled laboratory studies of age regression have demonstrated a tendency of hypnotized subjects to confabulate information spontaneously.*

... Experimental researchers have observed that even when memories are found to be fantasy or confabulation when checked against verifiable outside sources, hypnotized subjects experience all recalled memories as if they were equally real."

(Mulhern, p. 149)

Mulhern also points out that in studies of patients diagnosed as having multiple personality disorder virtually all fit the profile of Spiegel's Grade Five Syndrome. Yet, incredibly, this research which shows the connection between highly suggestible people, the unreliability of memories recalled under hypnosis, and fantastic recollections of satanic abuse while under the guidance of a therapist who specializes in MPD and satanic abuse, has been largely ignored in the mental health community.

Even though Mulhern's research provides a rational explanation for confabulations of satanic cult abuse, a growing number of "adult survivors" and their therapists continue to contribute to the satanic hysteria. Some therapists call themselves specialists in cult therapy and they suspect satanic cult abuse in every patient who walks into the office. In a similar fashion, as statements made in the *Interview With Therapist A* illustrate, some therapists are constantly on the lookout for childhood incest in certain patients – particularly those with eating disorders.

When such therapists have a patient who recalls satanic abuse, they believe the stories without too much hesitancy. It does not occur to them that the patient's memory may have been contaminated by stories heard or read or even seen on television or in a movie. Suggestible people pick up cues from all sorts of stimuli and have memories stored in their minds of such cues that can be confused with reality, later to be part of a confabulation that emerges in therapy. Many therapists do not even consider this possibility.

Some therapists believe that it is not necessary to corroborate their patients' unbelievable memories, but instead "validate" them no matter how outlandish they may be. They say the pain is the same whether the memories are real or not. By "validating" the memories, therapists are causing long-term damage to people who, because of their trust in their therapist, become convinced the false memories are accurate recollections. The traumatized patients are then ready to accuse their parents of abominable acts of childhood abuse – malicious accusations which are destroying families.

Conclusion

Our Conclusions

Countless adult children who go to therapy come to believe they have been victimized by their parents. SOME of these adult children are victimized – by their "therapy." No matter what the reason is for seeking therapy, they are led to believe they were sexually molested as children. They begin to believe they are incest victims and sever all ties after labeling their parents as "perpetrators" or "enablers" or both.

The horrendous abuse that these accusing adult children describe may not have happened to them in reality, but the abuse is real – it happened! Not in their cribs at six months of age, or when they were two or three years old, or from age two to fourteen as some claim. Satanists did not take these adult children from their beds in the middle of the night when they were young children and force them to witness the sacrifice of animals and babies. It is not likely that any of these adult children were given blood to drink in their baby bottles. But they have lived these experiences in their minds – so to them the abuse is absolutely "real."

They lived the experiences as they confabulated them with the aid of a therapist, books, tapes, groups, and seminars. The abuse became more vivid as they articulated it, visualized it, described it, relived it in therapy, wrote about it, had it validated by a therapist and a group, talked about it over and over again. The abuse became increasingly real as they grieved about it, confronted their perpetrators, told their friends and families about it, and performed rituals with their support groups. The hate they learned to express for the so-called perpetrators and enablers made the abuse even more vivid in their minds. The abuse became the center of their lives, so the abuse *is* real. If it happened or not, the abuse is now the most vivid memory they have. Most memories fade in time – they become fuzzy. These memories, that have been confabulated, are so vivid they will probably live forever. The adult children have lived with terror in their therapy and group for so long that it is real. They are programmed to direct the terror against their parents.

These adult children have different memories of their childhood than their parents do. They are told that their parents are "in denial." Their therapy has taught them to cut off all ties with anyone who does not believe their stories. Cut them off completely – do not accept letters, gifts, phone calls. Anyone who does not believe the stories is "dead" in the minds of the victims.

The therapy these adult children go to is a new type of therapy. The therapists believe in "body memories" and accept recollections of decades-long repressed memories as gospel without challenge or the need for confirmation. Therapists believe in reinforcement by books and groups and in focussing on the pain. Adult children are told the "family of origin" is disposable and a supportive "family of choice" is preferable. Grandchildren as young as five are being told their grandparents are evil and these children are often entered into "therapy."

These therapists are creating new definitions for the mind. They define the mind as a tape recorder with each memory firmly embedded to be brought to the surface with the aid of a therapist or hypnotist. They do not know or want to know that memory consists of fragments that are constantly reinterpreted. Therapists are exercising a tremendous power over their clients when they help them create memories and encourage them to act on the fabricated memories. When therapists encourage clients to focus on the pain, they are doing untold damage as they help create the pain.

What is going on? The Recovery Movement is a billion dollar enterprise. Hundreds of thousands of people are making lots of money in this growth industry. Many unqualified therapists are in this business. As soon as a victim accepts that she has been abused, she is told "recovery" will take two to six years, maybe a lifetime. The therapist has hooked a long-term patient.

Millions of well-meaning people are trapped in this widespread movement. The therapists may be well-meaning. Most people are sympathetic to anyone who has been abused and they have jumped on this bandwagon. State legislatures are being pressured to enact laws extending the statute of limitations on crimes discovered from repressed memories. Juries are sympathetic. Many journalists and talk show hosts accept the validity of repressed memories without question, and of course certain publishers are thriving in this area.

So many therapists now practice "inner child" therapy that they reinforce one another, validating each other's books and acting as "expert witnesses" to defend the concept of decades-delayed discoveries from repressed memories of childhood trauma. Most psychiatrists do not believe in repressed memories. According to David Halperin, psychiatrist at Mount Sinai Hospital in New York, trauma "is hard to forget." Sexual abuse is generally an indelible mark on a person. Post Traumatic Stress Disorder (PTSD) creates problems because the memories are impossible to forget. The victims of PTSD do not repress their memories – they cannot get them out of their minds, according to Dr. Halperin.

Therapists who rely so heavily on rediscovered memories do not take into account the traditional scientific knowledge about mind and memory. Memory is made up of fragments – often disjointed and contaminated – some bright and sharp, others murky and vague. Many memories are additionally contaminated by the images received from television, movies, radio, and books. How can it be determined if a recalled childhood memory is of an event that actually happened or is a made-from-TV image? Most rational therapists would treat stories of satanic rituals or crib rape as fantasy. Other therapists believe they must accept any story reported by their clients, however outrageous, as fact and even counsel their clients to take action against their families based on these unsubstantiated stories. To accept confabulations as accurate revelations is at best non-professional, at worst should be considered criminal malpractice.

Therapists must develop a code of ethics which recognizes that accused parents have rights, that repressed memories are not always valid, and that books, tapes and seminars that are programmed for specific objectives are improper tools for psychotherapy.

Legislators must become aware of the danger of passing laws that run roughshod over the rights of citizens regarding decades delayed discoveries based on repressed memories. And journalists better stop, look, listen – before accepting as valid, claims based on repressed memories.

If these agents for justice and opinion-making in our society do not become more responsible, many more abuses will occur, costing our society the very basic ideals it relies on in order to endure – fairness and justice.

It's time for an appraisal of this dangerous situation by professionals trained in the rational scientific method to look for data and facts about decades delayed discoveries and repressed memories.

It is absolutely unbelievable in this society, where justice is supposed to prevail, that parents can be vilified and victimized by their adult children without any recourse.

Of course, the adult children are the greatest victims of all. They are sacrificing families and inheritances and living in fear. New memories have come to dominate their lives.

Suggested Readings

Books

Baker, Robert. 1992. *Hidden Memories*. Buffalo, NY: Prometheus Books.

Gardner, Richard. 1991. *Sex Abuse Hysteria: Salem Witch Trials Revisited*. Cresskill, NJ: Creative Therapeutics.

Halperin, David A. (Ed.). 1983. *Religion, Sect and Cult*. Boston, MA: John Wright PSG Inc.

Kaminer, Wendy. 1992. *I'm Dysfunctional, You're Dysfunctional*. Reading, MA: Addison-Wesley.

Katz, Stan and Liu, Aimee. 1991. *The Codependency Conspiracy*. New York: Warner Books.

Lanning, Kenneth. 1992. *Investigator's Guide to Allegations of "Ritual" Child Abuse*. Washington, DC: Federal Bureau of Investigation.

Lifton, Robert. 1961. *Thought Reform and the Psychology of Totalism*. New York: W.W. Norton.

Loftus, Elizabeth and Ketcham, Katherine. 1991. *Witness for the Defense*. New York: St. Martin's Press.

Peele, Stanton. 1989. *Diseasing of America*. Boston: Houghton Mifflin.

Richardson, James T., Best, Joel, and Bromley, David G., editors. 1991. *The Satanism Scare*. Hawthorne, NY: Aldine De Gruyter.

Tavris, Carol. 1992. *The Mismeasure of Women*. New York: Simon & Schuster.

Articles

Alexander, David. "Giving the Devil More Than His Due." *The Humanist*, March/April 1990.

Alexander, David. "Still Giving the Devil More Than His Due." *The Humanist*, Sept./Oct. 1991.

Blau, Melinda. "Adult Children Tied to the Past." *American Health*, July/Aug. 1990.

Dawes, Robyn M. "Biases of Retrospection." *Issues in Child Abuse Accusations*, Summer, 1989.

Derus, Michelle. "She Says, They Say . . . " *Milwaukee Sentinel*, Feb. 26, 1991.

Drexler, Madeline. "The Lure of the 12-Step Fellowship." *Boston Globe*, Dec. 4, 1988.

Haaken, Janice and Astrid Schlaps. "Incest Resolution Therapy and the Objectification of Sexual Abuse." *Psychotherapy*, Spring 1991.

Holmes, David. 1990. "The Evidence for Repression: An Examination of Sixty Years of Research," in J. Singer (Ed.) *Repression and Dissociation*. Chicago: Chicago University Press.

Hughes, Robert. "The Fraying of America." *Time*, Feb. 3, 1992.

Jackson, Kathy. "Innocence Betrayed." *Dallas Morning News*, Nov. 16, 1991.

Keenan, Marney Rich. "Lost Souls." *Detroit News*, Oct. 20, 1990.

Loftus, Elizabeth F. and Leah Kaufman. "Why Do Traumatic Experiences Sometimes Produce Good Memory (Flashbulbs) and Sometimes No Memory (Repression)?" Unpublished paper, Jan. 1991.

Morris, Michael. "'False Memory Syndrome' Taking its Toll on Families." *Utah County Journal,* April 12, 1992.

Mulhern, Sherrill. "Satanism and Psychotherapy: A Rumor In Search of An Inquisition," in James T. Richardson et al. (Editors). *The Satanism Scare,* Hawthorne, NY: Aldine De Gruyter, 1991.

Rieff, David. "Victims All?" *Harper's*, Oct. 1991.

Sifford, Darrell. "Accusations of Sex Abuse, Years Later." *Philadelphia Inquirer*, Nov. 24, 1991.

Sifford, Darrell. "When Tales of Sex Abuse Aren't True." *Philadelphia Inquirer*, Jan. 5, 1992.

Taylor,Bill. "What If Sexual Abuse Memories Are Wrong?" *Toronto Star,* May 16,18,19, 1992.

Torrey, E. Fuller. "Oedipal Wrecks." *Washington Monthly*, Jan./Feb. 1992.

Toufexis, Anastasia. "When Can Memories Be Trusted?" *Time*, Oct. 28, 1991.

Whitley, Glenna. "The Seduction of Gloria Grady." *D Magazine*, Oct. 1991.

Whitley, Glenna. "Abuse of Trust." *D Magazine*, Jan. 1992.

Wielawski, Irene. "Unlocking the Secrets of Memory." *Los Angeles Times*, Oct. 3, 1991.

Citations to How Could This Happen? *(pp. 27-60)*

1   Names have been changed.

2   Electronic mail works like a fax machine.

3   During the past six months I have accumulated several hundred pages of family communications. Since this is my story, the excerpts of letters that appear in this paper are mine. I have edited only as seemed necessary for clarity.

4   Bass, E., & Davis, L. (1988). *The Courage to Heal.* NY: Harper. This book is a guide and manual for incest and sex abuse survivors and their families. It is our understanding that the therapist gave our daughter this book before Susan had her own revelation of sexual abuse. Could it have influenced her memories?

5   Widom, C.S. (1989). The cycle of violence. *Science, 244,* 160-166.

6   I have been told by two therapists who have experience with these sorts of issues that it is sometimes possible to show that events could not have taken place as remembered by the victim. It seems that there are few of these cases that make it through the legal system, however, because insurance companies almost always settle out of court.

7   Sgroi, S. (1988). *Vulnerable Populations, Vol. 1.* Lexington, MA: Heath. Sgroi does not mention why "late presenters" as she refers to them should be primarily from successful families. The book is poorly documented.

8   Maltz, W., & Holman, B. (1987). *Incest and Sexuality: A Guide to Understanding and Healing.* Lexington, MA: Lexington Books.

9   Maltz, W. (1990, December). Adult survivors of incest: How to help them overcome the trauma. *Medical Aspects of Human Sexuality,* 42-47.

10 See Yates, A. (1989). Current perspectives on the eating disorders: I. History, psychological and biological aspects. *Journal of the American Academy of Child and Adolescent Psychiatry, 28* (6), 813-828.

11 Wakefield, H., & Underwager, R. (1988). *Accusations of Child Sexual Abuse.* Springfield, IL: Charles Thomas.

12 Loftus, E., & Ketcham, K. (1991). *Witness for the Defense.* NY: St. Martin's Press.

13 Zehner, M. (1980, April). Treatment issues for incest victims. WOARPATH, pp. 2, 6.

14 Masson, M. (1984). *The Assault on Truth: Freud's Suppression of the Seduction Theory.* NY: Farrar, Straus & Giroux.

15 e.g., Woodall, M. (1991, March 26). Human services sued by couple over child-abuse case later dropped. *Philadelphia Inquirer,* pp. 3B.

16 Gardner, R. (1991). *Sex Abuse Hysteria: Salem Witch Trials Revisited.* Cresskill, NJ: Creative Therapeutics.